Escalation in Decision-Making

For Rachel

Escalation in Decision-Making

Behavioural Economics in Business

HELGA DRUMMOND
University of Liverpool Management School, UK

JULIA HODGSON
University of Liverpool Management School, UK

Routledge
Taylor & Francis Group

LONDON AND NEW YORK

First published in paperback 2024

First published 2011 by Gower publishing

Published 2016
by Routledge
4 Park Square, Milton Park, Abingdon, Oxon OX14 4RN

and by Routledge
605 Third Avenue, New York, NY 10158

Routledge is an imprint of the Taylor & Francis Group, an informa business

Gower Applied Business Research
Our programme provides leaders, practitioners, scholars and researchers with thought provoking, cutting edge books that combine conceptual insights, interdisciplinary rigour and practical relevance in key areas of business and management.

British Library Cataloguing in Publication Data
Drummond, Helga.
  Escalation in decision-making : behavioural economics in
  business.
  1. Decision making.
  I. Title II. Hodgson, Julia.
  658.4'03-dc22

Library of Congress Cataloging-in-Publication Data
Drummond, Helga.
  Escalation in decision-making : behavioural economics in business / Helga Drummond and Julia Hodgson.
    p. cm.
  Includes bibliographical references and index.
  ISBN 978-1-4094-0236-7 (hbk) -- ISBN 978-1-4094-0237-4
(ebook) 1. Decision making. 2. Economics--Psychological aspects. I. Hodgson, Julia, 1965-
II. Title.

  HD30.23.D78 2011
  658.4'03--dc22

                                                         2010048033

ISBN: 978-1-4094-0236-7 (hbk)
ISBN: 978-1-03-292882-1 (pbk)
ISBN: 978-1-315-58021-0 (ebk)

DOI: 10.4324/9781315580210

Contents

List of Tables

Acknowledgements

We warmly acknowledge the generous financial support received from the University of Liverpool, Management School and the Economic and Social Research Council. We also thank our colleagues in the Management School for their interest in the project. We are grateful to our commissioning editor Martin West for his help and enthusiasm. Janet Briddon proofread the manuscript with her unfailing eye for detail. Our ultimate debt is to the market traders themselves. We hope we have done justice to their stories.

Liverpool
April 2010

About the Authors

Helga Drummond, PhD (University of Leeds) has been part of the Faculty at Liverpool University Management School since 1990. She is now Professor of Decision Sciences. Professor Drummond is associated with a number of departments and agencies of the UK Ministry of Defence and is currently a non-executive director of the Service Personnel and Veterans Agency and a member of the Defence Scientific Advisory Council, the Finance Committee of the Royal Institution of Chartered Surveyors and the Disciplinary Tribunal of the Joint Council of the Inns of Court. Professor Drummond has lectured on risk and decision making at Cambridge University, Manchester University (UMIST), and the Defence Academy, Shrivenham. She has written 11 books and numerous academic papers and journal articles. She is frequently called upon to comment in the national newspapers press and broadcast media.

Julia Hodgson, MA, MPA, PGCE and is a lecturer at the University of Liverpool Management School. She has published academic papers and journals in the areas of decision making in organizations and consumer experience.

Introduction

It is afternoon on the market. Barrow boys are calling, 'Pick your own bananas! Twenty pence a pound! Come on now ladies! Pick your own bananas!' Another stall-holder shouts, 'Margarine! Plenty of margarine!' It starts raining. A trader grapples with plastic sheeting to protect his stock. His neighbour advises him not to bother. 'You can't damage damaged goods!' he jokes.

Anxiety lurks beneath the banter. Once, being a market trader was a sure route to prosperity, particularly on the indoor market where some traders became millionaires. 'Stalls were like gold dust,' said a trader. 'You couldn't get one for love nor money.'

Times have changed; January and February were known as 'kipper months' because of the quiet post-Christmas trading. Now almost every month is a 'kipper'. Gone are the days when flower sellers carried their takings home in buckets and spent all of Sunday counting out the copper and silver coins and when grocers could pile their counters high with pork pies and expect to be sold out by five o'clock. Now, hardly a week passes without another trader pulling down the shutters for good. Despite the poor prospects there is no shortage of new owners willing to 'give it a go'– sometimes taking a stall where the previous owner has just gone bankrupt. Most of these new hopefuls measure their tenure in months – sometimes only weeks. What makes them believe that they can succeed where others are so obviously failing?

Among the hardest hit were those who paid huge sums of money to acquire a business on the market when stalls were 'gold dust'. Among the last to arrive, they have frequently been the first to leave – particularly those who borrowed heavily to finance their expensive acquisitions. Yet no one is immune from the downturn. 'This stall is in a good position,' said Nana, a long-standing trader whom we shall meet later in this book, 'but what can you do when people aren't even stopping to look?'

Dangers of Escalation

What indeed? One of the most important decisions individuals and organizations may ever have to make is what to do when a venture falters. Do they cut their losses or do they reinvest and risk throwing 'good money after bad?' Economics teaches that market forces ultimately curb non-viable enterprises. The trouble is market forces can be slow to act. By the time it becomes plainly apparent that there is no hope of recovery, the damage may be well and truly done.

Yet behavioural theorists believe that decision-makers frequently make things worse for themselves by reinvesting in doomed enterprises – a phenomenon known as escalation of commitment. Escalation theory is important because it implies that many decision failures are avoidable. Individuals and organizations can learn to make better, that is, more economically sensible decisions.

There is certainly scope for better decision-making in both the public and the private sector. The UK's NHS electronic patient-record system is so far behind schedule that it seems destined never to appear, or if it does, will probably be obsolete by the time it goes into service. The London 2012 Olympic Games are well over budget. Yet despite the UK's precarious economic position, there is no question of cancelling the project. In 2000 Marks and Spencer (founded by Michael Marks from a stall on Leeds market) almost collapsed thanks to the company's persistence with an outmoded business model. Eight years later in 2008, Woolworths collapsed for similar reasons. In June 2009 National Express were forced to surrender the East Coast franchise, having failed to meet their hugely optimistic forecast of achieving a 10 per cent increase in passenger revenues. GNER had already failed to run the East Coast railway profitably – bankrupting the parent company Sea Containers in the process. As if one bad experience was not enough, in early 2010, National Express announced that they might bid again for the franchise! In 2010 Toyota suffered a huge loss in public confidence after being forced to recall of millions of cars with a potentially lethal fault in the accelerator. Recalls are actually quite common in the motor industry. If Toyota had acted earlier, instead of allowing the problem to fester, the company would have been spared much of the costly damage they eventually incurred.

Yet it is unclear what actually causes escalation. The main theories are explained later in this book. Suffice it here to note that part of the problem is that most of the research has involved experiments comprising paper and pencil tests that present decision-makers with reliable information and clear-cut choices – conditions seldom found in reality. In reality decisions must be made amidst the 'fog of war' where problems are often ill-structured and surrounded by ambiguity and uncertainty. Furthermore, whereas experiments demand instant decisions, in reality decision-makers can procrastinate – for a time at any rate.

Aims of the Book

This book has two main aims. One is to examine the relevance of the various theories of escalation to 'real-life' decision-making. The second is to draw lessons for practice. Indoor market traders were chosen as subjects to study escalation and de-escalation because they face economic extinction. Escalation theory is 'work in progress.' Each case in the present study is like a tiny piece of mosaic that contributes to the bigger picture.

Structure of this Book

The book is structured as follows. The main behavioural theories of escalation are explained in Chapter 1. The aim has been to present those theories in accessible language with examples from private and public sectors. This chapter also discusses some of the controversies surrounding escalation theory. Are decision-makers as reckless as behavioural theorists seem to imply? Or is escalation largely unavoidable, that is, just a normal business expense?

Chapter 2 takes the reader on a tour of an imaginary market. The purpose of this chapter is orientation. It sets the context for the research, by sketching some of the history of markets and the sights and sounds of a modern market.

According to behavioural theorists escalation typically starts with bright promises. Chapter 3 explores this proposition by analysing interviews with new traders. Assuming that no one starts a business intending to fail, what explains new traders' optimism when the odds are so heavily stacked against them? Also, why do experienced owners sometimes make obvious mistakes?

Not all new start-ups fail completely. Chapter 4 analyses interviews with traders who start new businesses that may not be completely successful but survive nevertheless. In each case the metaphorical bottle is simultaneously half-full and half-empty. Analysis focuses on how owners respond to such equivocal situations and why they may be tempted to escalate their commitment and risk overreaching themselves.

Chapter 5 focuses on established traders who persist with their failing business until forced to quit. Why did they not leave when they had the chance? Moreover, why do they keep the business open when persistence is only making things worse?

All theories are false because they are abstractions from the real world. Chapter 6 explores cases of traders who contradict extant theory by exiting sooner rather than later thereby capping their losses. What distinguishes them from those who remain to the bitter end?

Although not all established traders are in acute financial straits, persistence may be economically suboptimal nevertheless. Why do they not switch to more profitable lines of businesses or even change career altogether? Chapter 7 concerns another form of 'lock-in' known as entrapment. Whereas escalation results from a deliberate decision to reinvest resources in a failing venture, entrapment results mainly through the simple passage of time. Chapter 7 sketches the main theories of entrapment.

Chapter 8 examines the relevance of those theories by analysing cases of traders who have succumbed to 'lock-in'. The chapter includes a case that contradicts the theory. This outlier serves as a counterpoint to compare and contrast other cases. The focal question for analysis is what holds entrapped traders in place? Do they simply not realize what persistence is costing them, or is it because changing direction has become too costly?

Chapter 9 summarizes the main findings of the study. What do we now know about escalation and entrapment that we did not know before? The chapter begins with a resume of the main theories of escalation and entrapment and mentions some of the limitations of the research before addressing the central research questions. This chapter ends with suggestions for research.

Chapter 10 considers the implications for practice. The recommendations are aimed at both entrepreneurs *and* executives. This chapter includes a discussion of the role of options in limiting escalation and entrapment.

To preserve the narrative flow, the procedures used to obtain the data, conduct interviews, construct and analyse the cases and so forth are explained in a section entitled 'Note on Method' at the end of the book. It should be noted here, however, that names and contextual details have been changed to conceal owners' identities. Details concerning time and place have been kept vague for the same reason.

It is dangerous to try to summarize a complex and nuanced study into a few 'take-home' messages. Mindful of that caveat, the present study reveals that escalation and entrapment are by no means inevitable. If they do take hold, however, the results can be devastating. Decision-makers can best protect themselves by taking charge. That means reading the road ahead and erring on the side of caution by exiting sooner rather than later even though the cost may be high. The most dangerous response may be to live on borrowed time. Those who avoid painful decisions may end up facing an even bigger reckoning. On a more positive note, it is axiomatic that risk-taking is the key to generating wealth. In studying some traders it becomes apparent that the emotional behaviour which can produce bad decisions can also drive progress. There may be a fine line between success and calamity.

The Epilogue briefly reflects on one of the most successful gambles in business history.

A Note on Method

Discovery consists of seeing what everyone else has seen and thinking what no one else has thought.

(Albert von Szent-Gyorg)

The Role of Theory

The window nearest the north transept of the medieval church of St. Cross near Winchester is angled so that sunlight falls on the church cross on only two days of the year. Those days are 3 May, the day in the church calendar of the Invention of the Cross, and 14 September – Holy Cross Day. A theory explains and/or predicts something. The window at St. Cross is an enduring testimony to the genius of medieval astronomers. Without the aid of modern telescopes and computers, they could predict exactly where the sun would fall on two days of the year, although they were unable to explain why.

Theories are axiomatic systems of thought. More specifically, a theory may be defined as, 'A statement of relations among concepts within a set of boundary assumptions and constraints' (Bacharach 1989: 496). The role of a theoretical statement is to simplify the observed world by organizing parsimoniously and communicating clearly. Indeed, a good theory may make only one single prediction. For example, Festinger's (1957) influential dissonance theory predicts that people are motivated to resolve inconsistencies (Sutton and Staw 1995: 377 discusses this point).

Since they are abstractions, all social sciences theories are wrong by definition. Yet they can still be useful. Usefulness means that a theory changes how we think about things (Weick 1989). That said, the aim of the present study was not to generate new theory but to develop existing theory. Besides, completely new theories are rare as social scientists are inevitably influenced by what has gone before (for example, Bacharach 1989). More specifically, the present study pursues the middle ground as it examines the relevance of extant theorising and research and tries to fill gaps (for example, Pratt 2009: 859, Weick 1989).

More specifically, as the review of the extant theorising and research in Chapter 1 shows, researchers have already identified a long list of factors that are potentially conducive to escalation and entrapment. Thus, although the present study is concerned with *why* escalation and entrapment occur, the main scope for theoretical developments lies at the boundaries, that is, the *who*, *when*, *what* and *how* of escalation and entrapment. For example, what factors increase decision-makers susceptibility to escalation?

Why Case Studies?

Most research into escalation and entrapment has been conducted using experiments. Experiments have an important role to play, not least because they afford tight control over the variables studied. Yet that strength is also a limitation because so much depends upon the selection of variables in the first place. For instance, early experiments involving sunk costs found that the more money decision-makers had invested in a project, they more likely they were to persist (Garland 1990). Yet when the level of project completion was added to the equation, it became apparent that although sunk-costs may influence decisions about whether or not to persist with a faltering project, decision-makers are also influenced by how near the project is to being finished (for example, Conlon and Garland 1993, Moon 2001a).

In contrast, case studies allow the researcher to encapsulate a wide range of variables – including possibilities beyond extant theorising and research. More specifically, they allow researchers to probe decision-makers' perceptions, their emotions and to learn about contextual influences. Above all, case studies are grounded in reality. Experiments present decision-makers with hypothetical scenarios involving clear cut choices that can be made by merely ticking a box. Moreover, those choices are forced. Procrastination is not an option. Yet in reality, important decisions must be made amidst the 'fog of war' where issues are surrounded by ambiguity, uncertainty and 'noise'.

Why Market Traders?

Indoor market traders were chosen as study subjects because economic trends are driving many of them out of business and creating huge uncertainty for those who remain. Those who are being driven out of business have to decide whether to quit sooner rather than later. Those who are still viable but have seen trade decline, must also decide whether or not to persist with an economically suboptimal venture. These are precisely the issues that occupy escalation theorists.

Why Multiple Case Studies?

The development of escalation theory is like building a mosaic, whereby each study contributes another tiny piece towards a bigger picture (Weick 1989). The rationale for selecting cases in the present study is that each one contributes something (a piece of mosaic) to our knowledge and understanding of escalation and entrapment.

In more formal language, multiple case studies can be useful in elaborating theory, 'By piecing together the individual patterns the researcher can draw a more complete theoretical picture' (Eisenhardt 1991: 620). Emphatically, the present study is not a statistical survey and therefore it is impossible to generalize from the results. The criterion for selection of cases centres upon theoretical or as it sometimes called, purposive sampling (Glaser and Strauss 1968). That is, cases have been selected for analysis because they have something new to say about escalation and/or entrapment. 'New' means that a case either validates (or contradicts) existing theory and research, and/or offers new insight. There is no hard and fast rule about how many to include. To paraphrase Eisenhardt (1991: 622), that depends upon what is already known and what a new case can add.

Research stops when theoretical saturation is reached. In other words, when successive cases add little or nothing to what is already known about a particular phenomenon. In practice, true theoretical saturation is seldom achieved because there is always something new to be learned. Yet as the present study progressed, certain themes began to be being repeated suggesting that the research was approaching a kind of saturation. For example, interviews with new traders whose businesses failed pointed repeatedly to insufficient reality testing.

Not all interviews are reported in this book. More specifically, if an interview merely raised the same issues as another interview, there is no point in including it because it adds nothing new. Where there is little to choose between cases, the one that offers the richest and most interesting contextual detail has been selected.

Approach to Interviewing

New traders were mainly identified by public notices announcing a new tenancy, or sometimes by observation – seeing a new trader in situ. Established traders were identified from indicators such as 'closing down' sales, a 'to let' sign over the door or a notice saying 'business for sale' sign or signs of distress such as stocks running very low or an owner doing very little business.

Most of the interviews were conducted by the first author. The second author made visits to the research sites and conducted some interviews and informal conversations as a familiarization exercise. Requests for an interview were usually made in person. Some approaches were made by telephone, for example, if the owner did not actually work in the business or if the business was boarded up but the owner's telephone number was still visible.

If the owner agreed to be interviewed, there would normally be preliminary exploration of their history and present circumstances followed by a full interview. (Sometimes the first stage had to be dispensed with as the owner would invite the researcher to start the interview there and then.) The purpose of the initial exploration was to seek background information to inform the interview. For example:

H.D.: You said on the phone that it had been a hard decision to come out. Why is that?

Barry: Because when this one (shop) goes ... I am no longer self-employed. I am no longer my own boss.

The focal 'decisions' of interest in each case are the decision to open a business on an indoor market and, subsequently either close it down or reinvest in it when expectations are not being met. Or, it means a decision by an established trader either to close down a business or persist with it suboptimally. The unit of analysis in each case is the registered owner of the business.

All interviews were approached in a semi-structured fashion. A list of questions (see Table M.1) was used to guide the interview with supplementary questions to probe emergent issues. Owners were also encouraged to talk about what was important to them.

Table M.1   Interview schedule

1. Please tell me something about yourself.
2. Is this your first business?
3. How did you come to open it?
4. How long have you owned it?
5. Do you own any other businesses?
6. Are you the sole owner?
7. Why did you go into business?
8. How well did you know the market before deciding to open?
9. Why did you decide to sell, clothes/food/etc. as applicable?
10. How have you been able to finance your start-up?
11. Did you have a business plan?
12. What made you believe you would succeed?
13. What risks did you think you were taking?
14. What risks do you see now?
15. Can you give me an idea of what your outgoings are?
16. How is the business doing?
17. Is that better or worse than expected?
18. Have you had to put extra money into it?
19. How long you are prepared to persist with the business?
20. Are you able to draw a wage/salary from the business?
21. How do you feel about the business now?
22. What do you think you will do next?
23. What are you hoping to achieve in the longer term?

If applicable:

24. When did the business begin to decline?
25. How did you become aware of the decline?
26. How did you react to it?
27. Did you ever think of making changes to the business before it declined?
28. If so, what changes and with what result?
29. If not, why not?
30. What happened next?
31. Have you tried to sell the business?
32. Have you set any limits on how long you will keep the business?
33. What is it costing you to keep it open?
34. Why do you keep it open?
35. What made you decide to close the business?
36. Could you have closed it sooner?
37. If not, why not?
38. How do you feel the decision?
39. How easy or hard was it for you to make the decision?
40. Have you any alternative employment (or other option)?

All interviews were tape-recorded (latterly electronically recorded) and transcripts produced. Interviews ranged from 40 minutes to over 3 hours, generating anything up 60 pages of transcript. Quality should not be confused with quality. Long interviews were not necessarily more informative than short ones. Owners who gave longer interviews might repeat themselves or talk at length about the intricacies of their line of business. Some of this contextual detail is reproduced in the text as it adds colour and variety to the text, even though it is not strictly relevant to the subject matter. Owner's sometimes say 'we' when they mean 'I'. The original has been left to stand.

Owners chose the interview location. Some interviews were conducted in the owner's home, some in nearby cafes and others actually at the stall itself with the researcher variously perched on a spare stool, a box or a pile of carpet. One participant who had forgotten the appointment invited the researcher to conduct the interview from behind the counter while they served customers. One interview was held in a fish van. Owners might be interviewed more than once as the researcher tracked their progress.

Approach to Analysis

Eisenhardt (1989, 1991) urges researchers to start from clear constructs and testable propositions. In contrast, Dyer and Wilkins (1991: 634) argue that story is all-important for developing theory: 'Good story telling is what makes the most difference in the generative capacity of … studies,' they say.

The present study takes its leads from Dyer and Wilkins. The emphasis is upon presenting data holistically in order to further our understanding of the contextual realities and pressures of escalation and entrapment.

A case study is essentially a story, albeit told in a systematic fashion. The task of analysis proceeded as follows. Each transcript was summarized by the first author. The summarized version omitted extraneous material and repetition. Analysis proceeded using the summarized transcript but referring back to the original to retain a holistic perspective.

Theory determines what we see and how we see (for example, Glaser and Strauss 1968, Wicker 1985, Weick 1989). Ideally, analysis should ignore existing theories and research. In practice this is impossible, so a two-stage approach was used. Stage one involved analysing the data within the confines of escalation literature. Stage two involved stepping outside it.

To be more precise, stage one involved cycling back and forth between data and theory (Glaser and Stauss 1968) looking for 'goodness of fit' between the two. To guide the process, a list of pointers (see Table M.2) was compiled from the extant literature.

Stage two involved re-visiting transcripts to see what had been missed with a view to teasing out additional insights. This exercise revealed factors that are not prominent in the literature but are potentially relevant to explaining escalation and entrapment – for example, the impact of owners' prior commitment and subsequent disappointment in producing risk-seeking behaviour (for example, Anita), lowering expectations as a passive form of reinvestment (for example, Tony) and issues of decision-avoidance (for example, Carole).

In order to try to overcome the blinkered approach imposed by extant theory and research, 'playful' techniques of 'disciplined imagination' (Weick 1989, Mills 1959) were

Table M.2   Pointers for analysis derived from extant literature

- Alternatives (e.g., McCain 1986)
- Commitment (e.g., Salancik 1977)
- De-escalation – possible premature (e.g., Drummond 2005)
- Denial (e.g., Staw and Ross 1987a,b)
- Depression (e.g., Moon et al. 2003)
- Ego defensiveness (e.g., Staw 1981)
- Entrapment (e.g., Rubin and Brockner 1975)
- Escalation (e.g., Staw 1976)
- Experience (e.g., Langer 1983)
- Feedback: positive, negative, equivocal (e.g., Bowen 1987)
- Learning (e.g., Singer and Singer 1985)
- Loss (e.g., Whyte 1986)
- Limit setting (e.g., Simonson and Staw 1992)
- Myopia (e.g., Simons and Chabris 1999)
- Opportunity cost (e.g., Northcraft and Neale 1986)
- Options (e.g., Zardkoohi 2004)
- Overconfident (e.g., Taylor 1980)
- Prospect theory (e.g., Whyte 1991a,b)
- Quitting points (e.g., Simonson and Staw 1992)
- Rationality: prospective, retrospective (e.g., Staw and Ross 1978)
- Reference point (e.g., Whyte 1986)
- Relative magnitudes (e.g., Kahneman and Tversky 1982)
- Reinvestment: active, passive (e.g., Brockner, Shaw and Rubin 1979)
- Risk propensity (e.g., Sitkin and Weingart 1995)
- Risk perception (e.g., Wong 2005)
- Risk-seeking (e.g., Whyte 1991a,b)
- Salvage value (e.g., Staw 1997)
- Self-enhancement (e.g., Pfeffer and Fong 2005)
- Side bets (Becker 1960)
- Social pressure (e.g., Teger 1980)
- Sudden shock (e.g., Ross and Staw 1993)
- Sunk costs (Arkes and Blumer 1985)
- Time investment thereof (e.g., Coleman 2009)
- Vividness (e.g., Bazerman and Watkins 2008)
- Waste (e.g., Arkes 1996)

deployed. For example, what would be required for a perfect relationship to exist between two variables such as alternatives and de-escalation (Wicker 1985)?

To give an example of how this approach worked, Terry reinvested his entire life savings to maintain a failing business. Yet Carole, who had also spent her whole life on the market and might therefore have been expected to have been highly vulnerable to escalation, exited with her savings largely intact. Both recognized that persistence was hopeless: Carole when she had no surplus to invest, Terry when Christmas trade failed. How could this apparent conundrum be explained? Deploying Mill's technique of inverting the sense of perspective, in this case imagining near things as far and vice versa, it became obvious that what separated the two was time. To coin a cliché, Carole saw the future just before it had arrived, Terry only after it had arrived. This insight then led on to the role critical incidents could play in limiting escalation. Another playful technique was to deploy so called 'thought trials', that is, mental experiments (Weick 1989). One form of mental experiment deployed in the present study was to study the opposite of escalation and entrapment such as Mike's risky decision to completely revamp his businesses.

Reporting Protocols

The main aims in presenting the data were to reflect the world view of participants and to share as much as possible with the reader to enable them to judge the adequacy of interpretations reached. Inevitably this approach means some repetition and cross-referencing of cases. For example, some themes such as sunk costs and 'side-bets' repeat themselves across several cases.

To protect participants' identities, all names have been changed. Likewise, time and place have been deliberately obscured. Contextual details have also been changed where they do not affect the story. Where it is necessary to preserve those details, additional precautions have been taken to protect the participants' identity. Quotations are reproduced in participants' own words except for some minor editing to facilitate comprehension.

Researchers and Researched

None of the participants in the present study were known to us previously. No attempt was made to engage in participant observation, for example, by working on a market stall.

The first task on visiting a market hall was to gauge 'the mood of the market'. This not a recognized social sciences technique! It refers to an intuition about when to make an approach and (most importantly) when not to, as a clumsy or ill-timed opening could jeopardize the chance of being granted an interview. If the 'mood' did not seem right, no approaches were made and the researcher would return empty-handed. Experience, moreover, taught that Fridays and Saturdays were 'out' as regards holding interviews or even conducting informal conversations as most traders were too busy attending to customers. First thing in the morning was not a good time either; nor was late in the day. Traders were either busy setting out their stalls or packing them up. The best time to approach was early in the week, just after two o'clock in the afternoon. By then the lunch time rush had usually died down, aisles emptied, and with two hours to go before 'packing up' time, many traders were only too glad to speak. Another quiet time was on a Tuesday or Wednesday morning if it was half-day closing. A few new owners were too busy setting up their shops to participate in the research. A few new owners disappeared before they could be interviewed. One established trader leaving the market was too upset to be interviewed. Another was too engrossed in a book. Only one said 'Mind your own business.'

Research inevitably changes researchers. The present study disabused us of any notions we might have had of running a cosy cafe or even starting a business. Ownership may be a path to wealth creation but not everyone manages to travel along it very far. One case will stand for many. In an informal conversation about career opportunities and salaries a stall holder said, 'Eighteen thousand a year! That's a fortune! You can eat out every night on that!'

Suddenly we felt rich.

1 If at First You Don't Succeed – Then What? Introduction to Escalation Theory

If at first you don't succeed, try, try again. Then quit.
No use being a damn fool about it.

(W.C. Fields)

Introduction

In 1961 something remarkable happened in the Libyan Desert. Eight years earlier in 1953 an obscure entrepreneur named Bunker Hunt applied for a drilling licence. The prospects were exciting, as geologists advised Hunt that an oilfield recently discovered in Algeria would almost certainly extend into Libya. Unfortunately for Hunt the so-called 'Seven Sisters' (multi-national oil companies) were already drilling in the best sites. The only concession available to Hunt was so far remote from the Algerian border offering such miserable prospects that even the customary bribe to local officials was waived:

> *The story could have ended there … except for Bunker's instinct. As a gambling man, he believed that the more cards he could draw on, the better his chances would be, even if the cards were those no one else thought worth picking up. (Fay 1982: 5)*

Indeed Hunt drilled for years and found nothing. Moreover, despite their markedly better chances, the 'Seven Sisters' did no better drilling near Algeria. Eventually, one of the 'Sisters' – British Petroleum (BP) – gave up and went into partnership with Hunt:

> *The deal did not at first change Bunker's luck. In 1961 BP's experienced drilling teams struck out into the desert and drilled one well in Block 65. They reported that it was dry. So was the second well, and the third. (Fay 1982: 6)*

The rig superintendent was instructed by BP to stop drilling and return home. It was the final shattering blow for Hunt who had invested all his money in the venture:

Then, just for luck, the rig superintendent drilled another ten feet into the sand before withdrawing the bit from the third hole, and, in doing so, uncovered Bunker's ace. That ten feet was enough to pierce the cap of one of the world's largest oil fields. (Fay 1982: 7)

How Decisions Should Be Made

Any decision involving uncertainty runs the risk of failing. When it becomes apparent that a venture is not turning out as expected, decision-makers may face a dilemma. Do they cut their losses or risk 'throwing good money after bad'? We will probably never know what made the foreman decide to drill drown another 10 feet. Yet supposing that the decision had proved abortive – then what? It is not difficult to imagine the foreman drilling down another 10 feet, and then another 10 feet and so on.

Economics teaches that such futile persistence is wrong. To be more precise, decision theory assumes that decision-makers aim to maximize future outcomes. In order to attain that goal, decision-makers should invest resources only after careful and objective assessment of all available options. Assessment, moreover, should reflect future costs and future revenues and/or other benefits – not hunches or wishful thinking.

Why Decisions Are Not Always Made as They Should Be Made

Research by behavioural scientists suggests that decision-makers may not always behave so rationally. That is, instead of ending unsuccessful ventures, decision-makers may be tempted to reinvest resources in them, hoping of pull matters round but usually only to make things worse – a phenomenon known as escalation of commitment.

More precisely, escalation means persistence with a course of action beyond a rationally defensible point. In other words, beyond the point where feedback reliably indicates that expectations are unlikely to be met. For example, if marginal costs are consistently higher than marginal revenues. A typical escalation scenario is thus one where:

1. Resources are invested in anticipation of results.
2. Feedback progressively worsens until eventually it becomes clear that expectations are unlikely to be met.
3. There is an opportunity to quit or continue.
4. The precise consequences of quitting and continuing are unknown.

Almost any risky investment decision can result in escalation. For example, whether to remain 'on hold' on the telephone, whether to continue an unrewarding personal relationship, whether to repair a car that is in danger of becoming a liability or abandon a multi-million pound infra-structure project like Amsterdam's controversial metro system or the UK's multi-billion-pound faltering NHS electronic patient record system. The defining feature of escalation scenarios is that they involve a continuing cycle of *active* reinvestment in response to negative feedback (for example, Staw 1981, Ross and Staw 1986, Staw and Ross 1987a,b, 1989, Staw 1997).

What Causes Escalation?

Why should anyone want to 'throw good money after bad'? It seems bizarre. There are four main schools of thought about what drives escalation, namely:

1. Self-enhancement – needing to look good.
2. Emotional attachment to sunk costs.
3. Risk-seeking behaviour.
4. Uncertainty.

Each of these theoretical perspectives is explained in turn as follows.

Needing to Look Good: The Self-Enhancement Motive

Theories of self-enhancement suggest that escalation is primarily driven by the pursuit of self-esteem, that is, our innate desire, as human beings, to look good in our own eyes and in the eyes of significant others (for reviews of the literature see Pfeffer and Fong 2005, Staw 1997, 1981, Brockner 1992, Zhang and Baumeister 2006 and Crocker and Park 1974).

When it comes to decision-making, self-esteem means we need to be proved right. For example, in a consumer behaviour experiment, two groups received a sample of paint, 'try before you buy' as it were. One group paid a small amount for the sample. The other group got it free. When researchers compared levels of satisfaction, between the two groups they found paying customers were more satisfied with the paint than non-payers (experiment cited in Salancik 1977). Likewise, individuals who are free to choose from a variety of job offers subsequently reported higher levels of satisfaction and were less likely to leave than job applicants with less freedom of choice (O'Reilly and Caldwell 1981). Supervisors typically give higher performance appraisal ratings to staff they have personally selected than staff they did not appoint. It is as if supervisors unconsciously say to themselves, 'I chose them therefore they must be good' (Schoorman 1988; see also Bazerman, Beekun and Schoorman 1982).

PERSONAL RESPONSIBILITY FOR FAILURE

The risks of escalation may be heightened if decision-makers are liable to be held personally responsible for failure. In a seminal paper entitled 'Knee-Deep in the Big Muddy' (Staw 1976) observed:

> It is often possible for the decision-maker to greatly enlarge the commitment of resources and undergo the risk of additional negative outcomes in order to justify prior behaviour or demonstrate the ultimate rationality of an original course of action. (Staw 1976: 29)

The argument is that once resources are invested in anticipation of results, decision-makers tend to feel the need to justify their investment. What better way to signal that the decision was the correct one than by reinvesting in it? Staw seems to have had in mind

US embroilment in Vietnam. In 1965 George Ball, former Undersecretary of State, warned President Lyndon Johnson to think carefully before scaling-up US military deployments:

> Once large numbers of U.S. troops are committed to direct combat, they will begin to take heavy casualties in a war they are ill-equipped to fight in a non-cooperative if not downright hostile countryside. Once we suffer large casualties, we will have started a well-nigh irreversible process. Our involvement will be so great that we cannot – without national humiliation – stop short of achieving our complete objectives. Of the two possibilities, I think humiliation would be the more likely than the achievement of our objectives – even after we have paid terrible costs. (Memo from George Ball to President Lyndon Johnson, July 1965; source The Pentagon Papers 1971; cited in Staw 1976: 29)

This communication proved prescient. Three years later on 4 March 1968 a presidential meeting in the White House noted that even with the addition of another quarter of a million men the war might continue without accomplishing its purpose and with no end in sight.

The conflict in Vietnam overshadowed Johnson's presidency, eclipsing his achievements and, as we now know, driving Johnson to heavy drinking and depression as he found himself locked in to an unwinnable war. Likewise, to exit empty-handed from the military conflict in Afghanistan is tantamount to saying that troops have died for nothing.

Staw (1976) conducted an experiment to test responsibility theory. Two groups of undergraduates studied a scenario describing a company that had experienced a decade of decline due to problems in the research and development (R&D) department. Group 1 were given $10 million to invest in R&D and asked to decide which of the two major divisions to support, that is, consumer or industrial products. The group was asked to justify their decision in writing.

Notice what happens here. A clear volitional choice is made. It is a decision with potentially far-reaching consequences and is difficult to reverse. Moreover, responsibility for the decision is clearly pinned to individuals. Participants then received feedback. They learn that, five years on, the company now believes an even greater investment in R&D is required and therefore $20 million are now available. This time, however, instead of making an 'either/or' decision, participants can divide the money between the two divisions as they see fit. Again, written justification is required. Half of Group 1 subsequently learns that the divisions are now profitable. The other half of Group 1 learns that profits have fallen and that their decision has failed.

In contrast, Group 2 only participated in the second allocation decision. Group 2 did not decide which division to support initially, but were told that decision had been made by someone else. Both Groups, that is, those 'responsible' for previous decisions and those in the 'not responsible' category, again decided how much money to allocate. As expected, Staw found that participants responsible for an initially unsuccessful decision tended to direct more money to support ailing divisions than those who merely inherited the problem.

Research can never prove a theory. It merely fails to disprove it (Popper 1959). Subsequent tests of responsibility theory have produced mixed results. Whilst some studies have replicated the effect (for example, Conlon and Parks 1987, Kirby and Davis 1998, Schoorman et al. 1994, Whyte 1991a), other studies, including other Staw's own work, have found no effect for responsibility (for example, Staw and Fox 1977, Conlon and Garland 1993, Karlsson et al. 2002) – even when repeating Staw's original experiment (Armstrong, Coviello and Safranek 1993).

Two mathematical field experiments require special mention, however. Staw and Hoang (1995) found that team managers who paid large sums of money to recruit star players tended to use them more frequently than their goal-scoring record would warrant. Likewise, Staw, Barsade and Koput (1997) found that bank managers are more likely to perpetuate problem loans if they loaned the money in the first place than if they merely inherit someone else's bad-loan book. These two studies are important because whereas aforementioned laboratory experiments merely required respondents to give hypothetical answers to hypothetical questions, in these two quantitative field studies, researchers actually observed how decision-makers behaved in practice so they provide more powerful support for responsibility theory than laboratory-based studies.

LAPSING INTO DENIAL

Clearly, few people would reinvest in a venture if they knew for certain that it was doomed to fail. The trouble is, decision-makers may not realize how bad things are because when negative feedback arrives, they lapse into denial. Beleaguered decision-makers typically narrow down the range of information that they consider, paying more attention to feedback that supports their preconceived views whilst downplaying or even ignoring disconfirming (for example, Nisbett and Ross 1980, Kahneman, Slovic and Tversky 1982, Staw, Sandelands and Dutton 1981). Alternatively, or additionally, they may distort the magnitude of a setback, seeing it perhaps as a minor hiccup, or even a blessing in disguise (Staw and Ross 1978). Moreover, if decision-makers can blame failure on factors beyond their control such as the business cycle, currency fluctuations or even the weather they may feel justified in escalating their commitment (Staw and Ross 1978). Since these processes are thought to occur unconsciously, the decision-maker may genuinely believe that the problems are temporary, that success is close and so forth, and reinvest accordingly.

OBSESSION WITH THE PAST

Recall that optimal decision-making means maximizing *future* outcomes. Yet when a venture begins to unravel, decision-makers may be more interested in defending past actions than optimizing future possibilities (for example, Beeler and Hunton 1997). For instance, they may spend hours and hours going over previous decisions again and again, at the expense of addressing immediate problems and opportunities. In extreme circumstances, decision-makers may lose touch with reality altogether – just like Hitler who eventually retreated to his bunker to command armies and an air force that no longer existed.

Such obsession with defending past actions may be helpful psychologically because it enables decision-makers to reduce the dissonance created by the gap between prior expectations and actual results. Dissonance theory (Festinger 1957) predicts that we strive for consistency between what we believe and how we behave. For example, if an entrepreneur buys a pub knowing that all owners over the previous 10 years have gone bankrupt they may experience dissonance. Clearly it is nonsense to invest money in a business that is almost certain to fail. Dissonance theory suggests that the entrepreneur may persuade themselves that previous tenants lacked the requisite skills and experience to run the pub successfully, or that they underinvested in the business. Such self-serving attributions reduce the dissonance created by buying the pub. When the pub subsequently proves unprofitable, another way of reducing the dissonance created by the gap between expectations and results is to reinvest in it (Staw 1981 also discusses the impact of dissonance on escalation).

AUDIENCE EFFECTS

Admitting failure privately is hard enough. Admitting it publicly may be even harder – so the presence of an audience is potentially powerfully conducive to escalation. Socially instilled norms – to be consistent, to fulfil our promises, to be resolute in the face of difficulties, to finish what we have started – can also make it hard to reverse unsuccessful decisions (for example, Drummond 2001, Ross and Staw 1986, 1991). For example, Margaret Thatcher became so locked in to her 'not for turning' persona and so personally identified with 'Thatcherism' that she could not change direction even when her political survival was at stake.

Escalation may be driven by the simple desire to show off. For example, Tata Steel's questionable £6.7 billion bid for Corus in 2007 may have been driven more by hubris, a desire to become a global player in the steel industry and above all to impress rivals like Mittal Steel, rather than by economic logic.

The evidence for audience effects is not just anecdotal. In an experiment, two groups of participants were invited to set limits on their involvement in an investment decision before committing funds and before receiving feedback. One group set limits in public; the other group were allowed to set limits in private. Those who set limits in public stopped investing when those limits were reached even though their economic data said 'continue'. Asked why they behaved in such an economically irrational manner, participants said they thought it would 'look good' to be seen to adhere firmly to their publicly stated intentions (Brockner, Rubin and Lang 1981). Similarly, a study by Beeler and Hunton (1997) found that decision-makers who announced new ventures with a fanfare were more prone to escalation that those who did not.

The Royal Institution of Chartered Surveyors estimates that the cost of pursuing a boundary dispute involving a parcel of land worth £700 it is likely to exceed £70,000; that is, at least a hundred times more than the land is worth. Yet there is never any shortage of litigants. Behavioural scientists might say that such seemingly irrational litigation is pursued because although the land is worth very little, dispossession poses a threat to owners. Certainly empirical evidence suggests that people are more likely to perpetuate an ineffective course of action if failure either threatens their identity or reflects badly upon them – for instance, if failure could be seen as implying that they lack the necessary skills for a job (Brockner et al. 1986, Zhang and Baumeister 2006).

Competition is thought to be powerfully conducive to escalation. Imagine being invited to bid for a £1 coin. There is no reserve price so, in theory, the coin may be had for as little as one penny. There is only one snag: the second highest bidder must also pay the bid price and they receive nothing (Teger 1980, Shubik 1971). Would you bid?

When we run the experiment with large groups of undergraduates it is never difficult to attract bidders. Most students bid for fun and soon drop out. Yet inevitably two bidders become trapped in a mutually destructive spiral as the hammer price of the coin soars well above its face value – £4.15p at the last attempt. Bid prices tend to be even higher with MBA students as they have more money than undergraduates. The auction shows how decision-makers can become caught up in escalatory spirals almost by accident. Interestingly, when bidders are debriefed it is apparent that bidding is partly driven by unwillingness to lose face in front of an audience and desire for revenge. The experiment is a metaphor for potentially suicidal price wars between airlines and supermarkets.

Money Sunk and Lost: Sunk Costs as an Escalation Driver

Sunk costs are investments made in anticipation of a return. If the decision-maker quits, they merely become expenses.

Generally speaking, sunk costs should be ignored when deciding whether or not to reinvest in a venture, precisely because they cannot influence future outcomes. The following simple scenario will illustrate the point. You invest £30,000 to convert your living room into a corner shop. You work 70 hours a week. The business consistently generates £200 a week. If you closed the shop and took a job stocking supermarket shelves you could earn £350 for a 40-hour week.

Assuming your aim is to maximize your income you would be £150 a week better off working in the supermarket. Intellectually the decision makes itself. Clearly the economically optimal course of action is stacking shelves. Emotionally it may be difficult to change direction as you may be reluctant to 'waste' the £30,000 invested in the shop even though that investment is plainly irrelevant because the real choice is between earning £200 a week or £350. Even so, research by behavioural scientists has consistently shown that we dislike wasting things or even appearing to be wasteful. For instance, imagine that in your fridge you have two 'takeaway' dinners. Both have reached their 'use-by' date. The dinners are identical except that one cost £8 and the other was bought on special offer for £5. Which meal do you eat?

Logically it makes no difference which meal you choose but behavioural scientists discovered that some people chose the more expensive meal because it seemed less wasteful (Arkes 1996, Arkes and Blumer 1985). Research has likewise shown that the more we pay for a theatre ticket the more likely we are to use it (Arkes and Blumer 1985). In addition, the closer we are to finishing a project and particularly if a large portion of the budget has been spent, the more likely we are to finish it – regardless of whether completion makes economic sense (for example, Garland 1990, Conlon and Garland 1993, Boehne and Pease 2000, Moon 2001a).

It is not just money that gets 'sunk'. Time, effort and emotional energy are also sunk costs. Research into prices paid on E-Bay shows that sellers who start from low bids and avoid reserve prices tend to attract higher final bids than those who impose reserve prices (Ku, Galinsky and Murnigham 2006). We can infer from this study that early bidders are likely to outbid late entrants because of all the time and effort already invested in the auction. (The experiment also poses an interesting dilemma for sellers. Dispensing with reserve prices means they will probably achieve a higher price. The risk is being forced to sell cheaply if bidders are scarce.)

DEADLY COCKTAIL: SUNK COSTS AND OVER-OPTIMISM

The existence of sunk costs can undermine decision-makers' judgement in other ways. Consider the following scenario:

> As president of an airline company you have invested 10 million dollars of the company's money into a research project. The purpose was to build a plane that would not be detected by conventional radar, in other words a radar-blank plane. When the project is 90 per cent completed, another firm begins to make a plane that cannot be detected by radar. Also, it is apparent that their plane is much faster and far more economical than the plane your company is building. (Arkes and Hutzel 2000: 295; original experiments reported in Arkes and Blumer 1985)

If you were asked to tick on a scale of 1 to 100 the plane's chances of financial success, what would your estimate be?

Now suppose construction on the plane had not actually begun. No sunk costs, in other words. How would that affect your estimate? When the experiment was tried, researchers found that estimates were more optimistic if construction had actually started (Arkes and Hutzel 2000). Was this because:

a)   sunk costs produce over-optimism that in turn encourages additional investment, or
b)   reluctance to forgo sunk costs drives reinvestment and subsequent over-optimism, or
c)   do sunk costs simultaneously prompt reinvestment and over-optimism?

In other words, is over-optimism a *cause* or a *consequence* of the sunk cost effect, or *both*?

A further study based on an elaboration of the aeroplane experiment suggests that proposition (b) reflects the causal chain. That is, sunk costs prompt reinvestment and reinvestment then produces increased optimism. This discovery is consistent with dissonance theory in that inflating estimates of success can enable decision-makers to rationalize reinvestment in a questionable venture. Alternatively (or perhaps additionally) reinvestment could be an exercise in impression management whereby decision-makers reinvest in order to conceal failure (Arkes and Hutzel 2000: 295).

Risk-Seeking Behaviour: Impact of Framing

Another influential theory of escalation is that it is driven by how decisions are expressed (framed), that is, positively or negatively (Bazerman 1984, Whyte 1986). A negatively framed decision involves choosing between losses, specifically where the decision-maker is faced with a choice between either:

a)   accepting a definite loss now, or
b)   avoiding that loss but at the risk of subsequently incurring a much greater one.

Prospect theory predicts that when decisions are expressed as a choice between losses, decision-makers tend to become risk-seeking (Kahneman and Tversky 1979). To be risk-seeking is to take a bigger risk than objective conditions warrant. In the context of the present study that means selecting option (b). For instance, imagine you have lost £95 in failed bets during a day at the races. You have just £5 left. Do you place it on the favourite running at odds of three-to-one or on a twenty-to-one 'long shot'? Many people would be attracted to the 'long shot' because it offers a slim chance of recouping earlier losses. Indeed, most betting on long shots occurs during the last race (Bazerman 2004). The choice is risk-seeking because whereas betting on the favourite means we might emerge with £15, betting on the 'long shot' means we will probably lose everything.

Prospect theory was developed to explain decisions involving clear cut choices with defined mathematical probabilities. Yet it may be relevant to more amorphous domains such as Coca Cola's disastrous decision to change its winning formula. The decision was taken because Coke's market share had been declining. 'You can extrapolate that out and end up with zilch,' said Roberto Goizueta, Coke's president and Chief Operating Officer (Whyte citing Caminiti 1987: 48). Likewise, the fatal decision to launch Challenger in 1986 in risky conditions allegedly turned partly upon NASA's fear of losing funding if it failed to deliver (Whyte 1993). More recently, accountants Arthur Andersen may have been dragged down with Enron – the collapsed US energy firm, through making trivial concessions in year one, slightly more far-reaching concessions in year two and so on. It would therefore have become progressively harder to 'blow the whistle' on Enron because it would result in ignominy whereas, by staying quiet, those transgressions might never come to light.

Likewise, when a business falters decision-makers may see themselves as faced with a choice between losses. Do they close the business here and now and accept the loss of income, employment, prestige and so forth, or do they keep putting money into it, and perhaps pull through, but at the risk of compounding the problem? Like betting on the long shot, the temptation is to persist because subsequent investments represent opportunities to recover prior losses (for example, Arkes and Blumer 1985, Whyte 1986, Garland and Newport 1991, Northcraft and Neale 1986, Schaubroeck and Davis 1994).

Proponents of prospect theory argue that participants who reinvested in experiments like Staw's (1976) may simply have been reacting to how the problem was expressed (Bazerman 1984, Whyte 1986). We will return to this issue later in this book. Here we need only note that it is an important debate because prospect theory implies that decision-makers can learn to make better decisions simply by reframing the problem – much easier than getting them to ignore sunk costs and disregard fear of failure.

FOR BETTER OR WORSE: MODERATING AND HEIGHTENING FACTORS

So far we have considered what are thought to be the main escalation drivers. Later in this book we consider what might heighten decision-makers' propensity to escalation and what factors might reduce it. Meanwhile, just to give a flavour of the research, escalation is thought to be lessened if decision-makers have alternative investment opportunities (Aspinwall and Richter 1999, McCain 1986, Karlsson, Gärling and Bonini 2005) and/or if they keep careful records of expenses and/or set limits on their involvement and identify quitting points (Heath 1995; see also Simonson and Staw 1992, Tan and Yates 1995).

Evidently anxiety heightens escalation but not, interestingly, depression (Moon et al. 2003). Moreover, research tentatively suggests that decision-makers with high risk-taking propensity may be prone to escalation whereas decision-makers who dislike risk may be liable to err in the opposite direction and shun risks that they would be well advised to take (Sitkin and Pablo 1992, Sitkin and Weingart 1995, Wong 2005). People who are generally optimistic and/or who have high-self esteem and a strong belief in their abilities are more likely to persist with a potentially hopeless endeavour than people who lack these personality characteristics (Aspinwall and Richter 1999, Zhang and Baumeister 2006, Whyte, Saks and Hook 1997). Presumably this is because people who exhibit those characteristics find it hard to believe that they can fail.

In addition, more recent research suggests beleaguered decision-makers may look forward as well as backwards. Moreover, in looking forward and planning for the future, they may be reluctant to do something they will subsequently regret. Regret is defined as 'an emotion that we experience when realizing or imagining that our present situation would have been better had we decided differently' (Wong and Kwong 2007: 545 citing Zeelenberg). For example, we may experience regret if we decide against buying something and then change our minds only to discover price has gone up. It is thought that people are regret averse. We may therefore try to avoid selecting options that might induce regret. Since closing down a business is usually a virtually irreversible step, decision-makers may avoid taking it because of anticipated regret.

Conflicting Theories

ESCALATION AS A NORMAL BUSINESS EXPENSE

Recall that escalation refers to persistence beyond a rationally defensible point. Economists argue that behavioural theorists exaggerate human irrationality. More specifically, decision dilemma theorists argue that escalation is driven by uncertainty (see especially Bowen 1987; also Camerer and Weber 1999, Bragger et al. 1998). The argument is that in the real world it may take a long time for it to become plainly apparent that a venture has well and truly failed. Although, strictly speaking, decision-makers should invest resources only where marginal revenues exceed marginal costs, in practice this precept can be difficult to follow because much may depend on medium to long-term outcomes. For instance, for many years Woolworths depended upon Christmas takings to sustain them for the remaining 'kipper months'. It was only when Christmas takings dropped that business finally became non-viable. Besides, reinvestment may be defensible in order to give the venture every chance of success. In this view escalation is merely a 'real life' mistake made amidst the fog of war (Funder 1987) and should be seen not as a psychological aberration but as a normal business expense.

OCKHAM'S RAZOR

> *What can be accounted for by fewer assumptions is explained in vain by more. (William of Ockham [c. 1280–1349]) (Moody 1974: 143)*

Theories exist at the mercy of Ockham's razor – also known as the principle of parsimony which states that simple explanations are preferable to complex ones. Decision dilemma theorists acknowledge that psychological and social factors may influence decisions. Their argument, however, is that since feedback is almost invariably equivocal to some extent, social and psychological theories are redundant because persistence can be explained by uncertainty (Bowen 1987).

Indeed, research has shown that decision-makers do not always respond to negative feedback by escalating their commitment (for example, Jeffrey 1992, Singer and Singer 1985, Staw and Fox 1977). To be more precise, part of the corpus of the escalation literature suggests that decision-makers learn quickly from their mistakes. If a venture fails to turn out as expect, they may reinvest initially but then quit if reinvestment does not produce the desired results.

Most escalation experiments have been conducted with undergraduates with little or no business experience. Studies that have been conducted with professionals as participants show less of a tendency to escalate (for example, Jeffrey 1992, Garland, Sandefur and Rogers 1990). For instance, the chances of finding oil decline with each dry well encountered. In other words, exploration represents, 'A series of investment decisions made with decreasing uncertainty' (Garland, Sandefur and Rogers 1990). Explorers thus confront an interesting situation. Whenever they decide to drill another well, they incur further sunk costs knowing that the likelihood of success is not increasing but decreasing. When professional geologists were recruited to participate in an experiment, Garland and colleagues found that the more dry wells encountered, the less likely it was that geologists were to authorize funds for further drilling and, contrary to sunk costs theory, the lower their estimates of striking oil. Moreover, students who have attended courses in accountancy are much less susceptible to the sunk costs error (Tan and Yates 1995). Sunk cost effects may also be reduced if participants are provided with clear information about future costs and returns (Tan and Yates 1995) – but not always. Specifically, Karlsson, Gärling and Bonini (2005) found that escalation occurred even though decision-makers' information indicated that reinvestment would not be economically beneficial.

MONEY DOWN THE DRAIN: ESCALATION IN THE PUBLIC SECTOR

A possible explanation for conflicting findings is that escalation only occurs in the public sector organizations as they are shielded from the full rigours of market forces (Camerer and Weber 1999 discuss this possibility). The public sector has certainly produced many prima facie cases of escalation. Chicago's new sewer system was meant to improve the city's capacity to handle major storms. After repeated postponements amidst spiralling costs journalists dubbed the project 'Money down the drain'. More recently, a report on defence procurement in the UK noted that:

> There has been a long list of defence equipment projects that have experienced severe problems in terms of cost overruns and time slippage, including Eurofighter Typhoon, Astute submarines and Nimrod MRA4 aircraft. … Our armed forces in Afghanistan and Iraq desperately need heavy lift helicopters, yet eight such helicopters are sitting in hangars … and no one can tell us when they will be operational. (Defence Procurement 2006: 25 bold removed)

Indeed, the small handful of empirical studies of runaway projects strongly suggests that decisions in public sector organizations are not always determined by economic rationality alone. For example, the Canadian government agreed to host the international trade fair named 'Expo 86' only on the understanding that the venture would at least break even. It was an optimistic prognostication to begin with as trade fairs habitually lose money. For instance, in 1963 the projected loss for 'Expo 67' was $47 million but the final deficit was over six times this amount. As 'Expo 86' got underway and costs mounted well beyond initial estimates, the government considered cancelling the venture but were dissuaded partly by external stakeholders who had built hotels and made other large investments in anticipation of the fair being held, but also by the prospect of public humiliation (Ross and Staw 1986). The London 2012 Olympics are already well over budget but there is not even a question of cancelling the project.

'A YEAR HAS GONE BY': ESCALATION IN THE PRIVATE SECTOR

Yet the private sector is by no means immune from escalation. For instance, between 1991 and 1993 firms in the City of London invested over £400 million in TAURUS, an IT project intended to transport London out of the quill-pen era by enabling real-time settlement of securities transactions. After years of argument, a compromise was finally reached whereby the disparate needs of all stakeholders, banks, retail brokers, custodians, registrars and so forth were combined to create a hugely complex design. Complex designs are much more difficult to build than simple ones – particularly when people keep adding to them. Eighteen months into construction, there were doubts about whether TAURUS would ever be finished and, if it was, whether it would work. Former Chief Executive of the Stock Exchange Peter Rawlins said, 'The boys were having trouble with the technology … the regulations were getting more and more complex … requirements being built which were nothing to do with the original specification …' (Drummond 1996: 114).

Instead of cancelling TAURUS there and then, the Stock Exchange (with the support of the City) persisted for another 18 fruitless months. A member of the monitoring group said, 'I think they (the project team) were just optimistic and couldn't believe that it wouldn't work. They believed they knew how to make it work but it would just take longer and cost a bit more' (Drummond 1996: 141).

Eventually the monitoring group lost patience:

> Twelve meetings. A year has gone by and you said at the end of these twelve months, 'We haven't really made a hell of a lot of progress.' And at the end of eighteen months, 'We haven't made any progress at all.' And that is when we decided to do something. (Drummond 1996: 143)

That 'something' was to cancel the project and start again.

ESCALATION AND ENTREPRENEURS

Employees are agents. Agents are accountable; that is, they expect, at some time in the future, to be called upon to justify their actions to other people. Agents may well have nothing to lose by reinvesting in failing ventures because the organization bears the cost (Fox and Staw 1979 discuss this point). Logically we might expect entrepreneurs to be the last people to indulge in potentially destructive escalation precisely because, as principals, they would only harm themselves by doing so. Yet part of the corpus of the literature on new venture creation and outcomes argues that entrepreneurs are actually *more* prone to escalation than salaried employees because the emotional stakes are higher:

The motivation for managing one's own business is not simply personal profit; it also includes
... the need to prove oneself ... For members of a family business, the firm may not only be a
source of income but also a context for family activity and the embodiment of family pride and
identity. (Shepherd 2003: 319)

In other words, in practice, entrepreneurs may not see themselves as responsible only to themselves. Furthermore, such is the emotional significance of ownership that failure may be unthinkable:

It may be even more difficult for entrepreneurs than others to face the ridicule and loss of face
that can stem from admitting they were wrong in the first place; this would be especially true
with respect to bitter recriminations from friends, family and early backers- people who bought
into the entrepreneur's dreams and now find that these have crumbled. (Baron 1998: 228)

The very small corpus of empirical evidence is conflicting. McCarthy, Schoorman and Cooper (1993) found that entrepreneurs are more likely to sell businesses they have bought than businesses they started themselves even though they would be better off financially selling their start-ups. We can infer from this study that entrepreneurs are reluctant to forgo all the time and effort invested in starting and growing the business even though it would pay them to do so. Likewise, owners of dying businesses may exacerbate their financial problems by clinging to the trappings of status. For example, a sole principal solicitor insisted upon retaining a secretary even though there was hardly any work for her: 'I could do the work myself,' he said, 'but whoever heard of it?' (Drummond and Chell 2002: 212).

The owner of a hairdressing salon who hired a tardy assistant soon realized his mistake:

Say she (the employee) had an appointment at mid-day and somebody walked in the door at
quarter to [twelve] and said, 'Could I have my hair cut?' she'd say, 'We-ll, I have got someone
coming in shortly.' Then [the midday appointment] would come in at ten past [twelve], so she'd
spent the last 25 minutes doing nothing. (Drummond 1997: 104 owner speaking)

After six months, things were no better:

We actually looked at the hours worked, and for the eight hour day she was working four hours.
She said, 'Well I can't drag those [customers] off the streets can I?' I said, 'No, but when they
do come in you could leap up and be a bit more excited ... give them a card with your name on
it and say you look forward to seeing them again.' She said, 'Oh I don't agree with all that.'
(Drummond 1997: 105 owner speaking)

To make matters worse, the assistant was not a talented hairdresser and there were many complaints from customers. Yet the owner persisted with the appointment for over a year before finally dismissing the employee.

Yet owners may promptly reverse decisions if something important is threatened. Christine, a successful solicitor, decided to form a partnership with two other colleagues. Alarm bells sounded as early as day one, when Christine's new partners treated themselves to a long champagne lunch. Christine said:

It was my practice. These people were out at my expense ... time that they should have been in the office ... You would have thought that on day one they would have been very keen ... getting things sorted out. (Drummond 1995: 270)

Nor was it to be an isolated incident. Christine said:

As days went by my bookkeeper ... never seemed to find any of them there. People used to phone up and say I can't get a reply from your office in –. This is at three-thirty in the afternoon. (Drummond 1995: 271)

The crisis came when a solicitor from another practice threatened to report Christine to the Law Society. Christine said, 'I thought if I don't do something quickly, I am going to lose everything' (Drummond 1995: 272). Christine summoned her partners and sacked them on the spot. The arrangement had lasted barely six weeks.

DOUBTS RESOLVED?

In 1999 behavioural economists Colin Camerer and Roberto Weber re-analysed Staw and Hoang's (1995) aforementioned team-selection study using more rigorous controls. To paraphrase the authors, their intention was to show that escalation is neither common nor suboptimal. That is:

- escalation theorists exaggerate the problem of irrational persistence, and
- in so far as decision-makers do escalate their commitment, persistence is *not* primarily driven by self-justification motives.

The result was something of a surprise; that is, although the effects were weaker than those observed in the original study, nevertheless, Camerer and Weber found evidence of irrational escalation of commitment.

Aims of the Research

What emerges from this sketch of the literature is that it is unclear whether and to what extent escalation is simply a fact of life, and whether and to what extent it reflects systematic errors of judgement. It is an important question because if escalation is an unavoidable business expense then there is little that can be done about it. On the other hand if escalation does reflect systematic errors of judgement, decision-makers can learn to make better, that is, more economically rational decisions.

Emphatically, decision dilemma theorists accept that irrational influences may be present – an observation borne out by Camerer and Weber's (1999) aforementioned rigorous re-analysis of Staw and Hoang's (1995) mathematical field experiment. Decision dilemma theorists simply say that a parsimonious theory of escalation does not require mention of social and psychological pressures because uncertainty constitutes the overarching reason for persistence. The question is not whether emotional influences are present but what are those influences and what role do they play?

Self-justification theory has attracted most attention from behavioural scientists but critical reviews of the literature (for example, Sandelands, Brockner and Glynn 1988, Brockner 1992, Staw 1997) strongly suggest that the need to protect one's ego is by no means the whole story. For example, Sitkin and Pablo (1992) argue that risk propensity should be at the forefront of escalation research. Besides, we cannot assume that escalation scenarios are characterized by a single pressure to persist or that the pressures are all in the same direction. Decision-makers may be beset by multiple and conflicting forces, some making for persistence, others making for withdrawal.

The role of theory is to not just to explain why escalation happens but also to predict where and when is escalation most likely to happen, who is most susceptible to escalation and how escalation scenarios unfold (Bacharach 1989, Dubin 1976, Glaser and Strauss 1968, Suddaby 2006 and Sutton and Staw 1995 discuss theory-building). We know comparatively little about those conditions. Moreover, some of the evidence is conflicting. For example, contrary to what was suggested earlier, the availability of alternative investment opportunities does not always curb escalation (for example, Staw and Fox 1977).

Conflicting findings may owe something to the fact that most escalation research is based upon experiments. Experiments have many advantages, not least that they facilitate tight control over the variables studied. Those advantages come at a price, however. Experiments are artificial. They involve clear-cut decisions and forced choices whereas in reality decision-makers confront situations that are ill-structured and ill-defined. Moreover, it is one thing to tick a box and quite another to actually close down a real venture. Experiments, moreover, are open to interpretation. For instance, Staw and Fox (1977) may have found no effects for alternatives because the alternatives were not clearly specified. Participants were simply told that if they did not reinvest in the project funds would simply be returned to the company. Did participants see this option as an alternative investment opportunity?

The present study proposes to take conflicting findings as given. More specifically, the aim is to use multiple case studies to explore a wide range of issues. Unlike experiments, case studies allow researchers to probe multiple possibilities and to consider potential interactions between variables using extant theory as a guide for what to look for whilst being open to new possibilities.

Research Questions

Strictly speaking, case studies cannot test a theory. Case study research can, however, explore whether and to what extent a theory is relevant and useful. More specifically, the research questions are:

1. How does escalation start?
2. What drives escalation?
3. How are escalation predicaments experienced?
4. How are escalation predicaments finally resolved?

Question one explores why decision-makers embark upon ventures which, to any outside observer, seem to have little prospect of success. More specifically, what makes new owners believe they can succeed when the odds are plainly stacked against them?

Question two explores the driving forces for escalation. Do owners pour resources into failing ventures in the foolhardy manner implied by escalation theory, or is their response more nuanced and subtle? Moreover, to what extant are the factors thought to mitigate escalation relevant? For example, do owners who set limits and quitting points make better, that is, more economically rational decisions than owners who drift along? Question three focuses upon how owners perceive economic feedback. For instance, how do they recognize that the business is failing? How do they react to feedback that is intermittently bad and good? No one can reinvest in failing business indefinitely. Sooner or later owners have to stop. If they quit sooner rather than later, they may at least mitigate the damage and may even be able to salvage something from the situation. Question four focuses upon what is needed to persuade owners to give up and what may dissuade them from doing so.

Summary

Escalation refers to an active decision to reinvest in a failing venture beyond an economically defensible point – for example, when marginal costs consistently exceed marginal revenues. There are four main theories of escalation. Self-enhancement theory refers to the pursuit of self-esteem and audience effects. Sunk costs theory refers to emotional attachment to past investments of time, money and emotional energy. These investments may not be sunk psychologically. Prospect theory refers to risk-seeking behaviour arising from how decisions are expressed (framed). Decision dilemma theorists predict that escalation reflects uncertainty, namely the time it takes for failure to become well and truly apparent. Empirical evidence for these theories is conflicting. The present study aims to shed light on this conflict by conducting multiple case studies examining why escalation occurs, and also to explore the boundary conditions that heighten or lessen the effects.

2 *Shutters Up: A Walk Round the Market*

Where the ragged people go,
Looking for the places only they would know.

(The Boxer, Simon and Garfunkel)

Markets are covered places, indoors and outdoors, where people meet to buy and sell provisions (*Oxford Concise Dictionary*). Markets date back to antiquity. The market of Kirkby Stephen in Cumbria, for example, was established by a charter granted by King Edward III. Old regulations stipulate that:

For every bushel (Customary Measure) of potatoes exposed for Sale in the Market. One Toll-Dishful.

For each Person exhibiting Implements the Sum of Sixpence & upwards according to the space occupied.

For every Basket of Poultry or Fruit the sum of 1d per basket.

The Market Committee to Rule & Decide as to the size, position and fixing of Stall, Booth, Caravan or Space occupied in the Market Place and in the Streets and to have Full Control of all arrangements of the said Market.

There were also tolls for wholesale, sixpence for each horse sold, four-pence for all sheep except rams; carts laden with merchandise were required to pay a passage toll of one penny.

Markets have cradled many successful entrepreneurs. The supermarket chain Morrisons grew from a Bradford market stall owned by William Morrison, father of Sir Ken Morrison, former chairman of the supermarket chain. Sir Alan Sugar made money by boiling beetroot and selling it from a market stall. The most famous example is Michael Marks, founder of the retail chain Marks and Spencer. A near-penniless Russian émigré, Marks started as an itinerant peddler, travelling around villages in the vicinity of Leeds, exposing for sale buttons, mending wools, pins, needles, tapes, table cloths, socks and stockings, carried on a tray bearing a notice 'Don't ask the price, it's a penny'– a successful strategy, albeit driven by Mark's uncertain command of English. In 1884 Marks graduated to a small trestle table on Leeds outdoor market. He soon acquired a stall indoors which he named the 'Penny Bazaar'. The business prospered enabling Marks to expand into markets in other towns and ultimately to open a succession of shops.

'It's the Outdoor Market People Come to See': Getting a Stall

The easiest way for a would-be trader to start is on the outdoor market. Markets are controlled by local councils. Procedures for obtaining a stall vary but on the outdoor market the emphasis is usually on minimal formality. New traders may need to present themselves at the market office early in the morning, as vacant stalls are typically allocated on a 'first-come, first-served' basis. Rents are paid in advance, the precise sum depending on the location of the stall and the day of the week. A stall in a prime spot on one the bigger city markets on a Friday or Saturday can cost £30 or £40 to rent for the day. On a Monday or a Tuesday it might be £20 – half that sum for a stall in a 'tucked away' location. The small borough markets are cheaper – stalls costing as little as £6 or £7, even on a Saturday. After serving a qualifying period, usually three or four weeks, an outdoor trader becomes eligible for a permanent pitch – provided they continue to trade regularly.

Outdoor stalls are at a premium near Christmas. Not so the rest of the year. Stalls often stand empty, particularly in winter, even on a Saturday. It is depressing for other traders because without competition there is no market. Moreover, outdoor markets act as a magnet for the indoor market; 'It's the outdoor market people come to see,' said a trader, 'not the indoor.'

Outdoor traders comprise amateurs and professionals. Amateurs tend to trade on the quieter weekdays and Sunday markets. They typically deal in second-hand goods, selling for a hobby. Amateurs are easy to spot by the untidiness of their displays. Professionals work markets to make money – sometimes travelling hundreds of miles, sleeping rough and working seven days a week.

Life on the outdoor market is hard. Stock has to be unloaded from vans, transported to the stall, unpacked, displayed and reloaded at night and driven away. Market regulations typically require traders to stay at their pitch until closing time at 5.30. The rule is not always scrupulously observed. 'Packing up time' typically starts around 4 o'clock but it is often earlier, particularly if trade is quiet. Then there is the sheer discomfort of standing out all day and in all weathers.

'People Trust You More': Graduating Indoors

Like Michael Marks, many outdoor traders aspire to a stall on the indoor market. Rents are higher but so are the prices that traders can charge. A shoe seller said, 'People won't pay £30 for a pair of boots on the outdoor market. They don't trust you. They think that because you're on the outside, you're like here today, gone tomorrow.'

When stalls were like gold dust there was nothing for it but to wait until death or retirement resulted in a lease being offered for sale. A successful trader might own more than one stall on a market and even stalls in different towns. Renting indoors involves much more of a commitment and financial risk than working the outdoor market. Applicants may have to undergo credit checks, supply business plans and sign a lease. Leases may require exiting traders to give up to six months notice – albeit in return for security of tenure. Short leases requiring only a fortnight's notice are sometimes available – the corollary being no security of tenure. Indoor traders must also pay business rates and service charges. These can be almost a high as the rent. There will also be electricity bills plus other normal business expenses.

Prospective traders may have to specify exactly what they intend to sell. They may also discover that they are not allowed to vary their stock-in-trade without express permission. Traders spy upon one another. For instance, a trader who gave a red rose to customers buying a bottle of scent on Valentine's day was promptly reported upon and stopped. Applying for permission takes time, as notices have to be posted and applications may be routed through a committee. It can cost up to £200 and there is no guarantee of success.

Segregation may apply. For example, on the bigger markets, no two sellers of clothing or fruit may be located next to one another. Existing traders may also have the right to object to new tenants. Newcomers may thus be refused entry, or forced to compromise on location – sometimes with dire consequences.

Market bye-laws may be ancient, but most are commonsense. For instance, it seems reasonable to insist that anyone riding an animal (or vehicle) into the market must not exceed 5 mph and that every person using a water tap to cause the same to be turned off immediately after they have finished. More irksome are the rules relating to space. Traders may not place boxes, hampers or other articles on the roof of their stall or permit goods or receptacles to project beyond the limits of a stall. The last rule is not always scrupulously observed as traders sometimes commandeer empty stalls to extend their displays. If instructed to remove the offending articles, traders usually regard it as a 'fair cop'. Yet the rule can cause bitterness, for example, when a greengrocer is prosecuted for permitting a box of grapefruit to jut out a few inches.

'I DON'T OWE ANYBODY "OWT"'

There is no compulsory retirement age on markets. 'My mother was 86 when she died,' said a trader. 'She worked in here on the Saturday and died on the Sunday.'

Ada, aged 84, occupies a tiny pitch comprising a box that serves as a makeshift counter and a store plus a chair. She sells only three items, scouring pads, dish cloths and candles. With her money bag strapped to her, her walking stick close by, Ada calls out her wares. She has yet to be prosecuted for contravening the bye-laws. Other traders bring her cups of coffee. 'Does marvellous for her age,' said one.

H.D.: Why do you keep working?

Ada: Better than sitting at home, looking at four walls.

At Christmas time Ada also sells wrapping paper. 'I don't know if I shall bother this year,' she said, 'there's that many of them doing it.'

Although Ada's wares are limited, she attracts a steady trickle of customers who pass the time of day in conversation with her – though whether they actually need all the scouring pads and dishcloths they buy from her is uncertain.

Ada paid £150 a month for that tiny pitch. 'I don't owe anybody owt,' she said, displaying her rent book with its immaculate collection of receipts.

It is a claim that many market traders would envy.

'Ticked Off': Market Discipline

'Gone to take the rubbish out,' reads a notice on a stall in the indoor market, 'back in five minutes.'

As the notice implies, some indoor markets are rigorously regulated. Daily attendance and punctilious timekeeping are often strict condition of tenancy. Offenders (those not back in five minutes) may be liable to prosecution.

On some markets, inspectors take a register of attendance, morning and evening, literally 'ticking people off' – a practice that is frequently resented. A trader said: 'When you've stood there from 9 till 11 with hardly a customer, you feel like banging their clipboards over their heads.'

Yet things are not always what they seem to be. Owners conspire to thwart officialdom. For instance, if a trader wants to leave early they may leave the keys with a neighbour who will pull the shutters up just before the evening inspection to make it look as if the unit is open for business.

Today Michael Marks would be prosecuted, as waving rattles and open outcry are forbidden on most markets. Again, the rules are sometimes flouted, particularly on Saturdays as butchers and greengrocers vie with one another to clear stock. Rattles may be forbidden but not (apparently) the 'ghetto blasters' – used by some traders to attract attention by playing loud music. Gone too are 'fly sellers', the unlicensed street sellers who once hovered furtively on the fringe of markets, paying no rent, hawking handkerchiefs and socks from brown suitcases anxious to be gone 'before the Bobby [police officer] comes back from his breakfast'.

Ripping Off Arms and Legs: Tricks of the Trade

Legislation supported by Trading Standards Officers has stamped out the more blatantly dangerous or dishonest practices on markets. Gone are the days of shivering puppies offered for sale on outdoor markets and sheep's heads sold from under the counter. Flimsy plastic toys made in Japan 'batteries not included' have passed into history. So too has the practice known as 'nip and tuck' whereby butchers manipulated scales to give short weight or sold customers non-existent packets of stuffing:

> For years ... on his glass counter top he [a butcher] would have packets of sage and onion stuffing. A customer came in for several items, he's jotting them down with his pencil on a piece of paper, there might be four items – and he always used to add on a packet of sage and onion stuffing. Let's say it was 30p – he'd add it up – say 'That'll be £6.54. And they'd go away and never, never quibble. If they came back saying 'You've overcharged me 30p,' he'd say, 'Oh I am sorry. I thought you wanted a packet of stuffing ... '
>
> He'd covered himself – so 30p! I don't know how many people he cheated! (A market trader)

Yet regulation still has some way to go. Some butcher's offer 'English leg' and 'English shoulder' leading the unsuspecting customer to think they are buying lamb. It is actually a crafty way of selling mutton. On Christmas Eve, poultry dealers offer turkeys at a 'tenner' each 'to clear them up now' implying a bargain. Yet the same birds were on sale cheaper earlier in the day! 'They're fly those lads,' said a trader, 'they knock a pound off and put two on!'

What clothes stall would not be offering goods at 'Right Quality: Right Price – When Only the Best Will Do'? Very little fruit is offered for sale that is not described as 'Class 1: Sugar Sweet' – regardless of progeny. Sometimes customers are allowed to pick their own fruit and vegetables but those stalls are in a minority. The rule is still *caveat emptor!* Unwary customers may discover that the apples they receive may bear little resemblance to the shiny specimens displayed at the front of the stall. More seriously, markets are the place for 'knock offs' (counterfeit goods). Moreover, it is still possible to buy frozen 'takeaway' meals, and pies with their long expired 'use by' dates blacked out though still visible. Frozen cakes on display since early morning may be returned half-thawed to the refrigerator at closing time. Raw chickens can stand for hours on spits with no refrigeration.

Market traders have their own problems. Invoices arrive, goods don't. Not all wholesalers are trustworthy. Eggs bought in good faith as local, organic free range, turn out to be sourced from battery farms in Poland. A greengrocer may pay good money for the best strawberries, only to be swindled:

> *It's very difficult to get a consistent product in strawberries (because) it's a product that varies from plant to plant, from field to field. Out of ten pallets … you will only get three really good ones, four average ones and three poor ones. I've seen strawberry salesmen sell the same pallet of strawberries five times. You look at a palette and you say, 'I'm having that pallet … yes, that's the one, put the sticker on that pallet.'*

> *'Yes. Bang! Done!' Then when you get back to your wagon and it's loaded up, that's not the pallet you've got. That's where the mistrust comes from. (A greengrocer)*

Staff can be a headache. Seasoned traders reckon that two assistants do the work of one and three do none at all. Stealing is another problem. Traders tell stories of staff 'robbing tills blind'. 'I am convinced they were ripping off my arms and legs,' said a trader. 'In bakery there's always waste but I know what things cost [and] how many beans make five.'

All Day Sitters: Running a Market Cafe

Fancy a coffee? Market cafes may seem like cosy enterprises, but running one can be very stressful. Hours are long, as owners open early as 7 a.m. in order to catch the breakfast trade. The presence of hot plates and deep fat fryers can make it sticky work, even in winter. Customer preferences are unpredictable. Hot soup may sell better in summer than winter. The trade in baked potatoes may be inexplicably erratic; 'You never knew with baked potatoes,' said an owner.

Around two in the afternoon after the lunch time rush, there is a lull, and after about 3.30 it is usually cups of tea and coffee only, as owners dismantle and clean equipment.

The real strain is being polite to people who may not reciprocate:

It is very hard work in catering. You have to be very polite. We never cut down on food – we always give a good plateful. It's not like you nibbling (sic) and that's it finished. I make sure you have good food and plenty ... (Cafe owner)

A cup of tea made with PG Tips might cost about 60p; £1.90 will buy a bacon sandwich. A plate of chips is £1.50 – gravy costs another 10p – 'Sorry no pushchairs allowed inside.'

Much more annoying than pushchairs are the so called 'all-day sitters' – people with nowhere to go such as residents from a local care home who buy a cup of tea and try to linger all day. Cafes attract the poor and the dispossessed because they offer extra warmth and somewhere to sit. With low personal hygiene they discourage other customers and occupy tables needed for the more lucrative lunch time trade. 'It's not so bad when you aren't busy, but at lunch time paying customers walk away because there's nowhere to sit,' said an owner.

No one knew where Suzanne came from. A handsome woman, her camel-coloured raincoat lent her an air of distinction – contradicted by purple-coloured skin peeping from her heavily bandaged legs. Suzanne lived in her own house but gravitated to the market hall, alternating between the toilets (where she cut up newspaper) and a cafe counter-stool where kindly staff and customers discreetly paid for food and drinks. Sympathetic owners would leave clothes for her in a manner calculated to protect her dignity. 'If she wants them, she'll take them,' said a trader.

One day after devouring a plate of chips Suzanne wandered off. 'She's left her gloves,' said a customer.

'She'll be back before long,' said the manageress.

Suzanne is indeed back soon. It is Saturday and closing time is approaching. Suzanne is talking to herself: 'Cellar – half-past-four in the morning, snowing – door banging.'

The cafe owner interrupts her soliloquy. He reaches into the till and hands Suzanne a handful of pound coins to tide her over the weekend. 'Don't forget its Sunday tomorrow,' he said.

Shortly afterwards Suzanne was mugged. Security staff organized a taxi home for her and changed the locks on her door but Suzanne was seen less often. 'I think it was more her pride that was hurt,' said a trader. Then the cafe was sold and Suzanne banned. 'The new owner didn't want her hanging around,' said the manageress. Suzanne was last seen swigging from a miniature bottle of spirits and seeking such comfort as she could find – in an alcove.

'They Want Gold': Market Customers

'It can't be done!' shouts an exasperated haberdasher as two young Asian women challenge his prices. The cloth may or may not be sound in warp and weft but at a pound a yard (not all traders observe the law on metric measurements) he thinks it is cheap enough. 'It's not rocket science,' he shouts at the departing women.

Markets are the place for cheap mobile 'phone fascias, bingo pens at 25p each or five for £1, and greeting cards for 30p or four for a £1. Traders learn hard lessons about customer preferences. Cards must contain verse. A trader who tried to raise standards by investing in blank art deco style cards costing £1.99 each still has them. A newcomer who invested her precious capital in silver jewellery soon discovered that she had made a fundamental mistake. 'Lower working-class want gold,' she said. Even if it's the cheapest, nastiest gold they can get, *they want gold.*'

Trade is mainly in cash. Economists might say that the real test of an article's worth is the seller's willingness to buy it back. Significantly, few traders are willing to give refunds unless goods are faulty when they are legally obliged to do so. Many tell stories about customers trying to return goods, having decided, for example, that a roll of carpet cut specially to size does not suit a room or who try to return clothes having worn them:

Just before Christmas I sold a dress to somebody. I sold it for forty pound (sic). It was a Christmas dress. She had broken it. All the crystals have all come out. She had washed it. She said … the label wasn't inside … All the dresses have got labels inside with washing instructions. She want a refund!

I said, 'I'm sorry. You've worn it. You've washed it. All the crystals have come out. What do you want me to do?' I feel embarrassed to take it to the rails [return to display]. (A trader)

'Lovely Quality': The Goods

Markets have a reputation for being cheap but appearances can be deceptive. No one expects Patek-Philippe for £2.99, though that money does buy the word 'Geneva' stamped on the watch-face. Some items of doubtful utility can be enormously profitable for sellers. Toy eyepatches retailing for 99p, cost a pound for a gross (144) wholesale. 'I sometimes feel customers can read my mind and see what I bought them for,' said a trader.

An elderly woman fingers a nightdress. The owner looks up from reading a newspaper. 'Lovely quality', he says.

It is not lovely quality at all but a thin, skimpy garment, poorly stitched costing £7.99. For the same money or just a little more you can buy much better from a supermarket. In a cafe a customer orders a roast beef dinner costing £3.50. He leaves half the meat and most of the powdery mash. An assistant jerks the plate away without enquiry. Again, for just a little more money the customer could have had a pleasant meal in town. Markets cater particularly for people who do not have that extra pound or two that can make such a difference, and/or that have no access to large 'out of town' supermarkets and discount stores.

Yet there are bargains to be had. A toilet seat cover made from Chinese silk can be bought for £2.50 if one has use for it. New jeans may sell for as little as £1.99 a pair. The owner refused to disclose what he had paid for them but he did say they were surplus stock from a chain store. A condition of sale is that the buyer must take the whole carton and whatever sizes happen to be inside.

Coffee mugs of reasonable quality can be had for as little as 50p. 'I can't be doing with mucky pots,' said an elderly woman as she rummaged in her purse for change. 'You can't go wrong with these,' replied the seller.

Some traders are surly. Most are courteous and patient. Many are proud of the service they provide. The market is the place to find materials to restore a sagging settee and to seek advice on how to approach the task. Haberdashers will take pleasure in advising impoverished students on how to make a flat or a bedsit look attractive. Cancer victims suffering hair loss can buy a wig at an affordable price and receive discreet sympathetic service. A trader said, 'When people come here for a fitting they know that door is going to be locked. No one is going to walk in.'

Amateur traders add interest because of the eclectic nature of their stock – old silver cutlery (knives but no forks), plates, cut glass and old cameras jumble together. A crumbling top hat is offered for £10. A young couple buy a second-hand potato masher for 50p.

Occasionally rarities appear, such as a box of steel nibs, a heap of used postcards dating back to the 1950s; surveyors' instruments in rosewood boxes, and a spirit level, short and stumpy, with an inbuilt compass – apparently for use down a mine. A flute is offered for sale at £50. A leather wallet lies next to an old cigar box. It was once handsome, big enough to hold large notes in days when cash cards were unknown and cheques rare. Now it is torn and tattered with a sordid smell.

A pewter tray is on sale for a pound. It is heavy, presumably so that it would not flex dangerously under the weight of the tankards and glasses. The dents add to the authenticity.

Surprising how money could be made:

The (public) toilets were next to this little shellfish bar. Not that I think this was detrimental – in those days fellas used to go for a drink on a Saturday and probably when the pubs closed at 3 o'clock because they'd nowhere else to go, they'd come and eat some shell fish off a plate – waiting for the pubs to open again at half-past five. The toilet attracted them – I know it doesn't sound very nice but it worked very well. (Retired fish monger)

Was the pewter tray part of the fixtures and fittings of this long demolished market tavern? Did the wallet belong to a customer?

The little shell fish bar throve in the days when washing machines were demonstrated as novelty items on markets and when women bought work stockings at three shillings a pair (15p), and, if they had any money left at the end of the week, treated themselves to a handbag at 19s. 11d (99p). In those days a 15-year-old school leaver working on the indoor market would receive £2.50 for a week's work. In the market toilets, toilet paper holders were hung on the *outside* of the door.

Times have changed, but not that much.

CHAPTER **3** ## 'Maybe We Can Make A Go Of It': How Does Escalation Start?

We are never deceived, we deceive ourselves.

(Goethe)

Introduction

Contrary to popular business books, becoming an entrepreneur is not an easy road to riches. For example, over 80 per cent of new businesses in America collapse within two years (for example, Hmieleski and Baron 2009). What explains the high mortality rate?

It is axiomatic, and a theme of this book, that any decision involving uncertainty can fail. Opening a new business is a risky endeavour because it is a venture into the unknown. Prospective owners may have very little to go on. Moreover, even the most carefully planned and researched venture can fail. For instance, during the economic recession of 2008/2009 one of the few business models that prospered was the so called 'One Pound' shop retail franchises, selling items costing no more than a pound. Indeed the model was so successful that some supermarkets began to imitate the idea. Lee bought a franchise hoping to launch a career as an entrepreneur. Lee's reasoning was sound. 'I think people will pay if cheap. Five pound is too much for some people to pay – so I think that if I just charge one pound, people will buy,' he said.

On his first Saturday, Lee made £900 – enough to cover his rent of £500 a week and other expenses and replenish stock. Lee's success proved short-lived, however, as the novelty soon wore off. 'Now is Tuesday and people only look. They no buy. Already they ask, "When is new stock coming in?"' said Lee.

Lee made a mistake. He took a calculated risk that went wrong – bad luck, in other words. Yet according to behavioural theorists bad luck is by no means the only reason why so many businesses fail. Behavioural theorists believe that many failures could be avoided if decision-makers behaved more sensibly. Instead, say behavioural theorists, entrepreneurs invite failure by embarking upon poorly appraised ventures that any objective bystander can plainly see have little hope of success.

Indeed, although all new business ventures are risky, indoor market traders face a particularly challenging situation with long established traders closing down, others barely viable and new traders measuring their tenure in months and sometimes only weeks. Assuming no one sets up business expecting to fail, what makes owners believe they can succeed when the odds are so clearly stacked against them?

The remainder of this chapter is structured as follows. It begins with a case study of an extremely short-lived lived venture. The case is then analysed. This is followed by three more case studies of failures (and one vignette), again interspersed with analysis. Escalation research is like building a mosaic (Weick 1989 discusses this point). Each case adds a piece of insight that contributes towards the bigger picture. The chapter ends with a summary of the key findings.

Magic Thinking

DOING A RUNNER: DAVID AND THE VEGAN CAFE

David was a lorry driver. He left his job when the firm was sold and the new owners required him to make trips abroad. David decided to invest his life savings to open a vegan cafe – having discovered a gap in the market. 'I am a vegan and if you try to get a sandwich up in town there is nothing but cheese,' said David.

It was David's first foray into business. He gravitated to the market because the rent was relatively cheap. The premises were located in a quiet section of the market, modestly but adequately equipped with a few cheap trestle tables and folding wooden chair, plastic table cloths and a cheap music player. The first interview took place on a Monday lunch time in early December when David had been in business for only a week. The premises were empty. It did not seem hopeful even with the prospect of Christmas trade.

H.D.: How long will you be able to give to it for it to take off?

David: Till Tuesday!

Although David was joking, his resources were slim as he had used most of his savings to buy the fixtures and fittings. The second interview took place in mid-January. It was Friday lunch time. Again, the cafe was empty. By now, time was running out. David said:

Another month of this and I shall be struggling. There is a window of about three hours every day when we're busy but its cups of tea and teacakes – things like that. There's loads of vegan's in [the town] but people haven't flocked here in droves as I thought they would. Maybe it's the music that's putting them off!

H.D.: What will you do if it doesn't pick up?

David: I shall have to think about doing a runner.

We never saw David again. Three weeks later the shutters were down. Our first thought was that David might just be absent for the day but peering through the gap in the shutters we saw the fixtures and fittings were gone. The owner of a neighbouring stall confirmed that the premises had been vacated about 10 days before. Empty space was all that was left of one man's life savings.

THE ILLUSION OF CONTROL: ANALYSIS OF DAVID'S STORY

David's story is short but instructive. Recall that the focal question is why new owners believe they can succeed despite objective indicators to the contrary. The first point to establish is what those objective indicators were. David had indeed spotted a gap in the market. There were few wholefood sandwich bars in town. It is axiomatic, however, that consumers value their time. As Tim Harford (2007 Ch. 1) observes in his exposition 'The Undercover Economist', chains like Starbucks charge premium prices for coffee not because the rent is expensive but because they are ideally situated on consumers 'desire line'. The same coffee can be obtained round the corner for half the price but it means walking five minutes. Commuter's rushing to their offices, intent upon obtaining their caffeine fix, value time above money.

In David's case the 'hordes' are half a mile away in the town's main business quarter. Who is going to make a round trip of a mile for a lunch-time sandwich? Given the unfavourable location, the best David could hope for was that the business would grow as hungry vegans discovered his existence and that his food would be sufficiently compelling that people would go out of their way to buy it. Inevitably that would take time, if it happened at all. David's resources were insufficient to sustain him beyond a few weeks so the decision to venture into business was a huge gamble, particularly given the significance of the resources invested. This was not spare cash burning a hole in David's pocket but his life savings. Why did David take that risk?

Behavioural scientists believe that as human beings, we are over-confident to begin with (Langer 1975, 1983, Taylor 1980, Taylor and Brown 1988). The overconfidence trap refers to our innate tendency as human beings to overestimate our ability to control events and achieve uncertain outcomes – known as the illusion of control. (Illusion means seeing things as better than they are. Delusion means seeing things that are not there at all.) According to Taylor we are all too optimistic, forever believing that things will work out fine in the end regardless of the facts and forever overestimating our ability to achieve outcomes. Indeed, says Taylor, depression is not seeing things as worse than they are, but as they are! Taylor cites the daily 'to do' list as an anecdotal example of the illusion of control. Taylor notes that every time we compile a list, we almost invariably overestimate what we can accomplish in a day. Not that that ever stops from compiling lists! More importantly, empirical studies of gambling behaviour reveal that players often fall silent for a few seconds before throwing the dice then shaking softly if needing a low number on the dice, and vigorously when needing a high number – as if they can command fate by sheer concentration and will (Langer 1975, 1983). Overconfidence may be heightened when decisions involve skill as well as luck. This is because the exercise of skill imparts a sense of control, and feeling in control encourages risk-taking. For example, players tend to bet more if they are allowed to deal the cards (Griffiths 1990).

More precisely, optimism refers to an expectation of positive outcomes (Scheier et al. 2001). Overly optimistic people tend to hold unrealistic expectations, and discount negative information. Extremely optimistic individuals also tend to set unrealistically high goals and expect to attain them (see Hmieleski and Baron 2009 for a recent review of the literature).

Optimism and entrepreneurs

It is perhaps hardly surprising that entrepreneurs tend to be more even optimistic than the general population (Hmieleski and Baron 2009). They are often confident of realizing dream like ambitions even though they have no idea as to how they will actually achieve them (Scheier, Carver and Bridges 2001). To a point, optimism may be productive. If we are too grounded in reality, all too aware of the risks we would probably never venture into business in the first place. Highly optimistic individuals tend to exhibit a general level of confidence that allows them to respond enthusiastically to potentially daunting challenges, and to persist despite setbacks. For example, Richard Branson allegedly dispensed with expert analysis and advice when planning his aviation business because he knew that the answer would be 'Don't do it'.

But only to a point! As Hitler discovered when he invaded Russia, troops cannot fight without adequate food and clothing. Tanks are useless without fuel. Likewise, optimism will take owners only so far. It will not buy stock. Nor will it pay the rent. Indeed, Branson's optimism was tempered by realism as he was careful to de-risk his aviation venture as much as possible, for example, by leasing rather than buying planes outright. Not all entrepreneurs combine Branson's boldness with Branson's caution as over-optimism is thought to be the main reason for the high incidence of failure amongst new business start-ups (Abdelsamad and Kindling 1978, Gartner 2005).

David is a fairly extreme example of over-optimism. Extreme cases are valuable precisely because they are atypical (for example, Weick 1989). There are three fundamental mistakes a new owner can make as follows:

a) underestimate the costs of running a business,
b) overestimate revenues, and
c) underestimate the timescale for becoming profitable.

David's main mistake relates to (c), timescales. A rule of thumb in business is that it takes at least six months to a year for a new venture to become profitable. David's expectations of instant success were thus highly unrealistic even though he had spotted a gap in the market.

What explains such a high level of over-optimism? Inexperience may be a factor, yet as we shall see later in this chapter (and later in this book), experience does not guarantee immunity from error. Theories of risk-taking propensity may be relevant. Risk-taking propensity refers to our appetite for risk. It is thought that individuals with high risk-taking propensity tend to see less risk than is objectively true and vice versa (Sitkin and Pablo 1992, Sitkin and Weingart 1995). For example, owners with high risk-taking propensity are likely to pay more attention to opportunities than threats. David seems to have been imbued with high risk-taking propensity – investing his life savings in such a haphazard manner. What we do not know is what produces high risk-taking propensity in the first place.

Confronting Risk and Uncertainty

'MAYBE WE CAN MAKE A GO OF IT': FEI, BOB AND THE LUCKY DRAGON

Fei graduated abroad. Her degrees were not recognized in the UK, so she was unable to find employment that matched her qualifications. Fei therefore decided to open a business with her partner Bob. They invested about £30,000 to set up a small cafe-cum-takeaway business selling oriental food called Lucky Dragon. They rented premises on a short-term lease requiring only a fortnight's notice to quit. The premises were not their first choice as they were rather small with room for only three tables. Moreover, the location was away from the main thoroughfare. Fei and Bob decided to sign the lease, however, when the council offered them two month's rent free. 'We thought, maybe can make a go of it,' said Fei.

When Fei was first interviewed the business had been open for just two days. It was the couple's first foray into business. Bob worked as an electrical engineer and was largely a 'sleeping' partner. Fei did most of the day-to-day running of the cafe, helped by a friend. She was obviously very nervous and flustered in her new role. A customer had just returned his curry having received rice instead of chips. Fei struggled to open a metal storage cabinet and extract a large yellow-and-orange-coloured plastic bag of frozen chips. Two customers were seated at one of the tables, quietly eating with chopsticks.

The Lucky Dragon offered something new and over the next fortnight, customers began to discover it. Even so, Fei was beginning to have doubts. Previously, she and Bob had only ever visited the market on a Saturday. 'Saturday is busy,' said Fei, 'full of people.' Until they opened, they did not realize how quiet it was the rest of the week.

H.D.: What made you think you could succeed?

Fei: English people like something new and different. A lot of [oriental] places use chemicals. We cook fresh – that's why people like us.

H.D.: How long do you think it will take to build the business up?

Fei: I don't know. Maybe six months.

Fei planned to expand into selling bacon sandwiches, creating a breakfast trade. Too late she and Bob discovered that the market authorities would not allow it because another market cafe objected.

A fortnight later the business was quiet though two of the tables were occupied by diners. I asked how the business was doing. 'Location', replied Fei wistfully.

Over the next few weeks the cafe continued to attract new customers. Many of those newcomers were professionals, that is, non-traditional market customers such as social workers and health visitors attracted by the high quality, interesting and reasonably priced food. By now an exotic menu had appeared in the window supported by colourful photographs. One afternoon Fei was offering free samples of green tea. An almost empty jug of fresh orange juice suggested trade. The tables and surroundings were kept spotlessly clean as Fei applied an antiseptic wipe after every customer. Fei confirmed that business was growing but it was not enough. 'Is very quiet,' she said. 'Everyone says we will get there but.' Her voice trailed away.

Some days the business would take £100. On Saturdays, £200. 'But not good enough,' said Fei.

Fei's assessment was confirmed by a trader on the opposite side of the row. In an unsolicited comment during an informal conversation he said, 'There's a trickle of people in and out [of the Lucky Dragon] overall it's taking now't [nothing].'

Trade proved unpredictable: quiet when they expected to be busy, busy when they expected to be quiet. VAT was an unlooked-for burden. 'We're working to pay taxes,' said Bob.

There was another problem. Running a takeaway business demands gas cooking. There was a gas tap in the kitchen but only after installing the fixtures and fittings did Fei and Bob discover that it was defunct. Consequently, they were unable to produce food quickly enough. 'If people see a queue they won't wait,' said Bob. 'It's frustrating because we know the business is viable.'

H.D.: What will you do if it doesn't work out?

Bob: We would keep all this stuff [fixtures and fittings] and probably start again somewhere where there's a lot more passing trade.

The crisis came one Saturday when the cafe was extremely busy. The absence of gas caused chaos. Fei and Bob realized that even if they managed to build up enough trade, without gas, they were non-viable. 'If we get more people – cannot cope,' said Fei.

Accordingly they served a fortnight's notice and left. The venture lasted just 14 weeks.

ESCALATION AND A CRITICAL INCIDENT: ANALYSIS OF FEI AND BOB'S STORY

Although Fei and Bob did insufficient homework (saw the market only on Saturday and made unwarranted assumptions about selling bacon sandwiches), unlike David they recognized that they were taking a bigger risk than they had originally intended by compromising on location '*maybe* make a go of it' (emphasis added). That statement implies recognition of risk and uncertainty, but in this case sensibly counterbalanced by a short-term contract and rent concessions.

Contrary to escalation theory, Fei and Bob soon recognized that expectations are unlikely to be met. 'Every-one says we will get there *but* ...'. (emphasis added). The most striking feature of the case is the incident over the gas tap. It is thought that escalation may be curbed if something happens that shows beyond all doubt that persistence is hopeless. To be more precise, a critical incident is a significant occurrence, with a clear link between cause and effect (for example, Chell and Pittaway 1998: 25, Chell 1998: Ch. 3). For example, the explosion at Chernobyl destroyed the myth that nuclear power is safe and paved the way for the subsequent decommissioning of the controversial US Shoreham nuclear power station (Ross and Staw 1993; see also Drummond 1995). In the present study, the calamitously busy Saturday persuaded Fei and Bob that persistence was futile as expectations could never be met and, as decision dilemma theorists (for example, Bowen 1987, Camerer and Weber 1999) would predict, they promptly quit.

An experiment by Staw and Ross (1978) using scenarios involving major infra-structure projects found that where decision-makers could blame set-backs on external causes beyond their control such as currency fluctuations and unusual adverse weather conditions, they were more likely to persist than when failure was clearly attributable to problems within the decision-makers' control that could have been foreseen. The defunct gas tap may also have made exiting easier by protecting Fei and Bob from the ego consequences of failure.

'IT WAS LIKE "OH MY GOD"!': ANN AND THE CURRY HOUSE

What if there is no critical incident to precipitate a timely exit? Ann went into business because she was made redundant. She used her redundancy money to open a takeaway curry house. 'I saw there was a gap there and it was a good opportunity to open but unfortunately after the first four months I realized that we weren't going to survive in the market because it's very expensive,' said Ann.

H.D.: How well did you know the market before you set up?

Ann: My partner he used to have a stall in the market many years ago. So I was inspired by him really. And he said that the market can be a very difficult place, but, he was selling jewellery and I was selling food. And he thought food sells better than jewellery. So we thought, let's take a chance on it because its food.

Ann soon realized she may have made a mistake:

My first feeling of disappointment was the first Saturday I was in the market. And I thought, its Saturday today, I'll get a lot of people coming in. NO! And I thought, this is a bit strange. On a Saturday! And I thought, Nah! This isn't going to work. If you don't see people on a Saturday of all days, nobodies working, people can have more time to relax, but they're just shopping and going home.

H.D.: Does that mean that from the first Saturday, you could see it wasn't going to work?

Ann: Well, I wouldn't have said it wasn't going to work totally, I just thought if it's a Saturday and people are not coming in, then something's not right. I just thought this is a little bit strange.

Before Ann went into business she drew up a detailed business plan. Initially she expected to generate £250 a week surplus (her wage) after meeting all her expenses. Ann said:

I did the business plan I forecast you know so much for the overheads and so on, that should have covered it but in practice. it just didn't work out that way because the customers were just getting used to us being there; people were looking but weren't coming in – you know – they weren't sure about the food, so we weren't getting the money that were forecast in the business plan.

H.D.: Where did this expectation that you would be viable more or less from day one come from?

Ann: I assumed that when it come to food you would make more than if you were selling clothes, know what I mean? The expectation that people are hungry and they'll come in and buy the food yeah? But it doesn't always happen. There's many people just doing their shopping that walk straight past, that didn't come in and buy any food.

Ann also forgot to factor the costs of restocking into the cash flow equation:

I found that to replace the stock was actually taking the money back. And it was like, 'Oh my god! I didn't realize it would be so expensive' – just the meat alone because we do curry mutton. Mutton is not something that is easy to get hold of and when you do get it, it's expensive. And we were buying that every single day – even though you're selling it – every day you have to replace it; it's quite a lot of money.

Ann responded by increasing prices. Yet she realized there were limits to what she could charge to remain competitive against sandwich shops and the like:

Ann: We can't go in there with heavy prices because nobody's going to buy your food … So the prices wasn't (sic) reflecting what I was spending on the stock so that was the downfall. In the end I found that I had to quickly increase my prices. And I just thought, I can't carry on like this. Every month I'm adding 10p here, 20p there. I have to watch that.

H.D.: You said you realized after four months you couldn't go on like that. What made you realize it?

Ann: Because I weren't getting the rent. After say weekly I just looked at the money I was getting, well not even weekly, daily, and I weren't making the target.

H.D.: What was your target?

Ann: I was hoping to get over £2,000. But I weren't getting that. Even then that would only have covered – the rent was £1,400 call it. Then if I did get the rent I didn't have anything else for wages.

Ann also discovered that the takeaway business was not compatible with market hours. Most business is done in the early evening as people leave work and buy a curry to take home. Ann had to close by 5.30, so she missed the best of the market.

Early in the week Ann would be lucky to make £100 a day – much less on Tuesday's because it was half-day closing. On Thursdays and Fridays she might gross £180 and on Saturday's £200. 'Never past £200. Never: I don't know why – really strange,' said Ann.

That meant a total of around £810 – leaving a revenue shortfall of almost £1,200 a week on her target of £2,000.

Friends and relations helped to run the business without seeking payment. 'That's how we survived so long,' said Ann.

Eventually Ann paid one regular helper £100 a week rather than struggle to run the business single-handed.

Meanwhile, Ann's partner paid the rent. 'I weren't making it at all,' said Ann.

Ann opened in July. By November her partner could no longer afford to pay the rent which lapsed into arrears. Ann quit in early January.

H.D.: When did you decide to quit?

Ann: I decided before Christmas that I weren't going to survive beyond January because I just weren't going to see it happening (sic). And then in January ... I had meetings with them (council officials) twice and I told them I was struggling, but it was just spur of the moment that I decided to leave and just pack everything up because I couldn't let the rent go on any more. January, February are very slow months. I could not wait eight weeks till [things picked up] – all I could see coming in each day was like £30, £40. There was no money coming in.

GAMING: ANALYSIS OF ANN'S STORY

Intuitively Ann recognized as early as day one that the business would probably fail because of the sharp contrast between expectations and reality. Quite reasonably, Ann did not act upon that intuition but waited to see how things would turn out. Unlike many of the owners we meet in this book, Ann goes to the trouble of compiling a detailed business plan. Logically we might expect owners who compile business plans to do better than those who do not. This is because in theory, planning forces decision-makers to conduct reality testing before investing resources. Part of the purpose of compiling a business plan is to force owners to define their expectations and to identify a sufficient funding to meet expenses like supplies of mutton (for example, Chell 2001). Yet evidently entrepreneurs who compile business plans are no more likely to succeed that than those who do not (for example, Bhide 2000). Indeed, compiling business plans can distract entrepreneurs from more important things when it comes to launching a business (Carter et al. 1996).

Ann's story certainly suggests that business plans can be double edged. On the positive side, the existence of a business plan certainly helped Ann to recognize failure sooner rather than later by highlighting the serious revenue shortfall. Moreover, far from lapsing into denial, as escalation theory predicts (for example, Staw 1981) she addresses the problem by increasing prices. In addition, Ann is sufficiently realistic to see that this move could be counter-productive: 'Have to watch that'.

Yet planning is beguiling as it can impart an illusion of control (Mintzberg 1994 discusses this point in the context of large companies). Just as psycho-analysis addresses fears of the past, planning soothes our fears of the future (Brown 1989). By a process of classification, computation and extrapolation, planning gives shape and definition to that which does not yet exist (and may never exist) thus appearing to bring uncertainty under control. Yet planning is only 'dreaming with discipline' (Brown 1989). It is easy to forget that mere planning does not guarantee revenue streams. Moreover, predictions can be adjusted until the plan makes economic sense – a practice known as gaming. For instance, plans for 'Expo 86' assumed that every man, woman and child in Canada would visit the fair at least once. They didn't (Ross and Staw 1986). Nor did Ann's revenue projections materialize – but the elaborate planning may have made her feel more confident in them.

The financial damage could have been mitigated if Ann had quit when she realized that the choice of location was a poor fit with a takeaway business. That is counsel of perfection, however. More importantly, unable to pay the rent and seeing no prospect of immediate improvement, Ann gives up. Contrary to escalation theory (Conlon and Parks 1987, see also Staw 1981, Staw and Ross 1978), Ann looks forwards rather than backwards. By looking forwards she sees that whatever long-term future the business might have, the situation is going to get worse before it improves, if indeed it ever improves sufficiently. So she must quit.

Psychological Traps

THE EXPERIENCE TRAP

Again, Ann's failure was partly due to inexperience. An experienced owner might have anticipated the strain on cash flow that constantly renewing supplies would impose. Yet experience does not confer immunity from failure. Jim ran a small but thriving chain of wet-fish shops. He noticed that the shop next door to his main outlet always had a queue of customers waiting to be served. When the owner retired Jim outbid all competitors to buy this apparent goldmine. Having signed the contract for sale, Jim inspected his prize. The result was a shock:

> I walked up from my shop. I just stood there and I said, 'Right Frank [retiring owner], thank-you very much.' He shook my hand and I thought, Oh! Crikey! There's nothing here – we'll have to pull the lot down. We're going to have to put a fridge in, the duck boards are all broken, the knives are not worth it. Just [have to] throw everything away and completely rebuild it.

Worse was to come. Jim then asked Frank about turnover:

> Jim: I had said, 'What sort of money should I expect to be looking at for takings?'

> So he said, 'On a good week, £350 to £400. On a poor week say £300.'

> 'So', he said, 'Good luck with it in the future,' and off he walked, up the market.

> I remember standing there, I were looking at this feller walking into the distance – and I thought, what have I done here? I've bought rubbish. I'm going to have to refit it all out. I've got a shop in there that's doing £1,500, £1,600 a week and on a good week this one does £400 – if I'm lucky!

Vignettes like Jim's story can be theoretically significant (Dubin 1976 discusses this point in the context of theory building). Logically we might expect experienced owners to be less error prone when it comes to staring new ventures because optimism is likely to be tempered by knowledge and understanding of the realities of ownership. Experienced owners know what it costs to run a business. They know how long it takes to build a customer base and the implications of location.

Even so, Jim ended up buying rubbish. In order to save mental effort, decision-makers tend to simplify their worlds (Kahneman and Tversky 1979, Tversky and Kahneman 1974). Simplification speeds up decision-making but it increases the risk of making a mistake because we may be biased in what see and what we choose to ignore. One such form of bias is known as vividness. In a nutshell, decision-makers tend to notice information that is striking and emotionally appealing more than dull factual data. For instance, in a crowd of people we are more likely to notice those who are wearing bright colours like red and yellow than people who are wearing grey and black. If we happen to be a buyer for a fashion house and conclude that red and yellow are popular and stock-up accordingly, the result may be an expensive mistake! It is thought that if information is sufficiently alluring, decision-makers may dispense with analysis of facts and figures altogether (Schwenk 1986). This was Jim's failing. He saw the perpetual queues concluded that the business must be extremely profitable. In fact, the queues probably built up because service was so slow because of the state of the knives! Only after he bought the shop did he enquire into facts and figures. By then it was too late.

It is thought that the biggest danger of experience is that it produces hubris (for example, Langer 1983). For instance, Toyota recently admitted that the company had grown complacent and allowed standards to slip and suffered accordingly – and that was before the massive recall of millions of cars in February 2010, with a potentially lethal fault. Hubris results because success confirms our competence. To be more precise, people tend to attribute their successes to their innate skill and business acumen and failures to bad luck (for example, Taylor 1980). Past success may thus create an illusion of invulnerability. Recall that moreover, that being successful makes us feel in control. As perceptions of control increase, overconfidence increases (Stotz and von Nitzsch 2005). Overconfidence tempts risk-taking. For instance, studies of gambling behaviour have shown that players who experience a series of wins early on tend to increase their bets (Langer 1983).

'GO THERE AND YOU'LL BE IN TROUBLE': SILVIO'S 'HOT AND SPICY'

Silvio began working on markets in 1970. He started by assisting a long-established trader who became something of a mentor. In 1973, Silvio started working regional outdoor markets selling cheap electrical goods such as kettles and toasters. His mentor loaned him money to buy a van and supplied an introduction to a firm of wholesalers enabling Silvio to buy stock on credit. 'I used to do seven days a week,' said Silvio. 'It was marvellous.'

Eventually Silvio made enough money to buy stalls in the indoor market. 'I done about £3,000 a week. It was good money and rent was so cheap comparing to now. That time it was about £30 a week, everything included.'

When trade declined because of competition from supermarkets, Silvio closed those businesses down and switched to selling cooked food. He was the first person to sell spicy food in the locality. That business also prospered. After 10 years Silvio decided to transfer the business to his daughter and open a new outlet selling similar items called 'Hot and Spicy'.

There were difficulties, however. Silvio was refused his first choice of location. Silvio then applied for the tenancy of premises on a side-row, where another cafe had failed after only a few months of trading. Silvio chose those premises because he believed that as there had already been a cafe there, it would be hard for the council to refuse him the tenancy. Silvio's family were supportive but friends warned him against the idea: 'Oh is a dead place. Rent is too much. You're gonna go there (sic) and you'll be in trouble,' said a friend.

Silvio ignored the warning. 'You have to take a risk. If you can't take a risk, you can't do business. They [previous owners of the cafe] didn't last long anyway because they didn't spend money on it. They didn't even clean the window – dust on it – so dark,' said Silvio.

As he spoke, Silvio pointed to the light decor and cladding he had installed. He had spent about £20,000 on the fixtures and fittings. When first interviewed he had been in business for 10 days.

H.D.: Does it worry you that they [previous owners] didn't last long?

Silvio: No! I had a confidence (sic) I said, 'I'll do it because I know all the people [in the market] and the food will be slightly different from everyone else.'

H.D.: What are you aiming to achieve with this shop?

Silvio: Quality, peace of mind. Since I opened I've got more buying power. The two shops earning money – you've got cash flow. You can go to the wholesalers. You can have a bargain with him. I used to buy one, now I wanna buy four boxes, so you always bargain – so you can save money. Instead of 5.50, you can say, 'Look, I want ten boxes today.' So he say, 'All right, I give you 5.25.' So 25p pence less in ten boxes of one item – donner kebab, pita bread – so obviously the suppliers are quite happy – they always give you cheaper – better deal – they're welcoming you – they serve you first.

So far, Silvio was pleased. During the first week he had managed to clear all his expenses (including his assistant's wage), though at this stage there was nothing for him.

H.D.: Did you expect to clear you expenses in the first week?

Silvio: First week – for expense of the shop – yes. There's no profit yet – like the money I spent. I'm not expecting a miracle. Within a month, six months I'll get my money back – all of it.

H.D.: What makes you believe you can succeed?

Silvio: A feeling. A lot of people know me. If I go to the market, everybody knows me and I know them.

H.D.: What will you do, if you don't?

Silvio: If I don't, I'll sell it. Sell the business – then surely somebody will come up. But surely I will break even.

H.D.: In what ways has your experience helped?

Silvio: I learn quickly. The other thing is customer relationship. When the customer comes in I always give them a smile. I talk to them. I'm not here to make quick money and that's it 'gone'. So if a customer comes and says, 'What shall I get?' I'll say, 'I'll give you everything – meats – chickens – I'll mix them up for you so you can have a taste all of it – so next time whatever you like – we'll take it from there.'

H.D.: Would you expect to make a big profit in six months?

Silvio: It all depends on the public. At the moment, all the traders is (sic) buying from me. When passing trade, like public – when they start eating it will be very good.

As he spoke, Silvio pointed to the array of onions, tomatoes and lettuce, 'Look, is all fresh,' he said. 'A lot of English people they like my food because they taste the difference. You can see I've got mostly in here spicy food. If you go to the English shop is like all plain. There is no spice in – here is more like Chilli hot stuff.'

Wednesday was chosen as the day for the interview because it is a fairly quiet day. We had been talking for almost an hour. During that time Silvio served one customer with a can of Diet Coke.

H.D.: Tell me a bit more about that 'feeling' you mentioned.

Silvio: Well, first of all. I've been here a long time now and I know all the traders. That make me first priority for market traders, I'm happy about them because I know they are going to come in my shop, they're going to try my food because I've already done well and they like the food up there [other stall], they like the service. Even if you go on Wednesday, today is half-day, if you go in my unit up there you'll see the queue and I will do well here. I had a good, money target.

H.D.: What is your target?

Silvio: If I do £2,000 a week here, that's it, I'll be flying (laughter). Is good you know – four, five hundred pound extra; nice little income.

Free ice cream

About a fortnight later there was a small but telling development. A notice appeared in the window offering a free tub of ice cream with every main meal. Asked how the business was doing, Silvio waved his hands. 'OK', he said, 'new customer (sic) all the time but I'm not taking anything out of it'.

H.D.: Is it doing as well as expected?

Silvio: No.

Silvio had now been in business for ten weeks. He was still covering his expenses but he had been forced to cut his assistant's hours and was still not earning any money for himself. Silvio now planned to open a cafe in a different town in partnership with his brother-in-law. Silvio would contribute half the capital and the brother-in-law would take charge of the day to day running of the business.

H.D.: Why do you want to do that?

Silvio: Because I need the money. House needs things doing to it. If I sell this business I will expect three times what I put into it. I know this business will make money in five maybe ten years time.

Meanwhile, Silvio applied to the council for permission to sell chips. The cost of the new fixtures and fittings was an estimated £6,000. In the event, permission was refused. After searching for six months for premises, Silvio eventually opened his second cafe. 'My wife had a few jewellery (sic). She sold that. I had a few money (sic). You know. I wasn't totally skint.'

The venture failed. That failure prompted Silvio to apply to transfer to a more central location on the market. This time, his application was granted. The results were dramatic. 'Trade two times more,' said Silvio.

He may not have been flying, but at least the business was now viable.

THE COMPETENCE TRAP: ANALYSIS OF SILVIO'S STORY

Recall that it is thought that once decision-makers become committed to a venture, they are likely to downplay or even ignore negative information. Denied his first choice of location, Silvio succumbs to myopia. That is, he becomes more concerned with securing the premises than considering whether they are suitable. Consistent with escalation theory (for example, Staw 1981, 1997) Silvio rationalizes the recent failure of a cafe in those premises and ignores warnings from friends about the location: 'dead place'.

Silvio's professed self-confidence reflects previous success as an owner. He expects customers to follow him because he knows they like his food. Another psychological factor to consider is a mental bias known as the representativeness heuristic. Representativeness refers to our tendency to judge one thing by its resemblance to previous cases. For example, if a doctor makes an overly swift diagnosis and sees a 'sore throat' they may miss the subtle signs of the onset of a more serious illness such as diphtheria (for example, Kahneman and Tversky 1972, Kahneman and Frederick 2002, Bazerman 2004). Silvio sees the second business as an extension of the first. Indeed, there is some overlap as evidenced by the reference to bulk buying. The point is, whatever the similarities between the two situations, there is one big difference, namely the location.

As his friends predicted, Silvio is soon in trouble. The optimistic statement about selling the business at an inflated price may be ego-defensive. 'I know this business will make money,' but Silvio is hardly in denial. Moreover, the decision to invest in selling chips can be seen as a rationally defensible move to give the business every chance to work. The decision to open another outlet is tacit that the business has yet to live up to expectations. Like Ann he looks forward rather than backwards.

Speculatively, the ill-judged decision to open another cafe may have been risk-seeking. Like Coca Cola's disastrous decision to change the formula for Coke, Silvio may have extrapolated things out and decided that there was a danger of ending up with 'zilch' unless he acted. We will return to this point in Chapter 4. Here we need only note that the second failure finally prompts Silvio to address the real problem, and one that he has so far not admitted, namely location. Silvio reinvests in order to move to new premises. It turns out to be a good decision.

Summary and Conclusions

This chapter began with the question of why people start businesses when the odds are clearly stacked against them. More specifically, the aim was to elucidate what mistakes new owners make and why they make them. What emerges suggests that escalation may indeed start with bright promises. Magic thinking is the cardinal error. Moreover, the tendency towards magic thinking may actually be worse than escalation theorists predict. Escalation theorists predict that decisions are apt to go awry because planners' projections are extremely optimistic (for example, Ross and Staw 1986, Drummond 1996). The present study suggests, however, that what may be even worse is when decision-makers like David fail to think about what they may be getting into. Yet, as Ann's story shows, those who compile plans may not fare much better. A key theme of behavioural economics is that rationality produces better results than decisions driven by emotional influences. Perhaps – but emotional influences may enter the equation *sub rosa*, for example, if revenue forecasts reflect wishful thinking.

Although ultimately there may be nothing for it but for decision-makers to 'play their cards and take their chances' (Bowen 1987), there is no need to venture blind. It is not just that prospective owners are too optimistic. More importantly, their misplaced optimism may stem from a failure to conduct the most basic reality testing like visiting the market during the week. Inexperience may be partly to blame, but as the stories of Jim and Silvio show, experience does not confer immunity from error. Nor does 'sticking to the knitting' Davids and Waterman fashion (see also Deming 1986) guarantee success. Jim and Silvio stayed well within their comfort zones yet still came to grief.

Contrary to what escalation theorists predict, far from lapsing into denial when a venture fails, decision-makers soon recognize their mistakes. Moreover, far from becoming obsessed with vindicating past decisions (for example, Staw and Ross 1978), owners of failing business may be more capable of maximizing future outcomes than behavioural theorists predict. Although ego-defensiveness may be present, 'we know the business is viable'; 'I know this business will make money' decision-makers can nevertheless deal with failure rationally even if only to contemplate 'doing a runner'.

Recall that decision-dilemma theorists suggest that since feedback is almost invariably equivocal to some extent, decision-makers may find it hard to recognize when a business has well and truly failed (for example, Bowen 1987). The present study suggests that if decision-makers are prepared to read the road ahead and quit accordingly, they may manage to avoid the worst.

4 *Missing the Boat or Sinking the Boat? The Realities of Escalation*

He who hesitates is lost.
>   *(Proverb)*

Look before you leap.
>   *(Proverb)*

Introduction

Since the new traders in Chapter 2 soon ran out of money, their stories offer only limited insight into the realities of escalation. In this chapter we meet three traders whose new start-ups survive, though in at least two out of the three cases, expectations are only partly met. Strictly speaking, therefore, the venture has failed and the owner must decide what to do next.

Recall that decision-dilemma theorists argue that reinvestment may be wise in order to give the venture every chance of success. Yet behavioural theorists predict that decision-makers are likely to reinvest irrationally though it is unclear why. Is it because they are reluctant to admit failure (for example, Staw 1976, 1981) as part of the corpus of the behavioural literature suggests? Or is it because they are reacting to how decisions are expressed (for example, Whyte 1986, Bazerman 1984)? The purpose of telling and analysing the three stories is to consider these theories in relation to 'real life' predicaments.

'How Easy it Can Be To Make Money': Anita's Story

Anita left school at 16. She worked as a shop assistant in high-class chains selling gifts and cosmetics. After six years, a thirst for independence prompted her to start her own business. That, and 'Realizing potentially how easy it can be to make money,' said Anita.

Anita's long-term ambition was to become a serial entrepreneur and found a chain of shops. Her immediate four-year plan was to open a shop every year, 'selling beautiful things to people; unique things,' she said.

In the event, a market stall was all Anita could get. Disappointed, she decided to take it for a year and then graduate to a proper shop. Anita searched far and wide for suppliers, spending hours scouring catalogues and websites looking for high quality stock. She sourced perfumed soaps, perfumed candles, silver christening cups, and small ornaments containing semi-precious stones like amethyst and garnet. 'In the market we're not doing a market stall at all. We're offering something that isn't normally offered to people that want to be on the market. So, it's just a bit of a challenge,' said Anita.

In her first week Anita took £192. 'I remember being so excited that I'd taken the money and people were actually buying the goods,' she said.

Anita's excitement proved short-lived. She too had only ever visited the market on a Saturday. She soon discovered that few of her weekday customers shared her aesthetic aspirations. 'We foolishly weren't aware what kind of people were in there during the week,' said Anita.

H.D.: What is your best selling item?

Anita: (Looking embarrassed) Body jewellery: people that want holes in their bodies. The best selling item is belly bars followed by tongue jewellery and then we have a lot of lip jewellery. If they can put a hole anywhere, they do. I didn't want to stock it. One of my suppliers sold it. We went in one day and said, 'What's that?' And we got a few pieces, about one shelf; and from one shelf we have now gone to two cased dedicated to body jewellery.

The first year's turnover was £28,000 – enough to pay expenses, restock and to provide a small income for Anita. Contrary to what Anita expected, however, there was no surplus to finance another shop. Boredom was another problem. Whereas on Saturdays Anita might take £100 to £250, weekday trading was much quieter, particularly on half-day closing when Anita would be lucky to take £20 to £30 and might only take £4:

The worst thing is on a Wednesday when you're quiet. I know the first customer is going to spend 50p on a nose ring … They all buy the cheapest item they can find … We get a couple of school kids; they've lost their nose stud. One lady buys five or six at a time to get her through the week. It's quite disheartening when you say, 'Hello what can I do for you' and they say, 'Can I have a nose stud?' (Anita)

After a year Anita applied for a town centre lease. She was refused. She then tried for premises round the corner from the high street. Again, she was refused. In July, after 18 months in the market, Anita served notice to quit at the end of December. Having so far failed in her ambition to open another shop in her second year, Anita planned to redouble her efforts and open two after leaving the market. 'You tell me what business person will have a shop that's only there to pay a wage. There's no point. I want to get money in so I can build,' said Anita.

Anita kept applying for high street tenancies. Her applications were refused. In November she applied for a big stall in a prime location in the market. 'I'm exhausted with that [existing business]. I still want to keep taking money … but I've got no new ideas for it. It's just there. I want something else now,' said Anita.

In the event the vacancy was re-advertised because there were too few applicants. Anita reapplied. Her application was refused. Anita eventually left in March still hoping to obtain a tenancy or start a wholesale business. 'I'm leaving the market but staying in the game,' she said.

Impact of Frustration: Analysis of Anita's Story

Anita's expectations were high and clearly defined; namely, to open one shop every year. Negative feedback soon arrives as Anita discovers that making money is harder than she thought. Consistent with behavioural theories that suggest escalation starts with bright promises (for example, Staw and Ross 1987a, Staw 1997), when Anita is forced into the market, she tells herself that location is immaterial because her business model will succeed regardless. Yet Anita also behaves entirely rationally. She sets limits on her involvement in the market as she plans to stay for only a year. Moreover, reinvesting in body jewellery is a rationally defensible move because it gives the business a better chance to work (Bowen 1987).

Indeed, after a year Anita decides to exit. However, she is again refused first choice tenancies. Anita then considers two extremely risky moves. One was to rent premises off the high street. The other is to take a big market stall. Clearly we will never know whether Anita whether would taken those premises they been offered to her. The question is what drove her towards such potentially suicidal moves?

It is unlikely that Anita was affected by the psychological impact of a 'near miss'. Studies of gambling behaviour have shown that 'near misses' encourage risk-taking because the brain processes the experience as a 'near win' (Griffiths 1990, Reid 1986). (This is why lottery scratch cards frequently contain two out of the three winning numbers. It costs the organizers nothing to produce those cards and it encourages repeat buying.) This explanation seems improbable because there is little evidence that Anita felt tantalizingly close to success – quite the opposite as she had missed her first key target.

Sheer frustration is a more plausible possibility. More specifically, it is thought that equivocal feedback may produce an emotional reaction of frustration, and that frustration drives unwise persistence (Brecher and Hantula 2005 discuss this point, see also Amsel 1958). Although the experimental evidence is inconclusive, Anita's story suggests that frustration and escalation may be linked. The link may be that frustration may result in higher risk-taking propensity that may in turn lead to escalation. Anita did not want premises away from the high street. Nor did she want to stay in the market. She only considered those options because there was no alternative. Recall that people with higher risk-taking propensity are thought to see less risk than is normatively appropriate (for example, Sitkin and Pablo 1992, Wong 2005). Anita never mentioned risk. That may be a fluke of the interview but significantly, when Anita was refused the tenancy of the big stall she did not express relief she as might have done if she had been worried about the risks, but a determination to reapply.

It is thought that negative results eventually destroy decision-makers' commitment to the venture (for example, Bowen 1987, Drummond 1995, 1996). Latterly, Anita exhibits a form of burnout as she loses interest in the business. Her ideas exhausted, Anita exercises a form of lateral thinking (for example, De Bono 1990). She realizes that exiting from the market does not mean giving up her ambitions. It is simply a way of conserving energy and other scarce resources.

'I Have to Make the Next Move': Tanya's Story

Tanya opened a nail bar. She could only afford tiny premises with barely enough room for two people to work. With such poor facilities, it was hard to rent the second chair so Tanya was often lonely. Such tenants as she did attract, seldom stayed long and some poached her clients. 'Those five years were a waste of time,' said Tanya. 'We didn't really have the money to make the place nice enough to attract good people. For the first four years we didn't even have a door.'

Tanya then moved to much larger premises with five chairs to rent. 'The business had reached a point where I needed some staff,' said Tanya. 'Nobody wanted to work in a little hut so I took a bigger unit in order to get more staff and gambled that there might be more clients.'

The gamble failed. Tanya discovered that trade could only support four chairs, not five as envisaged:

> I thought the shop would be a lot busier ... I was wrong because only four staff can work in the shop at one time. It's not busy enough for five. Also I hadn't really thought it through. I didn't realize what the rent was going to be because it's increased already twice. And the rates and service charges (on top). If I'd actually realized how much I would have to pay out, I wouldn't have done it. (Tanya)

There were other problems. Tenants paid £50 a day rent; £14 for Tanya, the rest to cover expenses. Tenants did not always work, however, and could leave at short notice:

> It's the equivalent of two treatments [what I get] assuming they turn up for work but it's better for me to do it that way than to try for any more. You have to keep everybody happy because the staff have to earn a lot of money to keep their life style happy so you can't take from them ... so you've got to have a lot of people and hopefully offer them a situation that is better than most other places in order for them to stay loyal. (Tanya)

Because of the hugely increased rent, Tanya actually ended up earning less money than before. After a few months she decided to open another shop, this time in the town centre. 'It [present business] wasn't the best [move] financially ... because the rents are so astronomical,' said Tanya. 'That's why I have to make the next move.'

Determined not to repeat her previous mistakes, Tanya searched far and wide for premises. Eventually she found a shop to rent in a pedestrian shopping precinct, near to town office blocks. The landlord required three months rent in advance. Tanya took a five-year bank loan to pay it. She felt comfortable about it because the long timescale meant she could keep up with the payments. Even so, Tanya realized that the move was fraught with risk:

> Tanya: I worked it out if I open several shops and make a little bit of profit from each one it could work out quite good. But the big risk is the second shop. When you get to the third shop you've already got two shops full of staff and the chance of them going under is unlikely but ... if the staff walked out from this shop for instance I'd have to find £500 a week rent.

> H.D.: Does it worry you that you have to find £500 a week now?

Tanya: No, I don't worry about the one in the market because if all the staff went tomorrow I could run that myself and still make a profit. However, what I am worried about is the other shop. When I've got the two shops I am going to struggle (if all the staff leave) to make enough money to cover both shop rents and I'm tied into a lease. And also when you're not … in your premises the colleagues as nice as they all are could take all the clients and all the custom and move somewhere else. If you're not there you just don't see things like that – so there's a huge amount of trust.

Even so, Tanya decided to proceed. She made detailed plans for the decor, hiring additional staff and so forth. The week before she was due to sign the lease, Tanya rechecked the footfall in the vicinity of her new shop. Tanya the abandoned the plan, 'too risky – not enough people,' she said.

Instead, Tanya decided to wait a few months and then see what other possibilities might exist.

Anticipated Regret: Analysis of Tanya's Story

Tanya's first business failed because her expectations of being able to rent a chair regularly were not met. Consistent with behavioural theories of escalation, Tanya then made a risky and ill-considered decision to reinvest in bigger premises. The decision was risky because of the huge increase in expenses (even before the rent rises). It was ill-considered because Tanya had not researched it. The result is an even bigger loss. Tanya then reshapes her strategy (pattern of resource allocation) as she decides to become a serial owner, extracting a small surplus from each shop. This time she learns from experience as she attempts to de-risk the venture by researching the footfall, and spreading the loan repayments.

Was the decision to abandon the plan for the second shop irrational? In other words, did Tanya err in the opposite direction to escalation? It would only be irrational if Tanya saw *more* risk than was normatively appropriate (Drummond 2005 discusses irrational de-escalation). This seems unlikely because this time Tanya's assessment was grounded in analysis and experience. To be more precise, risk represents the probability of a given hazard materializing multiplied its impact. Tanya realized that because she would be geographically stretched, the probability of customer's being poached or some other hazard occurring was high. Moreover, since she would be paying two lots of rent, the impact would be severe as it could destroy not one but two businesses. Besides, she does not abandon the idea of expansion. Tanya's plan is to find a less risky way of achieving it.

'I'll Take Him on at His Own Game and I'll Beat Him': Howard's Story

Howard became a market trader by accident. After leaving school without any qualifications he served in the merchant navy for 10 years followed by a string of casual jobs. One day Howard visited a stall on an outdoor market. The stall sold outdoor clothing and camping gear. The customers included army and air force cadets, looking for pieces of kit. Howard was outraged to see dented mess tins priced £15. 'Some of these cadets haven't got two ha'pennies to rub together,' said Howard. 'Everybody's got to make a living, but at the expense of a little 12-year-old? Taking his hard-earned money he's saved up? I just thought it was wrong.'

Howard challenged the owner of the stall to justify his prices.

The stall holder said, 'What are you going to do about it?'

Howard said, 'I got a bee in my bonnet. I thought, right! I'll take him on at his own game and I'll beat him.'

Howard opened a stall on the same market not far from his rival. To his neighbour's consternation, the business prospered. 'When I first started he [neighbouring stall holder] started spreading rumours that a lot of my kit was stolen,' said Howard.

After a year, Howard moved to the indoor market. It meant that his expenses would rise from £70 a week to £250 a week, but Howard wanted a stable base, shelter from the elements and to stop stock becoming creased and damaged in transit:

> A lot of other traders were all 'doom and gloom'. They said, 'Why are you going in there when there's so many coming out?' Yes it was a gamble, but I was willing to take it because people have more confidence in you if you're inside [the market]. They know that you aren't just going to suddenly disappear. It is harder [being indoors] but every business has to expand. (Howard)

Howard opened on a Tuesday. He took £200 in one day alone – a remarkable start especially as it was half-day closing. Although trade subsequently levelled off, Howard's enthusiasm and willingness to advise customers about what kit to buy and how to use it meant he soon attracted a solid customer base.

After about three months, business dipped. Howard had had a similar experience on the outdoor market. 'People are saving up for their holidays,' he said. Even so, Howard considered moving to a half-size unit to reduce his expenses. He also devoted his evenings to selling to youth clubs, fishing clubs, cadet stations and the like – seldom arriving home before 11pm. 'I'm giving this a 150 per cent,' said Howard. 'You've got to do if you're going to get anything out of it.'

Howard's ultimate ambition was open a wholesale warehouse. 'Lads who start out where I am will buy off me,' he said.

Meanwhile, Howard applied for the tenancy of a much bigger unit on the market so that he could display a wider range of goods instead of keeping stock in a warehouse. His application was successful but in the event, Howard changed his mind. He was reluctant to be tied into a six-month contract, but the biggest worry was the huge increase in expenses: 'When I went back to look at it [the unit] again, just to see what the footfall was, it was too quiet,' said Howard. 'Lads might not find me. For me that was too much of a risk to take.'

Meanwhile, Howard's existing business prospered. For example, he built good relationships with local commanders who would advise cadets 'Go and see Howard. He'll sort you out.'

Howard was particularly proud when troops about to be deployed to Afghanistan came to him for kit.

Howard also planned to open a shop. Whilst he was looking for premises, a friend who already owned a shop offered to rent retail space to Howard. The plan was for Howard to supply stock and contribute £350 a month towards his friend's rent. His friend had ample product knowledge and would sell the stock. 'I've got three businesses now,' said Howard with pride.

The arrangement lasted for only six months. 'I'm going to pull the plug on that,' said Howard. 'It's not making any money. It's not costing a right lot but I'm going to cut my losses and bring the stock back down here.'

H.D.: How do you feel about the loss?

Howard: £350 a month's not to be sniffed at but it's not much in comparison to what it could be. It could be thousands.

H.D.: What made you think it would work?

Howard: 'There are a lot of scout clubs and cadet stations in the area. If it had paid out I was going to use that as a spring board to open a bigger shop.

After a year, Howard reckoned that his net earnings were about the same as when he worked outdoors. 'I'm about even,' he said.

By now, Howard had abandoned the wholesale project as being too risky and too big a commitment. He was determined not to borrow money in order to expand. 'Everything in here is mine,' he said. 'I don't want to be thinking, God! I've got to pay £1,000 in four weeks time.'

Instead he invested £1,700 to set up a web-based outlet. 'There's millions of people out there,' said Howard. 'That's where the future lies.'

The web business got off to a very slow start. Weeks passed with hardly a customer but Howard was relaxed as he had always assumed that it would take time to become established particularly as it meant competing with large, long-established businesses.

Fourteen months after setting up indoors, Howard moved to a bigger unit in a better location. The move meant more expense but that was compensated for by higher sales. Howard was also planning to employ staff. 'Slow but steady, that's me,' he said.

As for Howard's erstwhile neighbour:

He's still on the outdoor market working two days a week. I'm about to open my second shop. I'm still going. I've launched a website and started taking on the bigger boys. In the end it wasn't just his prices, it was his attitude. I spend time with my customers. I'm not there just to get the money off them and that's where I've succeeded. I've had a lot of job satisfaction out of helping people. (Howard)

Bottle Half-Full: Analysis of Howard's Story

Recall that competition, the presence of an audience, and linking one's self-worth with a venture (for example, Teger 1980, Brockner, Rubin and Lang 1981) are thought to be powerfully conducive to escalation. All these ingredients are present in Howard's story. Howard is determined to beat a rival. He likes the status of owning multiple businesses and the cachet of lads buying off him. Yet for all his pursuit of self-esteem, Howard is cautious and patient. He starts out the hard way, on the outdoor market. His story is then one of constant adaptation to circumstances. When business indoors falters he contemplates downsizing. When it improves he considers a bigger stall but then abandons the idea. He shelves his warehouse project deeming it too ambitious and is realistic about his web-based business. He limits his exposure to risk by renting space from a friend rather than opening a shop outright. Moreover, contrary to behavioural theories of escalation, when it becomes apparent that the shop is failing, Howard soon cuts his losses even though it means he no longer owns three businesses.

Howard starts from a slightly lower risk-taking propensity than Tanya because he will not borrow money to finance expansion. Recall that people with low-risk propensity are thought to see *more* risk than is normatively appropriate. Yet Howard's assessments seem reasonably accurate. Opening a warehouse would require volume sales. He does not yet have a big enough customer base to support it. Opening a larger unit in a quiet section of the market would most probably be a recipe for disaster. Conversely opening a web-based business was a low-risk enterprise that might prove rewarding.

Unlike Anita (and to a lesser extent Tanya), Howard is not burdened with precise expectations. He wants to expand but he does not set income targets and timescales. Moreover, his perceived success (for example, owning three businesses, challenging the big players) is largely a mirage. Yet that mirage may well be a steadying influence. For Howard the bottle is half-full whereas for Anita and Tanya, it is half-empty.

Summary and Conclusions

The title of this chapter is taken from a paper by Mullins and Forlani (2004) who suggest that entrepreneurs face two conflicting risks. One is missing the boat by not attending to a good opportunity in a timely fashion. The other is sinking it. Interestingly the authors found that entrepreneurs tend to be very cautious. Most would rather miss the boat than risk sinking it.

What makes decision-makers contemplate moves that could sink the boat? Dunegan (1993) found that decision-makers tend to be more cautious about reinvesting when decisions are negatively framed and vice versa. Not to be confused with prospect theory, framing refers to situations that are mathematically equivalent but may be expressed positively or negatively, that is, as bottle half-full or half-empty. The present study offers little support for this observation. If anything, the relationship is the other way round. It is because the bottle is half-empty that Anita and Tanya feel they need to act drastically whereas Howard, perceiving the bottle to be half-full, feels he can afford a 'slow but steady' approach.

A more plausible explanation for escalation may reside in frustration and disappointment.

Counter-intuitively, Brockner et al. (1992) found that it was often the most highly committed employees who left if the company disappointed them. The study implies that people with high expectations are likely to react more much more sharply to a disappointment than people with lower expectations. Significantly, Anita had the highest and most clearly defined expectations of all three. She was also the least experienced and therefore possibly the most unprepared for failure. In contrast, Howard's more amorphous aims enable him to interpret results in a self-serving manner. Contrary to what behavioural theories predict, Howard's positive illusions mean that he is *less* in danger of being driven to destruction by failure and frustration. Moreover, for Howard the status quo represents a gain, whereas in Anita and Tanya's case the status quo represents a loss. It is that loss rather than reluctance to admit failure that prompts Anita and Tanya to contemplate risks that could sink the boat – a response that is broadly consistent with prospect theory.

5 'You Think It's Going to Turn Round': Escalation

Fools learn from their mistakes. I prefer to learn from other peoples.
(Prince Otto von Bismarck)

Introduction

The last two chapters were mainly concerned with new traders whose new ventures failed to live up to expectations. This chapter focuses on more established traders who persist with failing business to the bitter end, only to seriously compound their losses. What explains such seemingly irrational behaviour?

To recapitulate, decision dilemma theorists argue that decision-makers are at the mercy of events. Closing down a business is virtually an irreversible step so they may decide to persist while ever there is a reasonable chance of recovery. In this view escalation is just a normal business expense (for example, Bowen 1987, Camerer and Weber 1999). In contrast, behavioural theorists believe that decision-makers deliberately reinvesting in failing enterprises rather than admit failure (for example, Staw 1976, 1981, Brockner 1992) and sometimes even when they know reinvestment will not make them any better off (Karlsson, Gärling, and Bonini 2005).

All theories are wrong because they are abstract models of a more complex reality. The question is what can we learn about the realities of escalation by comparing and contrasting cases? The three focal questions for analysis are:

1. How do owners recognize the business is failing?
2. What drives persistence with a failing business?
3. How are escalation predicaments finally resolved?

'Is No Good': Crystal's Story

Crystal decided to go into business when she was refused entry into university. She visited the market at Christmas and noticed that it was extremely busy. 'I thought I could do really well here,' she said.

Crystal opened for business the following September. She sold gifts and fancy goods like joss-sticks, perfumed oils and silk scarves from a small stall away from the main market thoroughfare, advertised by a single string of fairly lights hoisted onto the canopy of the stall.

At first business was good. But then came the post-Christmas lull and trade was very poor. Crystal drew on her savings to maintain herself and the business. She wondered if she should leave. By April the business had recovered so she decided to stay. In September, however, trade plummeted. The business generated barely enough money to pay the rent and other expenses totalling £800 a month and the rent on Crystal's home. Crystal had no money for housekeeping and leisure expenses. By early December Crystal decided she must quit. 'All my money has gone into this,' she said. 'I have no more'.

Her savings exhausted, Crystal asked the council to waive the requirement to serve a month's notice even though it meant forgoing part of the potentially lucrative Christmas trade. Besides, Crystal was not sure that Christmas would make much difference. 'I sell things that people no need every day,' said Crystal. 'So when they have no money – they no buy; is no good.'

That day, there was a bus strike in town. It was early afternoon and so far Crystal had taken nothing.

Early release was refused so Crystal was forced to stay until mid-January. By now, the stall was being left unattended for long periods as Crystal was spending her time with friends who also had a stall on the market. 'Saturday is the only day I take any money,' she said.

Escalation and Uncertainty: Analysis of Crystal's Story

Although a detached observer might say that the business had little prospect of success to begin with, initially Crystal's expectations are met. There follows a long post Christmas lull. Contrary to behavioural theories of escalation (for example, Staw and Ross 1987a,b, Staw 1997), Crystal does not lapse into denial. She recognizes that expectations are not being met. Marginal costs exceed marginal revenues forcing Crystal to dip into her resources to support the business so she considers leaving.

Trade then recovers and for about six months, expectations are met. The recovery might reasonably seem to suggest that the business was viable after all as Crystal decides to stay. Then there is another lull. Part of the corpus of escalation research suggests that decision-makers only persist with potentially failing ventures when feedback is intermittent, that is, a mix of positive and negative as distinct from when it is consistently negative (Goltz 1992, 1993, Brecher and Hantula 2005). Crystal's story shows how intermittent feedback can result in a costly real-life mistake that is hard to avoid. Crystal reinvests when trade dips again, but as it remains static as Christmas approaches Crystal recognizes she cannot survive. In the end, the decision almost makes itself. Her resources are exhausted.

'Christmas Never Happened': Tony's Story

Tony began trading in the early 1970s. He eventually acquired four stalls, two selling DIY items, the third selling greetings cards, wrapping paper and the like, and a 'flagship' unit, that is, a large shop with doors (unusual in markets) selling books and stationery. In its heyday, the big unit was lavishly decorated at Christmas with, lights, cotton wool and tinsel. At Halloween it was decked with pumpkins and broomsticks with staff dressed as witches. It was a small but thriving business empire. Yet within less than two years, Tony went from owning four businesses to owning nothing.

Trouble began when competition from chain stores like B&Q undermined the two DIY stalls. Tony decided that it was pointless owning businesses competing with one another so he closed down one of the DIY businesses. A few months later he closed the second DIY stall. By now the card shop was making very little money so Tony closed that too. Tony and his wife also moved to a smaller house in order to get rid of a mortgage. Then Tony decided that there was no future in selling books so he closed the flagship unit and moved to a medium size stall to reduce his rent. Within less than a year that too became unprofitable so Tony then moved to one the smallest of units on the market, measuring just 10 feet by 10 feet. He chose it because he and his wife could run it together without needing to employ staff. 'We did think that when moved here we would be all right,' said Tony.

It was not to be. Tony moved in November. To Tony's surprise and dismay, Christmas trading was extremely poor – an unprecedented event leaving Tony with nothing to tide him over the 'kipper' months of winter. 'Christmas never happened,' said Tony.

Tony decided that he could not afford to serve the full six months notice on the lease. 'If this goes on, we'll have the bailiffs in,' he said. As it was, he would still be liable for six months rent. However, at least he would avoid paying business rates and service charges. 'It costs us £24 a day to rent this unit and we aren't making it,' said Tony. 'We've no money to buy stock and when you've no stock you've nothing to sell.'

Tony and his wife took part-time jobs in a supermarket:

I said, 'You go first and I'll stay here awhile.' The money's no good but at least we'll have Wednesday's and Sunday's together. This job has been seven days a week because on Sunday you go to the warehouse. The wife had been coming home crying every night. She's a different woman now. (Tony)

Dangers of Lowering Expectations: Analysis of Tony's Story

Recall that a venture may be deemed to have failed when it becomes apparent that expectations cannot be met (Bowen 1987). The escalation literature has focused mainly upon the relationship between feedback and escalation. Comparatively little attention has been paid to decision-makers' expectations. Tony's story shows how escalation scenarios can unfold in practice. That is, decision-makers can end up persisting in a suboptimal fashion (and come to grief as a result) simply by lowering their expectations. By progressively downsizing both the business and his home, Tony tacitly accepts poorer returns. It is only when marginal costs start to consistently outstrip marginal revenues (the business is not making it), that Tony realizes he must quit. No stock means he has no business. No business means he cannot pay expenses. The business is imploding and failure has become a mathematical certainty.

Why did Tony not see impending failure sooner? Generally speaking, one of the biggest problems in decision-making is distinguishing between signal and noise. 'Signal' in this context means clues pointing to an impending crisis. Noise refers to 'Conflicting information that points to other critical problems or explanations for the threat' (Bazerman and Watkins 2008: 100). When the signal-to-noise ratio is low, it becomes difficult for decision-makers to identify real threats from spurious ones.

In Tony's case the signal-to-noise ratio was quite high. Strictly speaking, the moment one unit stood vacant on the market all businesses on that market were virtually worthless because stalls were no longer 'gold dust'. In fact several units stood empty. Moreover, Tony was by no means the first trader to downsize. Above all, competition from chain stores would not go away. In other words, there was writing on the wall to be read, even though the sentence may have been incomplete. Behavioural theorists might suggest thinking that he would be 'all right' having moved to the tiny unit, was a self-serving belief, that is, a form of denial. Yet if he was in denial, why move at all? Tony thought he was adapting sensibly to circumstances. With hindsight he misread the signals but at the time he had every reason to expect a good Christmas.

'You Don't Become Self-Employed to Give In': Sam's Paint Stall

Sam owned two stalls adjacent to one another. His first, he had owned for about 10 years. It sold towels, tablecloths and curtaining materials. The second, Sam had owned for about six years. It sold paint, wall paper and other decorating materials. Whilst the linen stall did fairly well, the paint shop was in decline. Sam's first move was to make the employee in the paint shop redundant and serve in both businesses himself.

Initially the paint shop yielded about £250 a week net of expenses. That figure fell to £100 a week. Sometimes the business made nothing at all. Sometimes it made a loss obliging Sam to make up the shortfall from savings. After a poor Christmas, Sam began to think about closing it down. 'I'll give it a year and see how it goes,' he said.

J.H: 'Why a year?'

Sam pointed to a row of boarded up stalls. 'It's hard but you don't become self-employed to give in,' he said.

Sam works all day in the market. In the evening he does his book-keeping. On his only half-day he has to drive 150 miles for stock. In bad weather the journey can take more than 10 hours. 'I'm sorry but if I'm going to stand here, work all them hours I want paying for it. I'm not standing here just to hand the council £1,000 a month,' said Sam.

Meanwhile, Sam decided to try stocking cheaper items on his paint stall, hoping that might regenerate the business.

A year later we visited Sam again. The depleted stock-levels suggested that Sam was indeed quitting.

J.H: Why?

Sam: My rent's gone up to £1,300 a month. That decision makes itself.

H.D.: Didn't your strategy of stocking cheaper stuff work?

Sam: It did – to an extent. But, how can I put it politely? People are coming into the market – yes, but a lot aren't buying. Fifty drug addicts and a hundred alcoholics a day – that doesn't do any good.

J.H: How do you feel about it?

Sam: Leaving the market? Great! (This is a figure of speech. Sam was not planning to exit altogether.)

The Rationality of Irrationality: Analysis of Sam's Story

Although most empirical studies of escalation assume the pressures to escalate are all one-way (Staw 1997 discusses this point), Sam's story shows that decision-makers may be torn between conflicting pressures. The main pressure to persist in Sam's case is that quitting is perceived as having failed. Recall that individuals may persist with an unrewarding task if their identity or self-esteem would be threatened by non-completion (Brockner et al. 1986, Sandelands, Brockner and Glynn 1988). Likewise, Sam is reluctant to quit for fear of giving in.

Yet Sam is also beset by pressures to quit. He has a clear expectation for the business, namely £250 a week, and, unlike Tony he is unwilling to lower his expectations. Sam is well aware that his expectations are not being met. Economics teaches that decision-makers should only allocate resources where marginal revenues exceed marginal costs. As Sam realizes, this precept can be hard to apply when short-term revenues fluctuate. He responds rationally by giving the business a year – enough time for a trend to emerge. The decision to restock with cheaper items means reinvesting in a potentially failing business but it is a calculated risk rather than a reckless response by someone in denial. The experiment with cheaper stock gives the business another chance to work, whilst recognizing that it may have no future.

Whereas behavioural theories of escalation focus upon the negative impact of emotional influences, Sam's story suggests that irrational sentiments can sometimes produce economically wise decisions. Sam is not working for the council. He is business exists for private appropriation. In plain language Sam works for himself. Yet when Sam speaks about 'wanting paying' it is as if sees himself as punishing the council by closing the business. It is an absurd idea but it probably helps to counteract the powerlessness of giving in (Taylor 1980 makes a similar point. See also Taylor and Brown 1988).

The conflict is resolved by a critical incident. Recall that sudden shocks can curb escalation if they clearly show that persistence is futile because expectations cannot be met (Ross and Staw 1986, Drummond 1995). The present study suggests that critical incidents can make it easier for decision-makers to quit by reducing the psychological pain and dissonance (Staw 1981 discusses dissonance). If justification were needed to finally close the business, an extra £300 on the rent supplies it. Sam no longer speaks of giving in. The decision has made itself.

'My Dad Paid £16,000 For the Stall': Omar's Fruit and Vegetables

Omar began his career as a market trader at the age of 15 working his father's greengrocer's stall. The business specialized in exotic fruit and vegetables like yams, sweet potato, okra, chillies, and green bananas. Omar's father immigrated to the UK in the early 1950s. He worked in a factory, saving enough money to buy a 'hot dog' stall. Eventually Omar's father owned several 'hot dog' stalls, a small portfolio of property, three corner shops plus the stall in the market. All of those businesses except the market stall were sold to provide dowries for Omar's sisters. When his father died, Omar took charge of the business with unpaid assistance from relations and his mother. 'She'll sit there, tell us what to do!' said Omar. Omar also had a stall on the outside market.

The indoor stall had been in the family for almost 18 years when business began to decline as their main customers, first-generation West Indian immigrants, grew older. 'Younger coloured people don't really eat their own food. They've been brought up in England so they're eating fish and chips and takeaways. They'd rather pay for some take-out than make a healthy dish for themselves. That's what we've realized,' said Omar.

Omar gave up working the outside market. He felt he was just competing with himself. It made little difference to business on the indoor stall. 'There's not much of a living to be made. They put the rents up. There's not as many customers. They're [council] trying to get us out of the market without paying anything for the stalls. My dad paid £16,000 for the stall. They don't want to pay him back,' said Omar.

To make matters worse, other hard-pressed grocers and greengrocers began to compete with Omar by stocking exotic lines. Omar could not respond by selling cabbages, turnips, carrots and the like because his customers shunned conventional fruit and vegetables apart from cucumbers, lettuce and tomatoes. Disputes ensued:

> I've put in a complaint because he [another trader] started selling packeted foods, but he didn't put it in the list [of application to vary trade]. I had to argue to sell salt fish. Every time I had it on display I got told, 'It's fish. You can't sell it.' After six months arguing they let him sell it. He didn't have to argue; they just let him sell it straight away. (Omar)

Fewer customers meant less money to buy stock so it became harder for Omar to offer a full range. 'I buy depending on how much money I have to spend,' said Omar. 'I like to buy a bit of everything so no one is upset – I haven't got this – I haven't got that'.

Omar also stocked rare fruits like bitter melon useful only as a medicine against high blood pressure and diabetes. Stocking such slow moving and perishable items could be costly.

> H.D.: Why do you bother?

> Omar: Because I don't like to upset the customers. They're ill people so you try to look after them. If they come here and they don't see it here they think, Aw! I've travelled all this way from — and they only come to me for it. That's the only reason why I buy it … But they only tend to buy a certain amount and [today] I bought too much.

When rents and other expenses rose to £1,000 a month, Omar decided to quit. 'You're making £800 and then you're having to go into your pocket,' he said.

The plan was to return to the outdoor market for three days a week and do odd jobs the rest of the time. 'I'll find something. I'm good with my hands. I can do anything, fix anything. Plumbing, joinery, electrical work – I can turn my hand to anything,' said Omar.

Omar advertised the business for sale. An adjacent trader keen to expand tentatively offered £9,000. Omar declined. He wanted £13,000 to £14,000 for the business, that is, close to what his father originally paid for it. That was in April. The weather was getting warmer, trade was improving and so Omar decided to await a better offer. That offer never came. In September Omar served six months notice to quit. In late November the bailiffs ejected him for non-payment of rent.

Escalation and Sunk Costs: Analysis of Omar's Story

The business was losing money for at least nine months before Omar quit. Dipping into his pocket to meet the shortfall was bad enough. Falling into in arrears made things worse for Omar because until he paid back rent plus penalty costs and interest, he was debarred from renting an outdoor stall on that market.

Contrary to behavioural theories of escalation, Omar does not bury his head in the sand. He recognizes that the business has no future, but is restrained by sunk costs (for example, Arkes and Blumer 1985, McCarthy, Schoorman and Cooper 1993, Coleman 2009). The offer of £9,000 for the business was highly fortuitous since the business had no value as a going concern as a would-be buyer could simply rent an empty unit. Yet Omar rejected it. There may also be a responsibility effect at work in Omar's case. His statement about the council not wanting to repay his late father could be understood as implicating the council in the failure of the business. In other words, Omar protects himself from ego damage by shifting responsibility from his own stewardship of the business, to the council – attributing blame to external causes, in other words (Staw and Ross 1978 discuss this point).

It is thought that the existence of alternative investment opportunities can reduce escalation (for example, McCain 1986, Karlsson, Gärling and Bonini 2005). Omar's story suggests that perceived alternatives may be double edged, that is to say they can also perpetuate costly persistence. Paradoxically, Omar believes he can quit anytime because his options are open and there is no expiry date on them. 'I can turn my hand to anything'.

'It's Hard': Sana's Story

Sana was a market trader for over 20 years. Her family once owned eight stalls in various towns and cities. Sana owned and managed three of those stalls. Over the years, all but one of those stalls closed down because of competition from cheap chain stores. Now Sana's remaining business was collapsing:

It's been every year it's been going down, down, down – just struggling along. I've noticed it about three years ago it was first going down. Last year it was bad, year before it was bad, but this year it's been really, really disaster.

H.D.: You said you were in debt. Why didn't you leave sooner?

Sana: I was thinking of giving six months notice and then someone wanted to buy it. OK give it a try – it's hard to give up as well when you've been here so long.

Ten weeks later the prospective buyer withdrew. Sana then decided to advertise the business for sale. After waiting for about six months for a buyer, Sana despaired. 'I put lease for sale, nobody wanted it; put up sale sign, nobody wanted it. So one day I got upset and I just gave my notice,' said Sana.

The notice period was six months. By now Sana could no longer afford to buy stock except for a few items for the Christmas market. It hardly mattered as she was unable to sell her existing stock:

But then you've got to give six months notice and you've got so much stock, you need time. I'm closing now [but] I've still got stock. I've got jackets which I bought for £20, I'm selling them for three pound. It's hard it's very, very hard.

As the business melted down, Sana became extremely stressed:

If I'm doing £50 a day I've got fifty pound a day rent. Then I've got electric to pay, telephone to pay. It's hard, it's difficult, it's very, very difficult. It's gone extremely down when you do £50 a day. Sometimes I do £20 as well but I still have to pay rent from my pocket. I have to pay electricity, telephone, and then I've got customers who come in and fight, 'Oh change me this and change me this' after they've worn it and put a stain on it – washed it, broken it, they want a refund. This is difficult.

At most the business was taking £80 a day. Sana decided that she could no longer afford to stay open for the rest of her notice period:

Standing all day, running for the rents, running for the rates, running for wages and stuff. If I sell something expensive [customers say], 'Why are you so expensive, you're not in town?' If I sell something cheap, they don't want to know. So, I'm nowhere. I can't sell cheap and I can't sell expensive. (Sana)

Behind with the rent, she had received a letter threatening legal action:

I haven't paid the rent for a few weeks, they sent me a letter saying, 'This (sic) is outstanding, £950. Pay within one week or else its going further.' So I pay that money, my income tax will be coming, my wages will be coming. I don't know where I am going to get the money. It's sad. It's so sad.

H.D.: How do you feel about leaving?

Sana: I would like to carry on if there was a business here but there is not. I feel sad I'm having to leave but I have no choice. I worked so many years here. Rents are too high here. Rates are too high … Good quality people don't come here. I get a lot of rough people. Times have gone very hard. Big stores have opened as well like Primark, that's killed my prices.

Salvage Value and Escalation: Analysis of Sana's Story

Ross and Staw (1991) urge decision-makers to keep watch on the salvage value of the business. The argument is that if there is little that can be salvaged from a venture, there may be an incentive to persist rather than lose the investment. The authors may have had in mind a scenario akin to the making of the film *Titanic*. The film had an initial budget of $150 million. Estimated box office returns were $200 million. Costs escalate to $200 million and the studio estimates that the film will cost $85 million to finish. Should the studio persist? Assuming that a partly completed film is worthless, the marginal cost of completing the film is $85 million as against marginal revenues of $200 – so it is worth persisting even though it means spending $285 million to earn $200 million? (Camerer and Weber 1999: 75). Moreover, that assumes that costs will not rise further and that the revenue projections are accurate.

Sana was thinking of giving notice when someone expressed interest in buying the business. That expression of interest suggested the business might have a salvage value, so when the sale collapsed Sana advertised the business for sale. She may have been optimistic but it was not a wildly irrational move to try to salvage something from the situation.

Persistence then becomes a waiting game (for example, Rubin and Brockner 1975). Escalation as a waiting game is discussed in detail later in this book. Here it is sufficient to note that Brockner, Shaw and Rubin (1979) suggest that this form of 'lock-in' can occur because the cost of *not* doing something is initially so low as to be almost invisible. Somebody wants to buy the business. 'OK', says Sana, 'give it a go.' Yet the passage of time involves cost. The longer Sana waits, the worse her situation becomes. Eventually the stress becomes too much for Sana. Stress refers to the difference between the demands placed on an individual and their perceived ability to cope (Ivancevich and Matteson 1980). In Sana's case the demands of 'running for the rent', meeting other expenses and dealing with impossible customer expectations, can't sell cheap, can't sell dear, become overwhelming so Sana despairs and serves notice. As her financial situation deteriorates Sana is held in place by a long notice period.

'You Think It's Going to Turn Round': Terry's Story

Terry bought his first stall in 1970. Within 10 years Terry progressed to owning three large stalls in different markets. Two sold frozen foods and ready-made meals. The third sold cheap perfume and makeup. He closed down one of the frozen food shops because it was losing money. 'We shall be all right now,' he told himself.

He was wrong. Over the next five years Terry habitually raided his life savings to pay the £3,000 a month rent on his two remaining businesses.

H.D.: Why did you keep putting money into the businesses?

Terry: You think it's going to turn round.

After a very poor Christmas, Terry decided to quit. 'If you can't make it at Christmas, what is the point,' he said?

Now, aged 64, Terry, had no money left. 'Now I'm struggling to pay the rent on my warehouse so the whole thing is just snowballing,' he said.

In January, Terry made economies calculated to save about £40,000 a year. He also decided to launch a 'closing down sale' on the perfume counter to stimulate trade and then serve six months notice to quit in June. 'Get rid of the whole lot,' he said.

H.D.: If the business is losing money why not quit sooner?

Terry: You just can't come out all at once – you wouldn't believe the amount of stock we've got in that warehouse. Otherwise I'd go at five o'clock tonight and never come back.

H.D.: Why not just get rid of the stock?

Terry: I'm not going to do that. It's what you've worked for all your life.

Terry felt bitter towards the council. 'I blame the council for everything,' he said. Terry particularly resented council officials enjoying comfortable salaries and guaranteed pensions and who seemed to have nothing better to do than make traders' lives even more stressful by imposing petty restrictions on displaying goods, and unfair time limits on parking. Terry related a whole catalogue of other grievances – some dating back years. He intended to sue the council for contributing to the demise of his business. 'This is going further,' he said.

Optimism Bias: Analysis of Terry's Case

Terry's is a clear case of escalation of commitment because he actively reinvests scarce resources in a failing businesses for five years in the futile expectation that trade will improve when environmental cues point in the opposite direction. 'To have an expectation is to envision something ... that is reasonably certain to come about' (Weick and Sutcliffe 2001: 33). The crucial question is, objectively when did it become fairly apparent that persistence was futile because what Terry envisioned would not happen? Terry sold food, that is, things that people need every day. Moreover, he sold cheaply. That might have been a rationally defensible cause for optimism. Yet the profusion of vacant stalls and collapsing businesses would or should have been equally obvious. It was also obvious that marginal costs were consistently exceeding marginal revenues.

Expectations are powerful realities, however (Weick 1989, 1995). Seeing is believing, but believing is seeing (Weick and Sutcliffe 2001). Moreover, expectations dictate how we act. For instance, Weick (1989) recounts how a group of firefighters were told to expect a so-called '10 o'clock fire', that is one that would be under control by 10 o'clock the following morning. In fact, the fire was much more serious. However, having been led to expect a 10 o'clock fire, when the fire crew flew over the burning area in their helicopter they unconsciously rationalized what they saw to fit the expectation of a 10 o'clock fire. Consequently, when they landed and began fighting the flames they were hopelessly unprepared for the danger they had to meet and were nearly all killed. Likewise, the Tenerife air disaster when two planes collided on the runway in 1977 killing 583 people in the worst accident in aviation history may have been caused by a stressed pilot (navigating in fog, late and running out of flying hours) mishearing an instruction from the control tower. The control tower said, 'OK, standby for take-off.' The pilot, expecting immediate clearance may have heard, 'OK, take-off.'

Disaster might have been averted when the pilot replied. 'We are now at takeoff,' except that the control tower probably heard what they expected to hear, that is 'We are now at take-off position' (Weick 1990: 572).

According to Weick (1995) we may only recognize something is seriously wrong when something happens that is so untoward that it cannot be rationalized to fit expectations. By then, however, we may well have few options for addressing the situation. Whilst it is unclear what Tony saw during the preceding five years, significantly the 'wake up' call is a poor Christmas. Perfume stalls tend to do extremely well at Christmas so the abysmal sales clearly contradicted Tony's expectation that things will get better. It is at that juncture he realizes persistence is futile. 'What is the point?' By then, however, his liabilities are spiralling.

Behavioural theorists have observed that even when failure is admitted, decision-makers' freedom of action may be restricted by closing costs (for example, Staw (1997 see also Staw and Ross 1987a,b). Terry has a huge stockpile to dispose of. That stock-pile represents emotionally significant sunk costs because the stock is what he has worked for.

It is impossible to describe the intensity of Terry's feelings towards the council. Blame is a social account – it is a way of making sense of untoward events. The act of blaming shifts responsibility. It is a form of denial that can be invoked to shield decision-makers from the ego consequences of failure. If Tony can identify £40,000 a year in savings, perhaps the businesses could have been better managed. He may actually have been angry with himself for allowing the situation to 'snowball'.

Shifting responsibility may be irrational but it can be productive if it allows the decision-maker to then deal with the problem. That might have been the case with Tony except for his plan to sue the council. Dissonance theory predicts that if an individual has suffered a loss but cannot do anything to restore the loss then there may be a large need to protect one's ego or self-esteem (e.g., Staw 1981). Yet the measures people take to protect their self-esteem can prove counter-productive (Crocker and Park 2004 discuss this point). For example, Zhang and Baumeister (2006) found that people who escalated their commitment frequently ended up feeling doubly bad about themselves, first for enduring the ego threat and then for losing their money. 'In other words, losing one's money is not generally an effective way to salvage one's self-esteem, and if anything, it tends to make things worse' (Zhang and Baumeister 2006: 991).

Tony has already suffered the huge loss of his life savings. Suing the council could turn out to be ruinously expensive thus further damaging his esteem.

'If You Don't Try You'll Never Find Out': Sally and the Blue Lagoon Cafe

Finally in this chapter we come to Sally and the Blue Lagoon cafe. The story is as follows. Sally and her friend Martha used to visit the Blue Lagoon (not its real name) during their Saturday shopping expeditions. One Saturday they discovered that the cafe was for sale. Sally's husband had recently had £2 million lottery win – shared between a syndicate of four. He bought the cafe as a present for Sally. Although Sally had no previous business experience, the plan was for her to run the cafe with Martha. Martha had previously managed a profitable transport cafe with a weekly turnover of £3,500. Sally had no such ambitions for the Blue Lagoon. 'I'm not bothered if it doesn't make a profit,' she said. 'It's just summat to do.'

The seller owned several businesses in the town. He said that the cafe was becoming too much for him. When Sally and her husband inspected the accounts they were impressed by the turnover of £85,000 a year. To make sure they showed the books to an accountant who pronounced the business sound.

Once Sally took up ownership she set to work. She sacked rude staff and staff who were 'robbing tills blind' and made other improvements. 'We've given the place a good clean, decorated, introduced new dishes and brought prices down – now it's up to them,' [customers], said Sally.

Customers began returning to the cafe, remarking upon how clean it was. After about two months Sally applied to extend into a vacant unit next door. It meant almost doubling their rent but the plan was to open the extension in time to capture the potentially profitable Christmas trade and also expand the relatively profitable lunchtime trade.

Sally's success was short-lived. After three months, she began to feel disillusioned about the business. Her efforts to introduce new dishes like curry had failed as customers would only eat pork dinners. A cabinet for chilling and attractively display a range of soft drinks was already *hors de combat*. 'That didn't do any good so it went back,' said Sally. Some customers were nice, 'You get a laugh,' said Sally, 'especially when the bus drivers come in.' Not so with the drunks, the 'all-day sitters' and aggressive people. 'You try to be nice,' said Sally, but then something snaps.

The make matters worse, the business was losing money. Sally's husband paid £28,000 for the lease. 'It were never worth it,' said Sally. 'If we put it on the market I reckon we would be lucky to get £18,000 – £20,000 for it.'

H.D.: In that case how risky is your plan to extend?

Sally: If you don't try you'll never find out.

Sally's husband was putting money into the business to keep it going. 'I didn't realize there would be all these expenses,' said Sally.

H.D.: How does your husband feel about it?

Sally: Oh he's not bothered. Money burns a hole in his pocket. He just says, 'If that doesn't work we'll try something else.'

BEYOND MARCH

It took the council until 15 December to approve the application for an extension. Sally decided not to proceed because there was no longer any prospect of catching the Christmas trade. 'Its too late now,' she said. 'We'll give it a bit longer after Christmas and if it [the business] doesn't pick-up, it's going on the market.'

Shortly after that first Christmas in the cafe, Martha died. Sally found it hard to run the business alone. 'Everything falls apart when she's [Martha] not here,' said Sally.

After a year, Sally put the business up for sale. The price tag was £18,000. 'You've got to give a new business time,' she said, 'but if you're not getting anywhere after a year …'.

Weeks passed and there were no takers. Then a council official noticed the sign. He pointed out that the lease stated that if the business was sold within the first three years of occupancy, there would be a penalty charge of £30,000. Down came the 'for sale' notice.

Next Sally and her husband tried to make the best of things. They bought new crockery, cheap but attractive. They repositioned the counter to create room for more tables. They installed a music player. They refurnished all the seats. They even went ahead with the extension after all. 'We're getting there,' said Sally.

Sally's optimism reflected a good Christmas. On one Saturday alone takings were £1,500. Again Sally's optimism proved short-lived as the 'kipper months' set in. 'It [Christmas] isn't enough to tide you over the rest of the year,' said Sally.

For example, on a bad Wednesday morning in February the cafe took just £58; the following Saturday takings were only £120. In contrast monthly outgoings were as follows:

- Rents, rates, service charges – £3,000
- Wages – £2,200
- Replenishment of stock – £800
- Electricity – £250
- Monthly total: £7,050

'And that's provided something doesn't go,' said Sally.

One day the fridge failed. It cost £400 to replace. A week later a microwave oven packed in. 'So that'll want replacing,' said Sally.

TWO YEARS ON

After two years, the long hours, lack of family life, the hard physical labour and the challenges of dealing with the public were telling on Sally. For example, staff falling sick at short notice. 'And I'm left struggling on a Saturday,' said Sally.

Sally decided that she could not continue for another year even if it meant paying penalty charges. She was about to leave when another member of the lottery syndicate offered to buy the business. He offered £26,000 for the business and to pay the £30,000 penalty charge. Sally warned the buyer that the business was losing money but he insisted on completing the purchase. 'If a buyer hadn't come along when he did, we'd have had to give three months notice and walk it,' said Sally. 'If my husband had said [a year ago], "Right; I'm not going to put any more money into this," I'd have been ready for going. He didn't so I felt I owed it to him.'

Sally stayed on to work in the cafe for a wage. The new owner kept the business for two years and then closed it having decided to move abroad. Sally's husband said he was thinking of buying the business back.

H.D.: Why?

Husband: Because we think we could make a go of it.

Sally: Not now. It's losing too much money.

Husband: But if you think it was only a couple of times I had to put in a thousand quid.

Sally: It were (sic) more than that.

Husband: It looked a fantastic business on paper.

Sally: Oh aye, on paper.

H.D.: What would you have wanted?

Sally: I would have been satisfied with a small wage and the cafe paying its way.

H.D.: Why did you expand when the business was already losing money?

Sally: We've tried all sorts … The hardest part is [accepting] that it's never going to work.

 In two years, Sally and her husband lost £26,000 (not including refurbishment costs) trying to keep the business going.

Risk Seeking Behaviour: Analysis of Sally and the Blue Lagoon

Contrary to behavioural theories of escalation, there is little evidence of denial. After barely three months Sally recognizes that expectations are not being met and might never be met as she is already contemplating the possibility of quitting. Moreover, after a poor year, Sally and her husband carry out their intentions. Contrary to sunk costs theory (for example, Arkes and Blumer 1985, Coleman 2009) they make no attempt to recoup the whole of their investment. They merely try to salvage what can by advertising the business for £18,000, that is, £10,000 less than they paid for it only a year before.

 Persistence was partly driven by Sally's perceived moral obligation towards her husband (Shepherd 2003: 319 discusses this point). The decisive factor, however, was the penalty charge. Quitting involved a definite loss of £30,000. Persistence offered the possibility of avoiding that loss altogether but at the risk of incurring a bigger one if trade worsened (Bazerman 1984, Whyte 1986). Having decided to stay, Sally and her husband then make substantial reinvestments in the business to try to make it work. There is a brief period when it looks as if the strategy may have worked. 'We're getting there'. Whilst such misplaced optimism is consistent with behavioural theories of escalation, it does not drive reinvestment. If anything it is the *product* of reinvestment (recall Arkes and Hutzel 2000 and the experiment with the radar blank plane) – that and a good Christmas.

 Reinvestment ultimately fails. Yet what actually prompts the decision to withdraw is the stress on Sally – left struggling on a Saturday. The gap between the demands made on Sally and her perceived ability to cope is widening, such that the costs of persistence are now higher than the cost of withdrawal – even though quitting means accepting that the business is never going to work and paying the balance of the exit charge.

Sally and her husband were saved by luck. Latterly ego-defensiveness comes into play as the husband states they could make a go of the business. His biased recollection about reinvesting only 'a couple of thousand' may reduce the dissonance created by the idea of buying this loss making endeavour back. Conversely, Sally revises her expectations of the business upwards. Initially she expected nothing. The cafe was just something to do. Now she talks about a wage. It may simply be that she has now experienced the difference between paid and unpaid work. Or, it may serve to reduce the dissonance created by quitting by helping to justify the decision (for example, Staw 1981). She dissuades her husband by saying the business is now losing 'too much' money. That statement may be ego defensive because it implies that under the previous regime, things were better.

Summary and Conclusions

This chapter has considered decision-makers who, one way or another, quit only when forced to do so. Crystal's story shows what escalation as a normal business expense can mean in practice. Market forces do indeed curb non-viable businesses. Crystal's story shows that besides being slow to act, those forces can play cruel tricks on decision-makers.

The other six cases are more complex and therefore offer more insight into escalation predicaments. Whereas behavioural theorists assume that decision-makers respond to negative results by reinvesting, the present study reveals another possibility, that is, they may simply lower their expectations. It is a dangerous strategy for two reasons. First, persistence can become seriously economically suboptimal. Second, it may address the symptoms rather than the disease. The strategy buys time but it destroys options. This is why Tony and Sana end up with nowhere to turn.

The present study also offers support for explanations grounded in prospect theory (for example, Whyte 1986, 1991b, Bazerman 1984) as it suggests that escalation may indeed be driven by reluctance to accept a definite loss, as evidenced by Sally and her husband's refusal to pay the penalty charge, and, Omar's unwillingness to forgo sunk costs. Terry's is virtually the only case in the book of continuous reinvestment in a failing venture in the mistaken belief that trade will improve. Emphatically, since this is not a statistical survey we cannot therefore conclude that irrational escalation is extremely rare – though it may be. What can be said is that when decision-makers hold such beliefs (and have resources to back their convictions) the results may be extremely destructive.

Emotional factors may not always drive escalation in the manner suggested by behavioural theorists. Rather their influence may be mainly to shield decision-makers from the ego consequences of failure and/or by reducing the dissonance created by failure. Yet the pursuit of self-esteem could become costly – if, for example, Terry and Sally's husband respectively carry out their intentions to sue and buy back a non-performing business. After all, dissonance theory predicts that we strive for consistency between beliefs and actions. If we really do believe that another party is to blame for our misfortune or that we can 'make a go of it' despite overwhelming evidence to the contrary, we may act upon that belief.

Conversely, seemingly irrational sentiments like Sam's attitude towards the council can facilitate economically rational decisions. In short, emotion can be double edged.

Finally, how are escalation predicaments resolved? Critical incidents like Terry's poor Christmas trading may signal that persistence is futile, and/or they may enable decision-makers to justify quitting – like Sam receiving notification of rent rise. Another possibility is when the decision-maker reaches a certain threshold. Crystal cannot continue because she has no money left. Tony cannot buy stock, so he has no business. Terry cannot pay the rent on his warehouse. The trouble is, by the time the critical threshold is reached, the damage is well and truly done. The present study also suggests that stress levels are also an important threshold. Tony's wife comes home crying. Sana finally gets upset and gives notice. Sally becomes so stressed that she is about to leave regardless. Recall the escalation literature throws the spotlight on the forces for persistence. The present study suggests that decision-makers may indeed experience conflicting pressures (Staw 1997 discusses this point. See also Drummond 1994). Rising stress levels may counteract the drive to persist with a failing venture.

6 Five Past Midnight: Introduction to Entrapment Theory

Either he's dead or my watch has stopped.

(Groucho Marx)

Introduction

One of the small pleasures of childhood was being taken to Woolworths on a Saturday afternoon to choose a toy. In 1961 half-a-crown (12.5p) bought such delights as plastic modelling clay, bubbles to blow and cap guns that gave a satisfying crack when fired. I can hardly remember visiting Woolworths as an adult, far less buying anything. Nor, it seems, did millions of other people. For in November 2008, following a series of profits warnings, the retail giant closed with the loss of over 3,000 jobs in the UK.

With hindsight, it is perhaps surprising that Woolworths lasted as long as it did. The reasons for Woolworths ultimate demise are complex and the global credit crunch that began with the fall of Lehmans in 2008 cannot have helped. Yet history might have been different had Woolworths not clung to its time-served 'pick and mix' business model.

Business history contains many examples of similarly maladaptive strategies. When cheap foreign imports of cloth began to arrive in the UK in the early 1950s, textile mill owners said there was no cause for alarm. In the 1950s the US produced most of the world's steel but the industry clung to old-fashioned technology and was eventually overtaken by Japan (for example, Schwenk and Tang 1989). The UK steel industry was even worse. The Victorian era lasted until the 1980s (for example, Tweedale 1995)!

Modern sophisticated companies should not make such elementary mistakes because they employ legions of highly qualified analysts and economists to scan the environment for threats and opportunities and to calculate costs and benefits. Yet Woolworths seemed to have learned little from Marks and Spencer near collapse a decade earlier. Kodak was likewise reluctant to manufacture 'new fangled' digital cameras. More recently, the once seemingly impregnable Microsoft has begun to trail behind firms like Google, Yahoo! and Apple who are rewriting the script for personal computing without the need for Microsoft's platforms.

Like dinosaurs, big organizations become extinct because they fail to adapt to change. By the time some organizations realize they need to change, it may be too late to reverse the damage. For example, by the time Kodak reluctantly entered the digital market, non-traditional competitors like HP and Sony had achieved a decisive lead and Kodak were eventually forced to exit.

The Subtle Movements

Paradoxically, big organizations may fail to notice important changes in the environment, thanks to their own environmental scanning. Environmental scanning is beyond the scope of this book. Suffice be it here to say that big organizations can miss signals because the protocols and programmes organizations use to filter information reflect what the firm sees as important (Starbuck 1983; see also Brown 1978 and Hedberg and Jönsson 1977). For example, at first Kodak paid little attention to digital photography because they saw it as none of their business. Likewise, IBM did not see the advent of the personal computer as a threat as they were mainframe producers. Early on, Microsoft's information gathering systems may well have filtered out information about firms like Google because search engines were nothing to do with Microsoft.

Contrary to what the popular turbulence literature suggests, the most important threats may not be the noisy developments that organizations expect, but the subtle shifts, like a trickle of cheap imports that are barely perceptible early on. Even when the signals become stronger, the looming threat may be missed because no one in the organization is looking for looking for it.

Signals, Noise and Small Businesses

In theory, small businesses should be almost immune from such dangers because owners tend to be in close contact with customers so they are well placed to notice developments. Small firms also tend to be more agile than big companies. Agility means they should be able to adapt quickly and effectively to environmental cues.

Yet anecdotal evidence suggests otherwise. My last glimpse of Woolworths as a going concern was in Blackpool, a seaside town in the UK and home to rows and rows of decaying boarding houses. Holiday makers have long since migrated to foreign destinations and many boarding house owners say they are desperate to quit but cannot leave. Likewise, many markets traders have ended up trapped in business that may not be failing outright, but make very little money. For instance, Mark said, 'I've built a successful business. But for the hours I work, it's nothing compared to industry. Holidays? I'm lucky if I get a week. That's another way I'm falling behind industry standards.'

Daley, a fishmonger, said, 'I have made a good living and we continue to make a good living but it's nothing like what it were. The trade just isn't there anymore.'

Five Past Midnight: Entrapment

ENTRAPMENT DEFINED

If the trade isn't there anymore, why do people like Jim and Daly stay? So far the present study has focused upon escalation of commitment. Escalation involves a clear and deliberate decision to reinvest in a failing course of action. There is another form of 'lock-in' however that results less from an active decision to reinvest and more from the simple passage of time – a phenomenon known as entrapment (for example, Becker 1960, Rubin and Brockner 1975, Drummond 2004).

To be more precise, entrapment happens because time itself becomes an investment. Entrapment may be more insidious than escalation as our theories suggest that it usually happens by accident. This is because decision-makers may not realize the significance of time passing and eventually end up, in the words of Tom Stoppard, 'drifting idly towards eternity' as decisions assume a life of their own.

'SIDE-BETS' AND ENTRAPMENT

In a seminal paper on the subject of entrapment, Becker (1960) asked why people pursue a consistent but suboptimal line of activity. For example, why do people not move to better jobs when the opportunity arises? Why do they accept poor returns and few holidays when they would be better off stocking supermarket shelves?

According to Becker, decision-makers can become locked into an economically suboptimal line of activity by mixing one's main interests with extraneous ones, that is, making what Becker calls 'side-bets'. Initially 'side-bets are inconsequential, but over time they mount up. For example, someone who contributes a tiny amount every month to a non-transferable pension scheme may eventually discover that although the decision to join the pension scheme was originally incidental to their employment, it becomes the main reason for staying because changing direction is now too expensive:

> The committed person has acted in such a way as to involve other interests of his, originally extraneous to the action he is engaged in. By his own actions ... he has staked something of value to him, something unrelated to his present line of action, on being consistent with his present line of behavior. The consequences of inconsistency will be so expensive that inconsistency ... is no longer a feasible alternative. (Becker 1960: 35)

In other words, if the decision-maker changes direction those 'side-bets' count for nothing. The investment merely becomes an expense. For example, Becker recounts how in the 1950s, Chicago operated a waiting list for teaching posts in middle-class schools. Consequently, many newly qualified schoolteachers took jobs in lower-class schools as a temporary expedient until they reached the top of the waiting list. Yet when they finally reached the top of the waiting list, many teachers decided to stay put after all. This was because having invested so much time and effort writing materials to suit lower-class children they were unwilling to start all over again and rewrite their materials for a middle-class audience.

Although Becker was mainly concerned with economic 'side-bets' he suggested that people make emotional 'side-bets' too. For example, an individual who assumes a certain persona ('tough guy', for example) in order to impress others may feel they need to maintain the impression even when it is no longer appropriate.

'DECISION-LESS DECISIONS'

According to Becker 'lock-in' happens because individuals fail to see the long-term implications of their decisions. Continuity begets continuity. For example, the lawyer who takes a job in one of the least popular areas of law, like mental health, social security and criminal law, because there is no alternative may eventually discover that this seemingly inconsequential decision shapes their entire career. Likewise, the motorist whose first car is a Ford may end up becoming a serial Ford owner because the best trade-in prices are to be had from Ford dealers.

Large organizations also enter into 'side-bets'. For example, once big projects like the London 2012 Olympics get underway, myriad stakeholders including hoteliers, restaurants and taxi firms invest in anticipation of the games being held – all adding to the pressure to persist with the project.

ENTRAPMENT AND CLOSING COSTS

Some projects can reach a point where it is almost as expensive to quit as it is to continue because of the closing costs. There may be penalty payments to subcontractors, redundancy payments to staff, costs of ripping out partially completed works and so forth. When those factors are weighed, decisions about whether to quit or continue may be finely balanced (for example, Staw and Ross 1987a, Staw 1997).

Entrapment as a Waiting Game

'Side-bets' theory focuses attention upon the pressure decision-makers may experience to persist. What about pressure to quit? In another landmark contribution to the entrapment literature, Rubin and Brockner (1975) imagined decision-makers being caught up in a conflict, confronted with pressures to persist with an economically poor decision and also pressures to withdraw.

The author's starting point is that the passage of time can represent both an investment and an expense. It is an investment in that it can increase the likelihood of goal attainment. It is an expense because of the costs incurred in waiting. Conflict arises because, as time passes, expenses mount but so does presumed proximity to the goal. Tension mounts, however, because we cannot wait indefinitely:

> The greater the passage of time, the greater the conflict. And the greater the conflict, the greater the pressures to act decisively – either by withdrawing or by committing oneself to remain in the situation.

> Of these two possible decisions (total commitment or total withdrawal), the former is probably more likely to occur. (Rubin and Brockner 1975: 1055)

For instance, having waited a long time for the bus to take us the railway station, we may reach a point there is no longer any question of walking because we would be too late to catch the train. The bus has become our only hope!

More specifically, drawing on Kurt Lewin's (1935, 1938) work, Rubin and Brockner conceptualize entrapment as a conflict between driving and restraining forces. The restraining forces reside in the mounting cost of persistence. The driving forces for persistence are thought to be:

a) the reward associated with attaining the goal,
b) presumed proximity to the goal, and
c) the costs of giving up on one's goal.

To take a very simple example, being kept on hold on the telephone at premium rates is an expensive business. So the costs of persistence mount as the minutes tick by. Yet if the call is important and the caller knows that they are next in line to speak to an operator and that if they give up they will need to start all over again (and perhaps take even longer), they may well decide to remain on hold. In other words, the conflict model of entrapment predicts that waiting begets waiting.

Yet supposing that the call centre does not actually operate a queuing algorithm? Just how long do we continue to wait? Supposing that although we know that being kept on hold is costly, we are not aware of precisely how much it costs per minute or exactly how long we have been waiting. How does that affect decisions about whether to persist or hang up? In order to explore those questions, Rubin and Brockner (1975) designed a fascinating experiment where participants were challenged to solve a crossword puzzle in return for a cash prize of $8. The exercise was time critical as the value of the prize dropped as the minutes ticked by. Respondents were told that a dictionary that would help speed up the task was available and that they were first, second or third in line for it.

Waiting for the dictionary meant that participants experienced the passage of time as both an expense and an investment. It was an expense in that the longer participants waited, the smaller the prize. It was an investment in that if participants obtained the dictionary sooner rather than later, they could win more money. Participants were divided into groups. One group of participants had 'real-time' information charting the precise rate at which the cash prize was declining. The second group did not have this information. Groups were organized so that for some participants the value of the prize declined slowly. For others it declined more rapidly. These were known respectively as low and high decrement conditions. All participants were free to stop the game during the first three minutes and take the $2.40 consolation prize lying on the desk.

In fact, there was no dictionary. Yet 87 per cent of participants stayed in the experiment beyond the critical three minutes where they could leave and take the consolation prize. More than half of the participants remained beyond break-even point, that is, where the value of the prize equalled the $2.40 consolation prize. Participants, moreover, spent almost a third of the time waiting for the non-existent dictionary and ended up earning less than half of what they would have earned if they had opted for the consolation prize.

Participants typically became entrapped because they believed that the dictionary would arrive soon and/or because or they believed that the dictionary would enable them to earn more money than they already had and/or because, having waited for so long for the dictionary, it seemed silly to give up. Furthermore participants tended to wait longer if they believed they were first in line for the dictionary, or if they were not acutely aware of the mounting costs of waiting, and when the value of the prize declined slowly rather than rapidly. In short, the longest waits were incurred when they goal seemed close to realization and/or participants were not acutely aware of the cost of waiting.

'Drifting Idly Towards Eternity': The Dynamics of Entrapment

The weakness in the phantom dictionary experiment was that participants had to decide whether or not to remain in the game. Yet in reality it is often possible for decision-makers to 'drift idly towards eternity', that is, to live with an economically suboptimal course of action indefinitely.

Brockner, Shaw and Rubin (1979) ran a sequel to the phantom dictionary experiment to see what would happen when decisions to persist with an economically poor venture could be made passively as distinct from when they must be made actively. Participants were divided into two groups. Group 1 had to decide whether to stay in a game and remain eligible for the jackpot prize. This was labelled the self-terminating condition. In contrast, Group 2 was labelled as the self-sustaining condition. In other words, unless participants in Group 2 decided to quit, their investments for the jackpot prize continued automatically. The purpose of the experiment was to see which of the two groups would remain in the game longest as the value of the prize fell.

In the result, participants in the self-sustaining conditions tended to invest more and remain longer in the game. We can infer from this experiment that where decisions to persist can be made passively, decision-makers are less likely to notice what persistence is costing them than where such decisions must be made actively. Indeed, Brockner and colleagues suggest that entrapment is inversely related to cost salience. To put it another way, this parsimonious theory suggests that decision-makers are *least* likely to succumb to entrapment when they are clearly aware of what persistence is costing them.

Research Questions

It will be obvious from the preceding discussion that the empirical evidence for entrapment is scant. Our general understanding of the nature of entrapment is also fairly thin. This is because our knowledge is mainly based on experiments. Just as the clock stands surrogate for the wider concept of time, experiments are basically metaphors (Brown 1978). Translating human entrapment into the language of an experimental paradigm enables predictions to be tested, but the results are inevitably narrow because experiments can only model the essential features of the situation. Experiments offer limited insight into important questions such as:

1. How does entrapment start?
2. What holds decision-makers in place?
3. How is entrapment experienced?
4. How are entrapment predicaments resolved?

The purpose of the present research is to put meat onto the skeleton. As owners are mainly responsible to themselves, we would not expect them to enter into many or even any side-bets. For example, owners do not acquire the type of seniority rights that might force salaried employees to stay in uncongenial jobs. In what other ways might entrapment start?

More specifically, Brockner, Shaw and Rubin (1979) suggest that entrapment may start because the cost of *not* doing something is initially hidden so it seems negligible. For instance, when digital photography was in its infancy and the quality of digital photographs was rather poor, Kodak lost little by adhering to conventional photography. Likewise, when search engines like Google first appeared, they were used mainly by IT-literate enthusiasts. As the revenue from advertising was therefore extremely limited early on, Microsoft may well have decided they were not missing anything. One of the very few field studies of entrapment (Drummond 2004) suggests that cost salience may indeed be relevant. Drummond studied a hairdresser's shop that had been a thriving business but had gradually declined to a point where it was financially worthless, a shadow of its former self. The decline happened very gradually simply as a result of Val the hairdresser doing what she had always done – 'perms' and 'shampoos and sets' – when other salons were offering new hair styles and treatments and re-equipping the business. As Val's customer base aged, died or drifted away for other reasons, Val had nothing to attract new customers. Eventually the business was generating only enough money to provide Val with a very modest standard of living.

Yet Drummond's study says little about *why* decision-makers opt for continuity in the first place. According to Zhang and Baumeister (2006) entrapment represents a paradox. That is, costly failure results from the pursuit of attractive benefits, but decision-makers reach a point where persistence *can only* make matters worse. The authors cite the dollar auction as an example. Bidders enter the auction for profit but once the bid price exceeds the face value of the coin, to paraphrase the authors, 'bad' can never be turned into 'good'.

Although part of the corpus of the literature depicts entrapped decision-makers as 'drifting idly towards eternity' (for example, Drummond 2001: Ch. 11) Rubin and Brockner (1975) discovered that participants in the dictionary experiment understood quite clearly how and why they succumbed to 'lock-in'. Yet it is unclear how decision-makers actually experience entrapment. For instance, if time can be invested passively and decision-makers are blissfully unaware of the mounting costs of continuity, entrapment may not be experienced as a conflict.

We also know very little about how decision-makers live with entrapment. For example, how do they rationalize falling turnover? Although it is analytically convenient to draw a distinction between escalation and entrapment, in practice there are probably few pure cases. Each may contain elements of the other. For example, Drummond and Chell (2002) observed that a solicitor who was a sole practitioner working in a dying practice insisted upon retaining a secretary even though there was hardly any work. The solicitor said he could do the work himself 'but whoever heard of it?' (188). This remark clearly suggests that the secretary was retained as a status symbol. Likewise Val the hairdresser kept an appointment book. Since she saw the same clients at the same time every week, the book was redundant as an aide memoir. It was retained more for its symbolic value, a totem of continuity and a relic from the days in the 1950s when the salon was bustling (Drummond 2004).

We also know comparatively little about how real-life entrapment predicaments are resolved. For example, what is the relative importance of driving and restraining forces over time and what ultimately binds decision-makers? Equally important, what finally persuades decision-makers to give up? Conflict-based models of entrapment are predicated upon the pursuit of an explicit goal like winning a prize. Moreover, the timescales are short and finite. Any conflict that decision-makers may experience must be resolved quickly as the game is over within minutes whereas in real life, many decisions do not need to be made in a hurry. In real life, decision-makers may not have explicit goals. Nor may decisions be as clear cut as choosing between a bigger prize and a smaller one – each with precise monetary values. This brings us back to the focal question. Does entrapment happen in real life and if so, why?

Summary

This chapter has focused upon another form of 'lock-in' known as entrapment. Whereas escalation results from a deliberate decision to reinvest in a failing course of action, entrapment results mainly from the simple passage of time.

It is thought that entrapment happens by accident. It can be the result of decision-less decisions, including side-bets. 'Side-bets' are investments that have nothing to do with the original decision to embark upon a course of action, but eventually become the main reason for persisting with it. Entrapment can also manifest itself as a waiting game where waiting begets waiting. It is thought that decision-makers are most likely to succumb to entrapment where decisions to remain can made passively as distinct from where they must be made actively; where the costs of waiting rise slowly rather than rapidly and where decision-makers are not acutely aware of the mounting costs of persistence.

7 *Entrapment in Practice*

We've travelled too far, and our momentum has taken over; we move idly towards eternity, without possibility of reprieve or hope of explanation.
(Rosencrantz and Guildenstern are Dead, Act 3, Tom Stoppard)

Introduction

It is nine o'clock in the morning on the market. The fishmongers have been busy for hours, shovelling ice onto their stalls then placing every piece of fish on their displays. The task takes hours. Even with thick rubber gloves it is cold work. Over by Mandy's Linens an elderly stall holder wields a long pole with a hook on the end to hoist her display of towels, cushion covers and tablecloths. At close of business the process will be repeated in reverse. Few of the items will have been sold, a small hand towel here, a length of net curtaining there perhaps. Tomorrow, the same items will be brought out again, and the day after, and the day after that.

Recall that entrapment happens less as a deliberate decision to reinvest in a failing course of action, and more as the result of the simple passage of time (for example, Rubin and Brockner 1975). This chapter examines the various theories of entrapment against a backcloth of six cases. The first two cases concern traders who avoided the pitfalls of entrapment. The other four have succumbed. Two of the traders interviewed became wealthy enough to own Rolls Royce motor cars but only one has sustained that success. What makes the difference? The others may not have been as wealthy, but all have seen better times financially. What could they have done differently, or is entrapment something that happens more or less by accident as the literature implies?

'Going to be a Disaster': The Origins of Entrapment

Henry had been a fishmonger for almost 40 years. The shop was consistently successful with an average turnover of £50,000 a week. When Henry's daughter started working in the business she urged him to stock exotic lines like bass and sea bream in addition to the staple lines like cod and haddock. Henry refused to hear of it. 'I can tell you exactly how I used to set the stall out. We maybe only had about 14 different lines. We'd kippers, then there was finnan haddock; then there was cod and haddock, herrings, plaice – things you would expect,' said Henry.

Henry went on holiday leaving his daughter in charge of the business. He returned to things he did not expect:

I left her in charge. All the time she's been saying, 'We ought to get all these [exotic] fish.'

'Oh! No! No! No! Too dear!'

I came back and the bill was about 25 per cent more than it had been the weeks before we'd gone on holiday. I looked at it and she'd bought all these things [exotic fish]. I didn't really know what she'd taken at that point, but I thought, Oh! Crickey! It's going to be a disaster is this. (Henry)

In fact, the experiment was a huge success. Henry again:

It hadn't been [a disaster]. And then you realized, people wanted other things. They wanted bass and they wanted squids and they wanted prawns. I would say now that without the Chinese, we wouldn't be able to survive at the rents and rates that we pay and the cost of staff. But the Chinese, they're very, very careful – they want absolute top quality stuff. So the days have gone when you could have gone down to the wholesale market and somebody would have sailed up to you and – you just couldn't do it now on a Saturday – 'Oh clear this up,' there might have been 20 stones of fish, 'and just return us a price.' ... If you brought it down now you wouldn't sell a stone of it ... You wouldn't get away with it any more.

Attitude to Risk: Analysis of Henry's Story

Henry's story is more a vignette than a full-blown case study. Again, vignettes from practice can contain important clues (Dubin 1976 discusses this point). More specifically, Henry's story suggests that entrapment may not always be accidental. It can start with maladaptive behaviour. Henry's daughter noticed important environmental cues that Henry was determined to ignore. Recall part of the corpus of the literature suggests that entrapment starts because the cost of *not* doing something is initially negligible (Brockner, Shaw and Rubin 1979). In the short-term Henry could almost certainly have confined himself to conventional lines awhile longer without incurring serious financial loss. Yet the fact that the new lines were an instant success, suggests that the business was already incurring a significant opportunity cost. Besides, in the medium- to longer-term, there would definitely have been repercussions because as Henry acknowledges, without the new customers buying exotic fish, the business would be non-viable.

Why was Henry so reluctant to experiment? Recall that decision-makers with low risk-taking propensity are thought to perceive more risk than is normatively appropriate (for example, Sitkin and Pablo 1992). Henry certainly exaggerates the risk involved. Allusions to 'disaster' were overblown. Buying a few extra boxes of fish was hardly going to ruin the business. If the venture failed, the turnover was such that the loss could easily be absorbed. Henry's reaction to his daughter's initiative might have been ego defensive. That is, Henry may have been incredulous that someone else's idea could work (see experiments by Bazerman, Beekun and Schoorman 1982 and Schoorman 1988). Another plausible possibility resides in prospect theory. More specifically, prospect theory predicts that when choices are positively expressed (framed), that is, as a choice between gains, a gain that is certain is preferable to one that is merely probable even though the latter is more valuable. For instance, it is thought that a definite win of £500 may well be preferable to a 50 per cent chance to win £1,000 or nothing at all (Kahneman and Tversky 1979). In Henry's case, the status quo represented a definite gain, whereas stocking exotic fish might prove profitable but could result in a loss.

Studying opposites, namely the conditions under which entrapment does *not* occur, can shed light on the phenomenon of entrapment itself (Camerer and Weber 1999: 80 discuss this point. See also Mills 1959 and Wicker 1985). Henry's story suggests that the seeds of entrapment may be sown when the business is going well because owners are reluctant to change direction for fear of jeopardizing existing gains. The trouble is that in business existing gains are often fleeting. Eventually, the without those new lines, the business would have become non-viable. As it was, the timeliness of the experiment enabled Henry to secure a local market lead in exotic fish. He still owns a Rolls Royce.

'You're Mad': Mike's Story

Yet even when a business begins to slide, entrapment need not be inevitable. Mike owned several market stalls in different towns and a wholesale business. As his mother and father grew older and became less able to help in the business, Mike found it increasingly difficult to manage such a geographically dispersed portfolio. Mike therefore decided to abandon the wholesale business and consolidate in and around a single market. 'In a way, it was the wrong thing to do,' say Mike, 'because all our eggs were in one basket.'

Three years later, one of the shops began to decline:

It was a good shop. Nice staff, good products, but we weren't doing the business. So, when you get to that stage you know you're selling the wrong lines, that's when you know you must alter and that's why it's got to be something that's going to make a big difference. (Mike)

The shop sold soap, shampoo and other toiletries. Mike decided to invest £40,000 to convert the premises into a fish and chip shop. 'Everyone wants fish and chips,' said Mike. There wasn't one near the market. So we kept 'humming' and 'hawing' – and then the last couple of years because trade's gone.'

Mike researched the project carefully. 'It took six months to find the best potatoes. Somebody will go, "Fish were nice," and you might not know that's not the best fish I've served you. But everybody will go, "Chips were good". That's the biggest thing,' said Mike.

Luckily Mike found an experienced fish fryer, recently made redundant. The discovery boosted Mike's confidence:

She [the fryer] taught me things I don't know. That's where you need people. We've done things before in business – we opened a restaurant – that didn't work because we weren't restaurateurs. We didn't get the right staff in. We got a good chef in but he'd no idea how to run a business. If he were working with you you'd say he's the best assistant we ever had. But put him on his own – he couldn't do it – and we couldn't do it. (Mike)

The equipment was expensive but state of the art:

Old fashioned style, you'd put a big bag of chips in, cook them through, put them in your holder. So if you don't sell all of them chips within half an hour, they've all gone soggy – hard luck. These new machines, you blanch chips first … and then finish them off in your hot pan, one and a half minutes at 180 degrees. So when staff shout, 'We need more chips' – you're only waiting one minute. (Mike)

The venture was an immediate success. Mike now wishes he had rented the vacant premises next door and created a restaurant but at the time, it seemed too risky. Mike was also pleasantly surprised to discover that fish and chips were a profitable business model. 'You've no chips left at the end of the day. At the end of the week – you've got a couple of boxes of fish left. You can work out what you've taken and what your expenses are. What you're left with is your profit,' said Mike.

Shortly after the new business opened, Mike's stall selling chicken legs, bacon and cooked meats like boiled ham began to decline:

> Butchers [on the market] only used to sell red meat and pork. When the BSE trouble started they went to the markets' authority and said, 'Look we need to start selling chicken and bacon.' So all the butchers were selling cheap bacon, cheap chicken and our trade slowly went down. And I wasn't prepared to sell rubbish – I wanted to keep it good quality. And we had our regulars – who had been shopping with us for years but they're not getting any younger. I thought if we don't do something that's going to make a big impact on sales and revenue we might as well shut down. (Mike)

Again, Mike 'hummed' and 'hawed' for months about what to do:

> If you sell raw food and cooked food together you have to have separate staff. How can you afford to have two people stood at £250 a week – if you can't cover your expenses? I thought, in another 12 months we aren't going to be able to afford to keep separate staff. That was a big factor – we need to do something that's cooked – something that takes the risk away of cross-contamination – 'Oh I've got it, give up raw!' (Mike)

Accordingly, Mike stopped selling raw meat and converted the business into a delicatessen. Again, he invested in expensive fixtures and fittings including good lighting to help create attractive displays. The new shop with its tempting arrays of salami, Polish bread and strings of continental sausage, supported by enthusiastic and knowledgeable staff, was another success. 'Nowadays you just can't stock something thinking [assuming] you're going to sell it. No one has the range like we have. People come from far and wide to shop there,' said Mike.

Another reason for Mike's success was his careful attention to food hygiene:

> It would be easy to skimp on things but I've just had my [food hygiene] inspection. He's [the inspector] come in and said, 'Fabulous that: you've done a really good job'. I could have waited until he came in and said, 'That's not right! You need this. You need that.' I could have saved myself ten grand. If I'd just one shop and it were just me to do it, you'd probably think well, I can get away with it. But when you're relying on staff you can't because you have to do it right for them because if it's not right, they can't do it. (Mike)

The reward was a five-star hygiene grading (known as Scores on the Doors) – a rare accolade particularly in markets:

> Mike: We've had to invest to survive. People are saying, 'You're mad.' The lad on the stall opposite me said, 'You're absolutely barmy. Why have you spent all that money when the place

is struggling?' And the place is struggling because people aren't investing a deal – putting the money in to make it better.

H.D.: What risks do you feel you are running?

Mike: If it doesn't go right at the end of the day it's me, my wife, my mum and dad will suffer because although we've leased the machine, you have to guarantee the money. You put your own business up – put your own livelihoods at stake. You just can't turn round tomorrow and say, 'I've had enough thanks very much – that it.' You've got machines to pay for. You've got creditors to pay … It's not easy. To move on, you've got to speculate to accumulate as they say. Now if I hadn't invested, I probably wouldn't have been any worse off than I am now but I probably wouldn't have a future. But now I can see some sort of future selling things that people want so you can see you are going to keep trading for a while.

H.D.: Where do you think you'll be in three year's time?

Mike: I want to get something away from the market on the fish and chip side. We do that job really well. Customers (keep) coming back saying, 'That were the best fish and chips I ever had. Your batter's lovely, how do you do it?'

It's because the machine is keeping the fat clean. If we can do that somewhere else and get more money for it.

With hindsight Mike wishes he had left the market altogether and specialized in fish and chips:

We'd probably have had six or seven shops in other places now but we didn't need to then. You should make the change while you're going well, not wait till you need to. When you're hands on involved in the business you don't see that. You're blinkered; you think done well today, that's great. You don't sit back and think, could have done better if we'd just done that. It's hard. The harder it gets you think, need a plan to develop the business. But … the harder it gets – the more you need to be on the job making sure it's right. (Mike)

Calculated Risks: Analysis of Mike's Story

In 2007 London's Savoy Hotel closed for three years to undergo a £100 million refit. It was a risky and decision but essential to bring the old building into line with modern standards. In real terms, Mike's decision to reinvest £40,000 to open and fish and chip was actually more radical and more risky.

But was it 'mad' to believe that reinvestment could overcome economic forces? It could be argued that reinvestment was motivated by ego-enhancement as evidenced by Mike's refusal to sell 'rubbish' and his allusions to exceeding food hygiene requirements. Yet unlike Anita in Chapter 4, Mike was keenly aware of the risk – that was why he hesitated ('hummed and hawed'). Moreover, unlike Terry in Chapter 5, Mike did not simply pour resources into a failing business – more of the same. Mike starts anew, a decision that appears to have been a calculated risk rather than driven by blind optimism.

Moreover, when the grocery business declines, contrary to behavioural theories of escalation (for example, Staw and Ross 1987a) Mike confronts reality. He recognizes that traditional business practices, selling raw and cooked food, indifferent quality and poor hygiene are no longer viable. Continuity is not an option – except perhaps in the very short-term. Even so, 'giving up raw' and implementing expensive food hygiene protocols was a radical change. Like the Swiss banks surrendering their long tradition of secrecy (as distinct from confidentiality), it marked a significant break with the past.

Of course, Mike may have merely succeeded in deepening his entrapment. Recall that Becker (1960) suggests that 'lock-in' can occur because decision-makers fail to recognize the long-term implications of their decisions. Although the decision was made for good reason, Mike regrets concentrating all his business activities within and around one market. He also regrets missing the opportunity to open a fish and chip restaurant. Yet both decisions were 'real-life' mistakes, not caused by systematic errors of judgement (Funder 1987 discusses this point). Mike erred on the side of caution.

More optimistically, the move into fish and chips creates a shadow option. Shadow options emerge unexpectedly (Janney and Dess 2004). Initially, the decision to open a fish and chip shop was a matter of survival. It now suggests a future – and an escape from possible entrapment in the market environment.

'When is That Day Going to Come?': Richard's Story

Not everyone avoids the pitfalls of 'lock-in'. Richard studied engineering at university. He was then offered a job with British Steel (now Corus) but decided that he was more likely to make a fortune if he went into business. He started by owning a suburban greengrocer's shop and subsequently 'dabbled' in fruit machines, pubs and nightclubs as side-lines. All of these sidelines gradually fizzled out. When supermarkets killed the suburban trade, Richard decided to buy a business in a market. 'And I'm still trying to make my fortune!' he said.

Richard may not have made a fortune but for the first ten years or so, the business generated a good living. For example, his income for 2000/2001 was about £50,000. Moreover, several competitors folded due to a back-dated rent rise that Richard had prudently provided for:

> The court ordered a 25 per cent increase – but because it took three years to go through the legal process, there were obviously three years of that 25 per cent increase owing to the council. Now anybody who couldn't pay that money, then they had to go. They were either evicted or they closed down … Because of that (I) became more viable and got a reasonable living out of it for about [another] four, five years. (Richard)

Richard also reinvested £60,000 to refit the shop as a high quality self-service business in order to reduce staff costs as Richard believed the business was living on borrowed time. The change helped, but self-service means quality is all important, making Richard more expensive than the other greengrocer on the market. Richard was determined to avoid a price war:

If I went through the shop and dropped everything by 10p a pound, within half an hour, if you walked on to the other [stall], he would be 10p down on everything because that's how it works. He sets his price just below ours … It's self-defeating as the supermarkets found out in the banana price war when bananas were on at 5p a pound. It's ridiculous – people get used to that price. It's very difficult then to get it back to a realistic figure. (Richard)

Sure enough, business began to decline. 'It wasn't a sudden decline,' said Richard. 'It's been a decline year on year for five years running and we're pretty much in a situation we were in 10 years ago facing another rent review.'

Financially, there was no question of making a further big investment in the business. 'If other traders have got it to invest, good luck to them,' said Richard. 'I haven't.'

H.D.: What about stocking a bigger range of exotic fruit and vegetables? Is that an option?

Richard: We've tried all sorts of exotic products. We do when we can get them but it's an expensive way of getting products to the market because most of the exotic things are flown in – so to get people to try something it's got to be first of all affordable and secondly appealing. If it's flown into the country it's too expensive and if it's shipped it's not very appealing. I know the stores do get bits and pieces in but the exotic side's died from the wholesale market.

After four to five years of diminishing returns, Richard considered quitting:

Three, four years ago, I wanted to get out, but it was complicated by going through divorce. If I had cashed the business in it wouldn't have helped my situation. While ever the capital was in the business she [ex partner] couldn't take my livelihood away. (Richard)

Four years later, the divorce was still pending. To make matters worse, Richard now faced the prospect of £12,000 a year rent rise. If it was implemented, Richard would earn less per hour than his employees. Moreover, by now, the business was virtually worthless:

You can't sell a business that's not viable. Nobody's going to buy it. The investment that I've got in this, which is the initial investment I put in 14 years ago, plus the refit and the new equipment and one thing another is quite substantial. I mean I'd have to walk away from this and that I won't do [said with emphasize. For the 15 years I've been here now it's intentionally been my pension. I know other people have lost pensions because of the stock market and one thing another but I'm looking at a loss of it all. The business has got no value. It's unsaleable so we're stuck here. (Richard)

Local wholesalers were also closing down, so Richard might need to buy a van which he could ill-afford and travel over 80 miles daily for supplies. If that happened, plus a poor summer, he would be finished.

H.D.: What will you do if they implement the rent rise?

Richard: I'll probably stick it for a year, but, I've got no capital to keep me going. If this (the business) can't pay the mortgage, then I'll have to look for employment. There's no alternative.

On reflection, Richard doubted whether he could even survive for a year:

It's a seasonal business this. The rent review date is April which is a month on. The bulk of the profits we actually earn between April and September. So if it is implemented, I'll probably give notice in April knowing that we could pay the increase – we certainly couldn't survive a six month winter on levels (rent) of £3,000 a month – it can't be supported by apples at 69p a pound. (Richard)

During his more optimistic moments Richard imagined a run of 10 good years in the business, culminating in an early and comfortable retirement at 55:

If we have a hot summer this year that might put a bit into the bank account and might let us survive a bit longer. There's lots of 'ifs' and 'buts' at the moment and 'don't knows' – supply side – that may go (sic) … It's a very varied job and when its going good there's nothing else I'd rather do. What crucifies is the stress of not knowing; the uncertainty of the future. (Richard)

In reality, Richard believed that the way the business was going, he would soon be better off stocking supermarket shelves than working 60 to 70 hours a week for less than the UK statutory minimum wage and no pension.

H.D.: What's holding you here?

Richard: What's holding me here is not being able to let go of the nearly £100,000 that I've put into it. It's very difficult to say 'goodbye' to that – although I know it's gone. [Tears] Because it's just not your money; you've put your heart and soul into it … [Long pause] I know it's not much to most people but it's very sad … When you've worked for yourself, you would like to see something for those 25 years – because that's why you've worked 70 odd hours a week. You're always working for the future. You're always working for tomorrow. And you get to your mid forties and you think, hang on a minute, when does this future arrive? At some time in your life you've got to take stock and think to yourself the future's got to be here – sooner or later.

Impact of Reward: Analysis of Richard's Story

Richard too made an expensive pre-emptive move by changing to self-service, but time caught up with him. Contrary to behavioural theories Richard does not lapse into denial when the revamped self-service business declines. He would have tried to sell it but was 'locked in' because of a 'side-bet' (Becker 1960). Although Richard's decision to marry originally had nothing to do with the business, it becomes the main reason for persistence. 'It would not have helped my situation,' he says.

The business is now worthless but Richard is restrained by his emotional attachment to sunk costs (for example, Arkes and Blumer 1985). Those costs are well and truly sunk because none of the effort and emotional energy Richard has invested in the business can influence future outcomes. Ultimately what holds Richard in place is the expectancy of a valuable prize. Evidently individuals who perceive a high pay-off may persist for longer with difficult tasks than those who perceive a lower payoff (Gatewood, Shaver and Gartner 1995, see also Wong 2005). Like those who waited for the non-existent dictionary (Rubin and Brockner 1975), the driving force for persistence in Richard's case is the valuable (if dreamlike) goal of making a fortune. He is still waiting for 'that day'. While ever he is in business, there is a chance (however remote) of making a fortune. If he switches to paid employment, that chance will most probably be gone forever.

Yet there are limits. Recall that Drummond (1995) has observed that owners may quit a venture regardless of any pressures for consistency, if persistence threatens something important to them. For all Richard's emotional involvement in the business and his hopes for the future, it is a means to an end. If it no longer pays the mortgage, then the business has out-lived its usefulness.

'I Have No Pension': Elaine's Story

Elaine held various jobs in retail over the years. After a traumatic divorce she took a career break and then began working outdoor markets with her new partner. 'I came into my own again,' said Elaine, 'I loved it. I thought, this is where I need to be. I need to be talking to people.'

Elaine's partner set up her up in business – a unit on a three month lease selling women's clothes offered. 'I thought, right! I'm going to have the best three months of my life!' said Elaine. 'That was eight years ago and I'm still here – struggling.'

At first the business prospered as Elaine decided to specialize in bridal accessories, evening wear and party attire. She worked hard to create attractive and striking window displays which she changed frequently, and acquired a good reputation for service and individual attention. Takings on a Saturday alone were around £3,000. Now they average only £250 a day:

> I used to love Saturday's. I used to get all hyped up for a Saturday. I used to get up early. I used to get all made up – all adrenalin going for a Saturday. It doesn't happen anymore; there were five of us in that little shop in a Saturday and we were packed. I took more (on a Saturday) than I take in a week now. (Elaine)

The business has three full-time members of staff to support – partly a reflection of the strategy of providing individual attention, partly because of personal loyalty as Elaine feels she needs to cut down on staff hours. Elaine said: 'I'm overstaffed, but I just haven't got the heart to say to someone, "Look! I need a day off you." I just can't do it …'.

Elaine has tried many tactics to attract customers including offering credit card facilities (unusual on markets) and fancy dress hire. Although those measures have helped to keep the business afloat, in real terms she earns less than when she worked as a shop assistant:

> Elaine: I'm still on the same wage now as I took when I started eight years ago … So yeah, I'm probably a lot worse off [than if I had stayed in employment]. I'm probably. I don't know. I daren't think about it. It's too frightening.

H.D.: How bad do things have to get before you quit?

Elaine: I won't flog a dead horse ... I won't get in debt. That would be my quit line ... If I found that I need more stock and I've no money, absolutely no money to pay for it, then I quit because I don't want to be one of these people that goes bankrupt and owes every supplier. A lot of them are friends ... I just couldn't hold my head up.

H.D.: What keeps you going?

Elaine: I like to be my own boss. I don't want somebody saying to me, 'You must be here at nine o'clock, why are you late? You can't go up for a sun bed at this time. And you can't do this, and you can't do that.' I've been there. I don't want that. I have always worked for other people but now I've spoilt it for myself.

Elaine's dream is to buy a rundown business abroad and renovate it:

I would get a dirty old bar that's cheap, and some cheap furniture and rip it apart, clean it up and start from scratch. ... I want to rip it apart and stamp my signature all over it and say, 'This is mine' ... And just be a beach freak.

The project is a constant source of tension between Elaine and her partner. Her partner owns his own business and is not therefore free to leave. He suggests that she goes and does it. Elaine's reaction is that one day, she might do precisely that.

H.D.: What would you do with the shop?

Elaine: Leave it. Walk away from it.

H.D.: Could you sell it?

Elaine: Sell the business? Nobody would buy it.

Meanwhile, Elaine manages the business, as best she can:

You need a certain amount of money to make money ... I'm stuck in a 'Catch Twenty-Two' situation now because the things I'd like to buy – I can't take too much out of the business because if I do I can't afford the other bills that are coming in. Last year the (display) cabinet was full of tiaras and I did quite well with that. But then people start saying, 'Have you got such and such for hen nights?'

Elaine's bigger concern is her pension. 'When you're younger, "Oh pension! What's a pension? Forget about pension; I don't need a pension." Now I think, God! I've no pension.'

Impact of 'Side-Bets': Analysis of Elaine's Story

Elaine's story shows how the paradox of entrapment (Zhang and Baumeister 2006) can play out in practice. A decision taken for good reason (setting up in business solves immediate financial problems) reaches a point where 'bad' can probably never come 'good' because every year in the shop costs Elaine a year's pensionable employment. The cost of not being in pensionable employment was initially low. When she was young, Elaine could not see the relevance. 'What's a pension?' It is only later that she sees the longer term consequences. Originally the lease on the shop was only for three months. But as the years pass, the opportunity cost of not making pension provision becomes increasingly apparent.

Evidently entrapped owners may practise denial by the opportunity cost incurred as a result of the passage of time (Drummond 2004). Yet although Elaine finds it frightening to think about the future, she is by no means 'drifting idly towards eternity'. Unlike Anita who became burned out when the business failed, Elaine still takes a lively interest in hers. For instance, she still changes her displays regularly and is keen to experiment with new items like tiaras. Moreover, Elaine knows exactly what persistence is costing her, namely a constant financial struggle and no pension.

Yet Elaine is only 46. She still has time to build a pension. What holds her in place, however, is the 'side-bet' of being self-employed. Elaine's decision to become an owner was originally driven by economic need rather than a desire for independence. Yet independence has become the driving force for persistence. Elaine's loyalty to her employees also limits her freedom of action.

Again there are limits. Much as Elaine enjoys being self-employed, she will not cross the threshold of getting into debt in order to stay in business. She too has a clear quitting point. Moreover, Elaine's story shows that 'side-bets' can be double edged. On the one hand Elaine's relationship with her suppliers contributes to her entrapment because it prevents her from taking the risk of borrowing money to buy stocks of high margin goods. Yet that 'side-bet' also defines her quitting point.

Elaine has invested substantial time and effort in the business but unlike Richard she exhibits little attachment to sunk costs. Her willingness to walk away may be because it is her partner's money and not her own invested in it, and/or because of the alternative of converting a bar. Alternatives are thought to be most effective in curbing unwarranted persistence when they clearly offer superior returns on investment (for example, Hantula and Crowell 1994). The idea of converting a bar invokes a vividness effect (for example, Schwenk 1986) as it offers an alluring escape from present reality. It would not, however, solve the real problem unless it was so profitable that Elaine could start her own pension provision.

'Can't Get Any Worse': Barry the Butcher

Barry started as a butcher's boy and became a shop manager in his early twenties. The pay was good. 'In those days I was so enthusiastic I used to come home and spend my evenings making up next day's price tickets,' he said.

Seeing how highly profitable being a butcher could be, in his mid twenties, Barry opened his own shop. It was a hugely rewarding enterprise. Barry then bought more shops on short leases, opening and closing them as leases expired. Within a few years he bought his first Rolls Royce. It was the first of many, with a life style to match. 'I couldn't have done better if I had won the pools,' he said.

After 10 years in business, Barry decided to consolidate his interests by buying three market shops. The purchase price was £150,000 – a huge sum at the time. 'It was my pension', said Barry, 'because you couldn't buy shops. They very seldom came up [for sale].'

For 14 years the acquisition was extremely successful. With turnover averaging nearly £50,000 a week, Barry become semi-retired appearing only in the shops in a suit to deal with paperwork like checking invoices. Then business began to decline, mainly because of competition from supermarkets and chain stores. Barry sold one shop for a token £1,000 in order to assign the lease. 'It was throwing me deeper and deeper … into the red. So, I was just glad to get rid of it,' said Barry.

Two years later Barry sold the second shop for a token sum as it too was losing money. (The new owners lasted for only a few months as they discovered they couldn't make the shops pay either.)

The third shop Barry kept. Two years later he received a shock, 'I had been very blasé,' said Barry. 'Its only when you get a bank statement you realize God! You are into an overdraft situation!'

The bank statement galvanized Barry into action:

> I took a close look at the books. Two staff who was in there and myself trying to draw a wage out of one shop … wasn't viable … I had to make redundancies which aren't cheap when you have so many staff working with you for so many years. And then we had a dreadful summer – months of hot weather. When its hot weather meat sales just drop. So … I was thinking about winding up this year end.

Barry immediately made one assistant redundant. He then donned an apron and started working in the shop himself alongside Pat, his remaining assistant. He planned to quit as soon as he had repaid the overdraft and accumulated enough money to pay Pat's redundancy. It was a hard decision. 'When this one (shop) goes … I am no longer self-employed. I am no longer my own boss,' said Barry. 'That's been the hardest decision, to give that up. I'm not going to be my own boss.'

Accordingly, in March, two months after receiving the fateful bank statement, Barry served notice to quit on 30 September:

> It [the business] has been going down slowly but surely – over the past seven or eight years. Weekly turnover is … £2,200 – £2,400. That shop used to take more than that on a Saturday – in one day! Unbelievable what the turnover was down there! But it's just gone and gone and gone. I kept saying, 'Can't get any worse. No, it just can't get any worse.' But it does. It gradually gets worst and worst. You look back at your books … and you can see it's on a slippery slope, its just going. You might be able to make a quick killing with a new line and then it fizzles away. There is no way its going to pick up. No possible way!

Meanwhile Barry sought work. He had always assumed that it would be easy to find a good job, given his experience of managing people and businesses. He was disappointed. 'They pay minimum wage and expect you to work all hours,' he said.

As 30 September approached, Barry changed his mind about closing. 'I have been self-employed for all those years. To give up in business, it is a hard thing to do. I said to Pat, "We've got the best trading months ahead ... so we shouldn't be walking away now. The shop should give us a living for another three months,"' said Barry.

Pat agreed to stay. "OK then". So Barry sought a three month extension to the lease. The council offered him a choice. Either take a contract for six months at the same rent, or, three months plus a 10 per cent rent rise. Barry opted for three months since that would take him to 31 December. He subsequently regretted that decision because as Christmas approached, he decided he might as well stay until the end of March – but certainly no later:

Barry: You've got May which is a terrible month because you've got a bank holiday beginning and back end of May; shortly after the Easter holidays as well. Once you get past March, that's it. That's why I've said, 'I'll stay till March ...'. The trade down there, definitely won't be there after March – that's for certain. I'll definitely not keep it any longer than the end of March.

H.D.: Have you tried to sell the business?

Barry: You can't sell them. There's units that are empty now and they've got the refrigerated counters and the walk in cold room. Anyone who wanted a butcher's shop, its there for 'em. All they've got to do is take a licence [lease] on it and just take their own knives and tackle and start trading. You can't sell them – can't sell them.

Having given up looking for a job, Barry decided he would either set up mobile business selling cooked meats like ribs and chicken, or, run a small hotel with his wife. In the event, those ideas came to nothing. In March, Barry tried to negotiate another three month extension to the lease. This time the council insisted upon six months. Although Barry still had hopes of starting another business, he saw no alternative but to acquiesce even though it would commit him to paying rent over the summer months. It was a galling prospect:

The clientele has changed. You might get a handful of students occasionally that might come down for a little bit of cheap meat. But the young housewife in her mid twenties, there are very, very few. Their mother's probably shopped there but their daughters aren't because they go into the supermarkets. So, I've seen some of my customers that we've had over the years suddenly not turn up and you find out that they've passed away. But their children that are growing up, they're not filling their place. The only people that are bringing new trade is the Asian, Chinese, Polish and what have you. And they're not the clientele that you can earn a living from. All they want is pigs' feet – trotters. They don't want to buy meat off you. Five pigs' feet for a pound. Then you've got to chop 'em into small pieces, cut the toe nails off for them, put them in a carrier bag which costs five pence and then they'll ask you for another carrier bag – by then you're arm aching (sic). Bloody pigs' feet! Cutting pigs feet in the winter and pork bones. Oh! My God! If somebody would have told me that I would have been selling pigs' feet and pork bones 10 years ago I'd have said, 'Never in a month of Sunday's! Never!' (Barry)

Three years later Barry was still in the shop. Trade had recovered slightly but on average he earns only slightly more than the UK statutory minimum hourly rate for employees. 'I don't have a sixteenth of the wealth I used to have,' said Barry.

He has cashed some of his pensions to maintain a semblance of his former luxury lifestyle. 'Seeing how the others have performed, I might as well have cashed the lot,' said Barry.

Barry's concern now is his failing health. 'Seven years to retirement: I just hope I can keep working that's all. One day you might ... find us all boarded up. The market's a candle that will burn to the end.'

The Dynamics of Implosion: Analysis of Barry's Story

The seeds of entrapment may have been sown when Barry (like Mike) concentrated his investments in the market because the decision narrowed Barry's options. Contrary to sunk costs theories of persistence (for example, Arkes and Blumer 1985, Navarro and Stolarz-Fantino 2008), Barry rapidly disposes of two shops even though they were his pension. Losses out of pocket are thought to be more keenly felt than revenues forgone (Northcraft and Wolf 1984: 233 discuss this point). Barry's willingness to forgo sunk costs may reflect the mounting costs of persistence as both shops were losing money.

Left with only one shop, Barry lapses into denial, insisting that things can't get any worse and, more damaging, avoids scrutinizing the accounts. Recall that behavioural theorists believe that a severe shock may be needed to force decision-makers to recognize reality (for example, Ross and Staw 1993). The critical incident in Barry's case is the bank statement, because it shatters his complacency. Again, Barry's response is entirely logical. He resolves to quit as soon he can pay the various closing costs. Meanwhile he makes economies.

Barry's resolve weakens as a key assumption about finding a job fails. Even so, by renewing the lease for only three months, he purchases a kind of immediate exit option that reduces the risk of being caught in a long notice period if trade suddenly melts down (Janney and Dess 2004 discuss the various types of real options). Recall that decision-makers may be less vulnerable to entrapment if they have to make an active decision to persist (Brockner, Shaw and Rubin 1979). This happens every time Barry renews the lease. He is held in place because he discovers he cannot afford to quit. First there is the 'side-bet' of self-employment (Becker 1960). Barry went into business on his own account to make money. Self-employment was incidental but it becomes a driving force for persistence. Yet what ultimately holds Barry in place is that there is no better alternative. Financially, he is slightly better off working for himself than working long hours for the statutory minimum wage, even though he has to endure the ignominy of chopping pork bones.

As regards how entrapment predicaments are finally resolved, Barry's story suggests that decision-makers may be held in place until events play themselves out. Three years after the arrival of the fateful bank statement, and in uncertain health, Barry either persists until his health fails, or retirement, or until trade in the market is finally extinguished, whichever happens first.

'What Can You Do?': Nana's Story

It is a summer's afternoon on the market. The indoor hall has a languid air. Traders sit on their stools. Some are reading books, others are doing crosswords. Cafe owners are wearing shorts. Ted, an iron-monger, leaves his stall to go and buy a cup of tea. 'You get so used to do nothing you can't be bothered to serve anybody,' he says.

Nana is showing an elderly customer a dress made of blue imitation silk. 'I've got it in other colours,' says Nana.

Nana wields her hooked pole and retrieves three more dresses. She spreads them out for the customer to inspect. Eventually the customer walks away. She probably never had any intention of buying and Nana probably knew it but it helps to pass the time for both of them.

Nana, a first-generation immigrant from Pakistan, has owned her stall since 1969. She sells women's cardigans made from acrylic and skirts, dresses and blouses made from viscose, bearing obscure labels like Alcatel. For many years the business was prosperous as Nana's customers included relatively affluent miner's wives. Since the closure of the pits in the mid 1980s and the demise of other local industries, business has declined to a point where it is 'just ticking over' said Nana. She now sells very little, even on a Saturday. Many of Nana's fellow traders have either left markets or downsized their businesses. 'When you see what's happening I think thank God I never wanted to spread my wings,' said Nana.

Nana makes only enough money to cover expenses. She can no longer afford to buy stock apart from one or two small items to vary her display between summer and winter. Her customers are mainly elderly. Young people want branded goods that Nana cannot afford. 'This stall is in a good position,' said Nana, 'but what can you do when people aren't even stopping to look?'

Just then, another trader interrupts the interview to hand Nana a Christmas card. 'God bless,' says Nana, 'I haven't done mine yet.'

H.D.: Have you ever had days when you have taken nothing at all?

Nana: I've had plenty of those. [Laughter] You hear of people paying 40, 50 pounds for a meal in a restaurant. I can't afford to do that … I bring my lunch from home.

Nana is now in her mid sixties. Twice in recent years she has been hospitalized for three to four weeks. She has also has suffered several shorter bouts of minor illness. It has meant closing the stall temporarily though Nana is still liable for rent and other expenses.

H.D.: Why do you stay?

Nana: My old ladies. They would miss me. And what do you do at home all day after you've done the housework?

Beyond The Continuity Trap: Analysis of Nana's Story

Recall that entrapment theory predicts that continuity begets continuity (for example, Rubin and Brockner 1975, Drummond 2004). There was a time when Nana's business was almost as novel as the so-called 'Dotcom boom' once was, and her wares as appealing as the Apple iPhone is today. Nana's business is now worthless because the world has changed but Nana has not updated her approach. She pays premium rent for a stall in a good position but no one even looks any more. Like Henry and the exotic fish, initially the cost of *not* updating the business model was probably negligible (Brockner, Shaw and Rubin 1979) but the decline is now irreversible. Nana can barely afford bits and pieces of stock. There is no question of revamping the business as Mike did. Indeed, since Nana has reached state retirement age why would she want to revamp it? Yet persistence is risky because if trade suddenly deteriorates (as happened to Tony and Sana in Chapter 5, or if Nana's health fails, she may find herself liable for six months rent and no takings to pay it.

The statement about not wanting to spread her wings may be Nana's way of reducing the dissonance created by the gap between past success and present poverty (for example, Staw 1981, Drummond 2004). Likewise, Nana's claim that her old ladies would miss her could be seen as rationalizing persistence with an unprofitable venture. Yet her customers would probably miss her and she would probably miss them. It seems reasonable therefore to conclude that Nana is held in place by her relationship with her customers – a 'side-bet' (Becker 1960) that has built up over the years.

It is more than that, however. Concepts like entrapment and side-bets are as man-made as acrylic and viscose. We invent them to try to make sense of our world. Entrapment is a figment of our imagination. Becker's starting point was why people persist with a suboptimal course of action? We impose the question on those we study and our theories dictate what we see. Can we really say that in Nana's case persistence is suboptimal? The stall is may no longer be a money making entity that it was, but the market has become the epicentre of Nana's life. She has attempted to integrate with the local community ('God bless'), and gained acceptance as evidenced by the Christmas card. In short, over the years the business has assumed a new significance.

Summary and Conclusions

Entrapment may be partly accidental, that is, the result of 'side-bets'. More importantly, the present study suggests that decision-makers are not always victims of circumstances. They make their decisions and their decisions make them. More specifically, the origins of entrapment may lie in ignoring important environmental cues, like a growing market for exotic fish or changes in fashion. In other words, entrapment may indeed start because the cost of consistency, that is, of *not* adapting to environmental cues is initially miniscule and therefore largely invisible (Brockner, Shaw and Rubin 1979). Entrapment can also start because of decisions that are initially beneficial but which ultimately destroy options. Barry puts all his eggs in one basket. Mike too could become tomorrow's entrapped trader for the same reason. Elaine puts short-term financial expediency before longer term pension considerations. To put it another way, entrapment may result from discounting the future. Discounting the future means a bias towards short-term advantage at the expense of bigger gains in the longer term. For example, would you prefer £10,000 now, or £12,000 in a year's time? The second choice clearly offers a much better return than would be achieved by putting £10,000 in the bank, but people are often tempted to opt for instant gratification (Bazerman and Watkins 2008: 85 discuss this form of bias).

As regards how entrapment is experienced, recall the theory that entrapment is inversely related to cost salience (Brockner, Shaw and Rubin 1979). That theory implies that entrapment only happens if decision-makers are unaware of the costs of persistence. Yet in the present study, far from 'drifting idly', Richard, Barry and Elaine are well aware of how they have become entrapped and what persistence is costing them. Mike too recognizes he has made mistakes.

What holds them in place is the cost of changing direction. Mike can only diversify as resources permit. For Richard quitting means forgoing sunk costs and giving up the dream of a valuable prize 'that day'. For Barry and Elaine there is the 'side-bet' of self-employment.

Yet there are limits. The present study suggests that entrapment predicaments may be resolved if the costs of persistence reach a certain threshold. Richard may have invested his heart and soul in the business, but paying his mortgage is his overriding priority. Elaine refuses to get into debt. In other words, entrapment is a dynamic entity. It depends upon the cost of persistence versus the cost of giving up. That observation is hardly new. What the present study suggests, however, is that while ever the costs of persistence are containable, and the cost of quitting is high, decision-makers are quite likely to continue until events play themselves out.

8 *'I'm Getting Out': Escalation and Entrapment Avoided*

The curious incident of the dog in the night-time.
The dog did nothing in the night time.
That was the curious incident.
                    ('Silver Blaze', Memoirs of Sherlock Holmes, Arthur Conan Doyle)

Introduction

The dog that did nothing in the night illustrates how exceptions can be enlightening. This chapter considers four cases of owners of failing businesses who, unlike many of their colleagues, largely manage to avoid destructive persistence. Again the rationale for studying opposites, namely the conditions under which escalation and entrapment do *not* occur, is because it can shed light on the phenomena of escalation and entrapment (Camerer and Weber 1999: 80 discuss this point. See also Mills 1959 and Wicker 1985). More specifically, the purpose of telling and analysing the four stories is to identify what distinguishes those owners apart from traders who persist suboptimally. For example, is it because they recognize failure sooner rather than later and if so, why? Or is it because they are less emotionally attached to the business so it is easier for them to accept the ignominy of failure and forgo sunk costs? Or were they just lucky in the timing of their exit?

'Would Like to Give Business a Whirl': Karma's Story

Karma could not afford to go to university. After working in retail, she moved into sales – working for a foreign timber company. In her mid twenties, Karma came into a small legacy and decided to use the money to open a delicatessen. 'This was my money going into it,' said Karma. 'I didn't want to speak to banks which everyone suggested you should … I don't want to owe anyone any money.'

The idea for delicatessen came from her parents who ran a mobile business. 'I reckoned I could give that a whirl, said Karma. 'I knew it was now or never. I was 27 and that time was passing and I was thinking I would like to give business a whirl.'

H.D.: What was the attraction?

Karma: Just the knowledge from what mum and dad were doing. It sounded exciting and a bit different. When we looked into it a bit more it did seem maybe there was a slight gap [in the market], but, to be fair it was more a case of, 'I want to do this. I will make a gap.'

Karma considered doing her own mobile round of outdoor markets, 'But I saw my mum and dad go through hell during the winter months … and such long hours, I thought I'm not sure if I could sustain that.'

H.D.: What happened next?

Karma: It was a lot of to-ing and fro-ing; six months of sleepless nights. I was so worried that it wasn't going to succeed.

Dealing with market authorities proved a trial of patience. 'You have to submit [plans of] exactly what you are going to do structurally,' said Karma. 'Food: so, sink; hot water. What the hell did they think we were going to do? Have a bucket? It was all basic stuff.' It took eight months to obtain final approval. Then Karma had to get the workmen in to build the stall:

We didn't just knock something up one weekend with a hammer. We just made it look fab. We wanted to make it look right. It wasn't a case of trying to be better than anyone. We just thought we would have to go the whole hog. The sort of customers that we do get and did expect to get aren't exactly your market goer. We couldn't afford anywhere else. Also I wanted to do it because it was where mum and dad started from. (Karma)

Finding suppliers was another challenge:

Karma: It was such a struggle to find suppliers. Apart from the ones my mum and dad had. We were going for quality. We're either doing this properly or we're not and I didn't feel comfortable doing anything other than good quality stuff.

H.D.: What do you remember about your first day?

Karma: I can absolutely remember everything about it. I was so nervous. I got up so early, I was so nervous I must have got there about half past seven which is when the main doors are open. I had been in all day Sunday. The lounge was stacked up. [I remember] opening up the shutters that had been a nightmare to fit. We had quite a promising day – people were stunned.

H.D.: Do you remember your first customer?

Karma: Yes! They spent about 20 quid and I thought, cor! I love you. The first day I didn't have lunch or go to the loo or anything. I got home and then thought, My God! I have to do it all again tomorrow.

The business opened in September. Although it was located in a fairly quiet corner of the market, it was such an arresting presentation that it soon began to attract custom. Everything about that stall was different; from the professionally lettered sign in red and gold cutting a striking contrast with the faded lettering and paintwork of adjacent stalls. The rich presentations of salamis, sun-dried tomatoes, black olives and crusted loaves were a far cry from the more traditional market fare of white teacakes and boiled ham. In the run-up to Christmas the business was very successful. All the customers were nice, and many sent pleasant emails saying it was good to be able to buy such nice food at lunch time. Karma even set up a website to promote the business and succeeded in attracting a small but significant custom from local restaurants and bars:

> Nothing major but quite regular and we save on packaging and all sorts of things like that. We know we are providing them with good quality stuff and they can just wander in, send a chef to pick some up so they don't have to worry about big orders and big deliveries. (Karma)

'I DON'T THINK I WANT TO DO THIS ANY-MORE'

Karma hoped that the business would expand though she was content for it to remain as a small but thriving market stall. 'We hoped it would develop in to something, but at the same time if it developed enough in there, we were happy to stay there. I didn't have any big ambitions. It just seemed the right thing to do,' said Karma.

As winter set in, however, Karma's enthusiasm waned. To her dismay she discovered that the long opening hours specified in the contract were strictly enforced. Consequently, when business was quiet she was forced to spend long hours with little to do. Karma also discovered that she was not allowed to vary the list of items that she had applied for permission to sell. For instance, Karma had assumed that, as the business developed, she would expand the range of bread on offer and sell sandwiches. 'We started getting some samples of some bread from some bakeries but someone complained, [and] the inspector came along,' said Karma. 'I thought, God! I'm selling a few slices of walnut bread so someone can take some away for their lunch. I was stunned that there would be such a problem.'

Winter took its toll in other ways: the tensions in the market, the drunks, the homeless and the drug addicts plus the sheer boredom also undermined Karma's morale. 'Customers fell off," said Karma. 'And it is really hard work. You're on your feet all day; you've got a big responsibility in your mind because you've got to make the money to pay the rent.'

One evening in June, after she had been in business for about nine months, Karma was having supper with her partner. She suddenly burst into tears:

> I had sort of been thinking; something had been on my mind for a long time. I said, 'I don't think I want to do this anymore'. I had a gut feeling that this wasn't going anywhere ... there was going to be a big rent increase ... we weren't just moving anywhere ... and I didn't want to get stuck there like I hear constantly every day. Everyone's complaining because they're stuck there. I just thought, God! Almost putting myself in a box, restricting myself and I don't really want to do that. I'm 28 and I don't want to get to 30 and think, God! If I'd only left two years ago! But then I start to think, if I ... stay, but there was nothing positive to go with, 'If you stay well this might happen. It was all 'if you stay this might happen'.

Shortly afterwards Karma served six months notice to quit. That meant she would leave at the end of December, thus avoiding another winter trading lull. Although by now the business was actually paying Karma a small wage, revenues were well below the business plan forecast. 'OK I'm making money at the moment which is good, but … we really need to make progress to make it worthwhile … It wasn't that I wanted to make loads of money. It was just the fact we were supposed to increase customer numbers,' said Karma.

Karma's business plan was based upon data from her parent's business as it was the only information she had. 'Things were and probably almost still are pretty much as we thought, but we've struggled to get many new people in since. I think we've almost levelled off too soon but I think that's because not many new people coming in. It levelled off quite quickly … after six months or so,' said Karma.

H.D.: What prompted the decision to leave?

Karma: What triggered it was I thought bloody hell! I could go back to college! That's what made my decision. Also, its late twenties … do I need to get myself a career? I've never really been conscious of that.

Karma duly obtained a place in college and started studying whilst the business was quiet. She sometimes wondered if she should withdraw notice to quit:

I felt I was ducking out, was I being a bit pathetic … giving up, taking an easy route out. On good days I think wouldn't it be nice if we could get someone in and keep it going even if it is just breaking even. I still almost think that it might be better if there was no alternative, it would almost be easier to stay in. (Karma)

Karma advertised the business for sale. The decision was partly prompted by money but also the thought of her beautiful presentation being ripped to the ground. She hoped she might raise £2,000–£3,000 for it but recognized that it was unlikely to happen. Besides, she doubted whether it was ethical. 'I almost feel … I shouldn't do that. It's not very nice for someone … if it doesn't work out,' she said.

Karma felt that the council had exaggerated the footfall. Moreover, it had declined since she had opened for business. Besides, footfall, Karma had discovered, does not automatically translate into paying customers. 'Maybe it's my own stupidity, my own naivety from not looking into it more thoroughly, not understanding about the market. But my enthusiasm normally takes over from my brain anyway, maybe I wouldn't have listened,' said Karma.

H.D.: How do you feel about the money invested in the business?

Karma: I should feel really gutted. But I feel if I hadn't given it a go I would be kicking myself. I wasted it, but I don't think I could have done it any other way. I think we gave it a really good shot. I wanted to do it properly, hoped it would lead to something else. It hasn't and I just see it as a lesson.

Trade in the run-up to Karma's second Christmas in business was good. Many customers said they were disappointed that she was leaving. Yet Karma had few second thoughts. 'Maybe we haven't given it long enough, but then you just can't tell … whether things will pick up. I just don't feel like hanging round and finding out,' said Karma.

Analysis: Impact of Expectations and Alternatives

Karma has a clear set of expectations for the venture. First there is the general expectation that ownership will provide congenial employment: 'exciting and a bit different'. That expectation is severely dented on day one as Karma discovers the sheer physical effort involved in running a business.

Experimental evidence suggests that escalation may be curbed if decision-makers track expenses against plans (Heath 1995). The present study offers field confirmation of this experimental discovery. Karma has a clear set of plans and monitors the results. A major factor in Karma's decision to quit is that although she succeeds in building a customer base, she fails to achieve the target increases forecast in the business plan. She monitors the situation very carefully so it becomes obvious that, although the business is making some money, the results are consistently below expectations. Karma is also conscious of the costs of persistence. Her commitment to the venture is further weakened as she discovers the realities of being a market trader – the boredom, the hostile environment and the responsibility.

Instead of lapsing into denial as behavioural theorists predict (for example, Staw 1976, Staw 1981), Karma confronts the situation, the implications of a possible rent rise, and decides that expectations will probably never be met. Moreover, whereas in Crystal's case progress was intermittent, Karma's business reaches a plateau so there is no positive re-enforcement to encourage her to persist (for example, Goltz 1992, 1993).

Recall it is thought that alternative investment opportunities curb escalation (for example, McCain 1986). The second major factor in Karma's decision to quit is that she could go to college. McCain suggests that alternatives limit escalation by highlighting the opportunity costs of persistence. 'Bloody hell!' says Karma as she sees what she could have instead.

Unlike some other traders we have met in this book, Karma is conscious of the passage of time, and what it is costing her. She needs a career. She also learns from the negative experiences of other traders. She exercises foresight and realizes that if she stays in the market she may share their fate.

Quitting clearly has negative implications for Karma's self-esteem. She feels 'pathetic'; that she has usurped social norms for persistence by 'ducking out'. Yet contrary to behavioural theories of escalation (for example, Brockner et al. 1986), those forces do not hold her in place. This is because the costs of persistence far outweigh the emotional pangs of quitting.

'Definitely Coming Out': Bev and Sue's Story

To put it another way, McCain (1986) predicts that escalation will occur in the absence of alternatives. Intuitively this may seem obvious. Surely no one is going to persist with a failing venture if, like Karma, they can switch to something better. Yet what if the decision-maker has no alternative lined up? What might prompt them to quit in those circumstances?

Two friends, Bev and Sue (both in their early twenties), left paid employment to become owners. They rented a tiny market cabin in a good location (rent £200 a month exclusive of business rates and service charges) where they sold speciality silk scarves and other fashion accessories. Both had previous experience in fashion retail. The shop opened in September. Business got off to a slow start. 'It's quiet,' said Bev who had been sitting doodling, 'but we've only been open six weeks. I love it.'

H.D.: *You say the rent is £200 a month. Isn't that a lot of scarves to sell?*

Bev: *It's not really.*

A month later business was still quiet.

H.D.: *Are you making any money for yourselves?*

Sue: *Not yet. It doesn't bother me. You get used to having nothing.*

Bev and Sue's optimism proved short-lived. In mid-December they decided to leave at the end of January rather than sign up to a six-month lease and because they knew from previous experience of working on markets that the winter months are financially dire. 'We've built up a bit of business,' said Sue, 'but it's nowhere what we need.'

The plan was to move the business to move to an 'out of town' shopping centre. Although it meant paying much higher rent (£500 a month), Bev and Sue believed that the increased trade would justify it. By mid January Bev and Sue were still waiting to hear if their application for a tenancy had succeeded. Yet they were resolved, however, to leave in any case. 'We're definitely coming out even if we've nowhere to go,' said Sue.

'I just want to get out of the market,' said Bev. 'It's horrible. People are ignorant – they drop litter in front of your stall.'

They were required to give a month's notice but they were trying to negotiate it down to three weeks because of financial pressure.

H.D.: *Are you managing to pay your rent?*

Bev: *Yes, just. We did all right up to Christmas, but it's been very, very quiet after Christmas.*

They had taken just £30 that day. But, said Sue, 'We've learned a lot. It's been a very useful experience; we've changed suppliers and learned how to live on very little wage. I don't feel bad about it. Everyone's in the same boat.'

Confronting Options: Analysis of Bev and Sue's Story

Unlike Karma, Bev and Sue do not have clearly defined expectations for the business. Nevertheless they soon recognize failure. That recognition prompts a search for alternative premises. The decisive factor in Bev and Sue's case, however, the lease on their existing premises. Recall that it is thought that decision-makers are less likely to persist in an economically suboptimal fashion where the decision must be made actively than where it must be made passively (Brockner, Shaw and Rubin 1979). Needing to sign up to a permanent contract forces Bev and Sue them to confront their options. Contrary to behavioural theories (for example, Staw 1981, Staw and Ross 1978), Bev and Sue eschew denial. Yes they have built some business but not enough. Moreover, they look forwards, not backwards and realize that the business is unlikely to survive the winter. They decide they must quit even though they have no definite alternative premises.

Again, impending failure is accompanied by rising levels of stress. Bev and Sue's story also sheds light on the direction of the relationship. To be more precise, whilst the stress of being in a market may contribute to a sense of failure, Bev and Sue's story (and to a lesser extent Karma's) suggests that impending failure may add to stress. Initially they love the experience. It is only when the business falters that they become aware of people dropping litter and other stressors that were there from the start.

Living on Thin Air: Peter and the Model Aeroplanes

Karma and Bev and Sue were new traders. They might find it relatively easy to quit because they have less of themselves invested in the market. Yet contrary to what we might expect, established traders can avoid the pitfalls of escalation and entrapment. Although they may not emerge completely unscathed, they at least succeed in limiting the damage to themselves.

When Peter was 30, he was made redundant for the third time. He bought a toyshop and enjoyed a small regional monopoly selling model railways and airplane kits to enthusiasts. After Peter had been in business for about six years, the council announced a large rent rise. Peter was not unduly worried. He was single, had a modest life-style and lived with his mother so his expenses were low. 'I can live off thin air,' he said.

Peter's main selling day was Saturday. During the week he mainly sold small items like tubes of glue. In summer, if he arrived early, he would sit out in the sun, never entering the market before the official opening time. 'I don't like work,' he said.

During the day Peter passed the time fixing laptop computers for other traders, chatting to neighbours and reading newspapers.

In October, a few months after the rent rise was implemented, Peter did his annual accounts. As a result, he began to think about closing the business. Part of Peter's problem was a shift in the market. Children now prefer computers to toys. 'I sell all these things and I'm still poor,' said Peter pointing to the wide variety of items on his stall. 'Selling tubes of glue to middle-aged men is no good. Turnover's what you need.'

Expenses were the main problem. Not just the rent but the cost of bus fares into town, and rising costs of stock as many suppliers closed down. When Peter did his accounts the following October things were worse. 'Turnover's static. Expenses are going up. I'll give it six months and see how it goes,' said Peter.

Six months later, Peter served notice to quit. 'I'm getting out while I can still see what my liabilities are,' said Peter. 'The business was going down eight years ago when I bought it. That's why Kathy [previous owner] sold it. I haven't broken the news to my customers yet.'

The day before Peter was due to close, he still had a lot of stock left.

H.D.: What about all your stock?

Peter: I'll just hire a van tomorrow and clear it out.

H.D.: How do you feel about leaving?

Peter: I'm used to being redundant – having no pension. Anyway, I've never been one for work.

Setting Limits and Quitting Points: Analysis of Peter's Story

Part of the problem that decision-makers face, and what leads to escalation is that failure seldom emerges full blown. The present study suggests, however, that decision-makers can use a period of grace to their advantage. At first Peter responds to the downturn by explicitly lowering his expectations resolving to live on thin air. Recall that it is thought that escalation may be curbed if decision-makers set limits on their involvement and identify quitting points (for example, Simonson and Staw 1992). Like Sam, Peter takes control of time as he too sets limits. Moreover, again like Sam, he does not wait until the ship starts to sink before quitting. When he sees the trend, he decides that the business is approaching a threshold and that it would be unwise to cross it. Unlike Tony and Sana, he reads the road ahead and makes a timely exit.

Peter's observations on Kathy's motive for selling may be ego-defensive, his way of saying that it is his fault the business has failed. Alternatively, if we take them at face value, they may mean that now that he is exiting, Peter can confront the truth about the business.

Peter's remarks about redundancy may also have been ego-defensive. Yet again if we take them at face value, they suggest that another function of alternatives is that they reduce fear of the unknown (Fisher and Ury 1983 Ch. 6 also discuss this point). Redundancy may or may not be a desirable alternative to ownership but, for Peter, it is certainly nothing new.

'Writing on the Wall': Carole's Story

The presence of a crowd around Carole's stall was strange. March is one of the quietest months of the year on markets, and Tuesday is the quietest day of all because it is half day closing. The unexpected clamour was explained by a notice 'Closing Saturday' written in crude capitals with a black marker pen.

'FOR SEVERAL YEARS IT WAS BRILLIANT'

Carole was born to markets. Her great grandparents owned a small shop and her mother was a market trader. Her husband also worked the outdoor markets – travelling up and down the country sleeping rough. Carole opened her first business in the late 1960s on the outdoor market, quickly graduating to a small stall indoors. Clothes were her main stock in trade with a special line in dresses. The business prospered. 'We had some beautiful things, really, really beautiful things from Korea and other parts of the Far East – beautiful quality things,' said Carole.

Times changed, however:

After a year or two, the big shops ... cottoned on to what was going on and they then started taking all the quotas that were coming in, so all our goods dried up. And then we were reliant, mostly, on English made goods from English sweat shops – which wasn't a patch on the quality. ... So life was just getting harder and harder. (Carole)

To make matters worse, the council decided to demolish the old market hall. For two years, whilst construction of the building was underway, Carole was shunted from pillar to post. Business plummeted and Carole's plight became desperate. 'We were down to our last fiver and that isn't an exaggeration,' she said.

Eventually Carole was allocated a permanent unit in a good location. She switched into selling refurbished consumer electrical goods, including micro-waves, televisions, videos, and washing machines. Again, the business was hugely successful – but only for a while:

For several years (it) ... was brilliant. And then, you find that all the electrical products are going down ... Videos, when they first came out for sale there was Betamax VHS and they were about £700 or £800 apiece – you can get them for £99 now. Electrical goods are coming down and down in price but in comparison all your expenses are going up and up and up – they never come down ... We got to the stage that you could buy a brand new television for £150 with three years warranty – so who is going to buy a second hand television for the same price when you can get a modern TV with everything you want? (Carole)

Carole decided that she needed to regenerate the business. Accordingly she borrowed £100,000 to buy equipment to enable her to start a 'one hour' dry-cleaning business. Carole was sure that the venture would succeed because she would have a monopoly locally plus a thick stream of passing trade including office workers en route to and from work. She was wrong:

I have to be honest and say that the people who sold it did not promise that it was going to make a fortune. They said that it was a good thing to augment a business that was already established. Everything that they said was true in actual fact. But I believed that being in the market where the footfall was so great, we couldn't fail. I felt that we were really onto a winner.

But we forgot the main thing about people. They'll walk through the market, or the city centre, or their local shopping area, and they will see what they expect to see. And we were invisible. The product that we were trying to promote they didn't see because they didn't expect to see it. And you will get people coming to you, after four years [Carole's emphasis] regular market customers – people that you see day in day out. They would bring me a skirt to clean and they would say, 'Never noticed you here – didn't realize that you did dry-cleaning.' This piece of machinery was huge and it was there for everybody to see and I had all the adverts round the shop and goodness knows what, but they don't see. (Carole)

Carole reinvested because she recognized that the business could not survive by selling small items like light bulbs, batteries, plugs and computer leads. Even selling more specialized items shunned by big high street retail chains like bags for vacuum cleaners, replacement plates for microwaves, and hoses for washing machines would not suffice. Carole said:

I decided that we would expand on these items – we did a very extensive range (and) – people would be sent down to us from the Town centre because ... we would go to the trouble of getting things that people wanted. They [big stores] would sell the machinery and we would supply all the bags and belts. So we were expanding in that – but that was not huge money and I thought that (dry-cleaning) would be a good money-spinner. In actual, fact it wasn't – it was poor. It's very labour intensive for little return ... That was a huge gamble which did not pay off.

In fact, the dry-cleaning business generated just enough money to enable Carole to repay the loan. 'I got £1,500 for [the dry-cleaning equipment] when we sold it. So that was a major blow to our finances. But you have to put it behind you and move on.'

'IT HAPPENED GRADUALLY ...'

Move on where? Carole kept meticulous accounts. She drew £100 a week from the business for housekeeping and general expenses. At the end of every financial year she would pay outstanding Value Added Tax (VAT), pay off any outstanding supplier's bills and calculate her income tax liabilities. 'And then you find out how much money you've made for the year,' said Carole.

The surplus Carole invested in savings accounts.

H.D.: What made you decide to leave?

Carole: It happened gradually I think. ... We had got to the stage – year on year – we were getting less profit. Originally we were able (to save) but [one year] we were not able to put anything away ... So it was really at that point I could see the writing on the wall – that I had to make some kind of decision about this because things were not going to get any better and eventually we would have been faced with dipping into our savings to pay our expenses. So that was what pushed us.

H.D.: How are you aware that trade is going down?

Carole: Well you look at your previous year's figures and realize that you are not taking the same kind of money but your expenses are going up. Electrical goods are coming down and down in price but in comparison all your expenses are going up and up and up – they never come down. Your wages expenses go up; your overheads go up and your products are coming down and your wages are going up.

Even so, it was another seven to eight months before Carole finally decided to offer the business for sale. 'I had decided – that our turnover was not going to increase and as year on year followed lower turnover, we couldn't hope to hold onto the business too much longer without losing any hope of selling it,' said Carole.

H.D.: How hopeful were you of being able to sell it?

Carole: We wondered if we would still be able to sell the stall. We were hopeful because it has always been our expectation that the stall would give us something for our retirement. We hadn't over the years been able to invest heavily in pensions. Our money has always been ear marked for the business.

Carole duly instructed an estate agent. 'And then the bombshell hit,' said Carole.

Rents on the market had been static for over a decade. As the agent was finalizing sales literature and arranging advertisements, the council announced that it intended to almost double the rent. For Carole it was the last straw:

> We pay £25 per square foot and there are add-on (sic) for two frontages and for the location. I pay just short of £500 a week for that stall for rent and my rates are nearly £800 a month for 10 months of the year and then there are wages and electricity and everything else I pay out on top. Rent of course has been up ... and on our unit they want to increase it by 90 per cent which brings our expenses to £1,000 a week. Without any hope of increasing our turnover there is just no chance that we could meet that kind of expense. We're really not meeting the expense now with the falling sales.

Traders decided to challenge the council's decision through the courts – an action that would take many months to resolve. Meanwhile, rents were frozen. Carole decided that until the case was concluded, there was no hope of selling the business so she gave six months notice to quit. 'No one in their right minds would take on a business that they had no idea what the rent was going to be,' said Carole.

Meanwhile the council told Carole that if she agreed to the pay the rent rise, she would not be liable for any back rent accrued during the notice period. Carole refused to sign – a decision that subsequently cost her £6,000. 'I know the value of solidarity and I won't break the ranks on this. I would rather pay what other people are going to be paying. I support the traders and I feel I've put my money where my mouth is,' said Carole.

Whilst Carole was serving notice, things got worse, 'The business just dropped like stone,' said Carole, 'absolutely dropped – nothing – it was just flat – very, very poor.'

It was, she observed, the same everywhere.

As the last day of trading dawned, Carole grew anxious. '[At first] I felt euphoric thinking I'm going to love walking in the countryside and then I suddenly had a panic the other week as I thought, we're not going to have any income. What are we going to do' she said?

Yet there was no question of turning back. Recalling the days when she was down to her last 'fiver' Carole said:

> Having experienced that, we didn't want to get to that pitch that we were desperate and we had nowhere to turn. We felt that if we made the choice now then we do actually have some choices. We haven't put every last penny into the business; we've still got savings and if we want to invest those savings in another business then we can do that.

Carole was not sure what those other businesses might be. One possibility would be to offer her services as a locum manger to enable other traders to take a holiday. She also wondered if she might open a small stall on the market selling computer accessories:

> It's looking less and less likely. I don't really want to be tied five days a week, 52 weeks of the year. ... When you work for yourself, whatever you're working for, you're working non-stop. The week never finishes. You're always working – everything you do is work. I do my paperwork every Saturday night, unless we happen to be going out, but we don't go out very often. Most of our life is work.

H.D.: Why did you not leave sooner?

Carole: You get into a rut … It's like people who have a paid job, they've been there 20 years and they can't imagine themselves anywhere else … Everyone has this crisis of confidence and once you're into this rut it's so hard to break out of it. You're paying your rent week by week and you're going in everyday at a certain time, and you're leaving at a certain time and you have your routine and you buy your goods and even though you're not getting the returns that you need to get, you're still in that rut and it is very hard to break that cycle.

'MY LIFE IS IN THAT SKIP'

H.D.: How has the 'closing down sale gone? Have you sold everything?

Carole: No, we're still packing away. Tomorrow is our final day and it looks like rubbish. This actually is the heartbreaking piece of it all. Everything that you're packing away, hoping that you are going to be able to sell at some future date is your life. You're finding things that have been there 20 years – that got tucked away somewhere – that might have been in a box from the last time you moved. Everything in that skip – that's your money. That's what you've been working for all this time … We've been selling goods for less than they've cost us and they're still on the shelves, people aren't buying them.

Carole planned to keep some unsold stock to start another business or sell off at a 'car boot' sale. Some goods she sold below cost in order to generate ready cash:

We need some cash to pay our bills. … Some of the goods I have let go very, very cheap in order to not have to store it and because there is only so much that we can sell cheap somewhere else. Things that are broken lines – that you don't have a full display of, its' very hard to sell … So those kind of things you have to say, 'Right! Forget it. Let's get rid.' I would not give it away. I would put it in the rubbish before I would give it away because that is what I have to work for … My life is in that skip.

H.D.: Isn't it better to get something, than nothing at all?

Carole: No! We have been very adversely affected by all the charity shops. People give things to charity shops. They don't have to pay the same kind of rates that we do. A lot of their staff are volunteers. They have all kinds of tax breaks because they are a registered charity. And they are selling goods in competition with people like ourselves who are finding it very, very hard. And it's a difficult situation. No one wants to say anything about the charity shops – they're doing such good work … But they are raising cash at the expense of legitimate businesses and I would not give it to something like that because I know how hard it is trying to earn the money.

H.D.: Did you get to a point, where you'd say we'll give it so many months to pick up?

Carole: We knew it's not going to pick up. Trade is not going to pick up.

H.D.: Did you ever hope that it would?

Carole: When you work for yourself you have to be optimistic. You always hope that things are going to get better, particularly when things have been better in the past. You hope they're going to return to that. But your common sense tells you they're not going to.

Analysis: Distinguishing Signal from Noise

In theory, Carole might be expected to be highly vulnerable to escalation and entrapment because she has invested her life in the market. Yet unlike Terry, she desists from raiding her savings and makes a reasonably timely exit. What explains the difference?

First it necessary to estimate at what point Carole's business actually failed. The critical juncture arrives when she has nothing left to save. Although Carole believes that the business has probably been losing money for years, having no surplus is a tangible event and one that signals a clear failure of expectations.

Carole then looks forwards. Whereas 'signal' means signs pointing to an impending crisis, 'noise' refers to conflicting information that suggests other explanations for a perceived threat (Bazerman and Watkins 2008: 100) such as a dip in the business cycle. Carole succeeds in distinguishing 'signal' from 'noise'. She sees only too clearly the downwards trajectory and what it implies. Above all, persistence would mean crossing a critical threshold.

Even so, seven months elapse before Carole instructs an agent. It is a delay that works against her overarching goal of keeping her savings intact. A possible explanation for the delay is anticipatory grieving (Shepherd, Wiklund and Haynie 2009). The argument is that, just as when a person is dying, bystanders prepare themselves for death by mourning the individual whilst they are still alive, owner's need time to accustom themselves to the prospect of losing the business. Since the paper by Shepherd and colleagues was not published until after the interview, this possibility could not be explored with Carole. Besides, the data suggests the opposite. Mourning involves cognitive effort whereas Carole refers to being in a rut. She persists through sheer force of habit. Such indecision may reflect a psychological bias towards the status quo, that is, putting short-term convenience first whilst discounting future costs (for example, Lowenstein and Thaler 1989; Gatley 1980). The difficulty with this explanation is that Carole does not really discount future costs. She is well aware that takings are insufficient. Rather, Carole's behaviour is not so much decision avoidance as procrastination, that is, having an intention but then acting against that intention by stalling (Sabini and Silver 1982). Procrastination seems to provide Carole with temporary psychological shelter (Anderson 2003: discusses this point). Doing nothing enables Carole to remain within her comfort zone – but at a price.

Unlike Terry, Carole's career has not been smooth. She vividly recalls the experience of being down to her last 'fiver' and she does not want to repeat it. Evidently if we can vividly imagine an unpleasant event, our belief in the likelihood of it actually happening is sharpened (for example, Bazerman 2004, Schwenk 1986). How much more vivid is our imagination if we have already experienced it? In addition, unlike Terry who drip fed money into the business, Carole made a substantial reinvestment in the business that failed. (Incidentally, the decision to invest in dry-cleaning bears all the hall-marks of irrational escalation. Faced with a failing business, Carole suddenly sees a solution to her problems. The result is myopic vision (for example, Schwenk 1986, Nisbett and Ross 1980).

Was it irrational to try to sell the business? Again, strictly speaking the business became worthless as soon one unit in the market hall stood vacant and there were several. Even so, the decision was reasonable given the size of the unit and prime location. Moreover, unlike Omar who had fixed ideas about what the business was worth, Carole's ambitions were flexible. She merely hoped that the business would contribute 'something' towards her retirement. The risk lay was whether the cost of keeping the business open would negate any proceeds from the sale. There was also the risk of becoming locked in to a long notice period if business plummeted – as indeed it did latterly. Besides, Carole promptly reversed the decision to try to sell following the announcement of a rent rise. That too was an ominous signal. Carole was also concerned about the opportunity costs of persistence. She saw that persistence would destroy options, whereas exiting sooner rather than later would preserve options even though she had no definite alternative investment opportunity in mind.

Unlike Terry, Carole does not really blame anyone for the failure of her business though she allows herself a swipe at charity shops. Emotionally it is painful disposing of stock because it reminds Carole of how much she has invested in the business. Consistent with behavioural theories of escalation (for example, Teger 1980), Carole would rather throw stock away than sell it too cheap. This relatively inexpensive gesture helps preserve Carole's self esteem. Having been at the mercy of economic forces for so long, she controls the one thing she has left to control.

A more expensive decision was her refusal to sign the rental agreement – the result of a social-side bet (Becker 1960). Having previously pursued traders' interests vociferously, Carole felt she had to be consistent by matching words with deeds (for example, Brockner, Rubin and Lang 1981). This might have been because Carole knew she might want to return to the market. The gesture may also have reduced the emotional cost of quitting.

Summary and Conclusions

This chapter considered traders who largely avoided the pitfalls of escalation and entrapment by making a reasonably timely exit from a failing business. Their timing may have been partly fortuitous, but their stories are instructive. They suggest that decision-makers are less likely to succumb to escalation and entrapment if three conditions apply. One is if they set clear expectations for the business. Two, monitor the results. Three, set quitting points and adhere to them even if it means erring on the side of caution by quitting sooner rather than later.

Recall that decision-dilemma theorists argue that decision-makers are often driven to escalate because it is unclear whether a venture has well and truly failed (for example, Bowen 1987). Expectations enable decision-makers to recognize failure sooner rather than later – particularly if they are made explicit. Karma has a clear plan for the business. Within six months she sees that expectations are not being met. Within nine months she has sufficient information to reliably conclude that expectations will probably never be met so persistence is futile. The others have tacit expectations that crystallize as their financial situations worsen. Bev and Sue recognize that they have not built up anywhere near enough business. Peter lowers his expectations initially but stops as he reaches a critical threshold. So does Carole: she expects to generate savings.

Monitoring results enables decision-makers to track progress against expectations. All of the traders in this chapter keep careful accounts. Unlike Barry who receives a shock when he opens a bank statement, they know where they stand financially. Setting quitting points implies being willing to read the road ahead. Reading the road ahead stops decision-makers from taking refuge in denial and forces them to think about what *will* happen if the business continues on its current trajectory. Karma cannot see the bright future she had hoped for. Peter fears being swamped by liabilities. Bev and Sue realize their resources are insufficient to survive the winter. Carole sees her savings being eaten. Setting limits on one's involvement buys time before making a decision that is virtually irreversible. More importantly, everyone in the present chapter exits before the ship sinks though all could have continued awhile longer.

In conclusion, although escalation and entrapment may be surrounded by an air of inexorability, they are by no means inevitable. In a nutshell, the present study suggests that what differentiates those who avoid those pitfalls from those who succumb, is the exercise of responsibility. No one is completely immune from the perils of persistence but it is the decision-makers who take control rather than wait upon events who emerge relatively unscathed.

9 *Escalation and Entrapment Theories Revisited*

The essence of the ultimate decision remains impenetrable to the observer – often, indeed, to the decider himself. There will always be the dark and tangled stretches in the decision-making process – mysterious to even to those who may be intimately involved.

(John Kennedy, former American President)

Introduction

The present study has focused upon economic behaviour and decision-making. More specifically, when a venture seems to be failing, decision-makers may be torn between cutting their losses and 'throwing good money after bad'. The main purpose of the present study was to explore how decision-makers respond to that dilemma. In particular, the concern was to understand why some decision-makers exit sooner rather than later, whereas others persist to the bitter end, only to compound their difficulties – a phenomenon known as escalation of commitment.

Escalation was studied from three main theoretical standpoints. Behavioural theorists suggest that persistence with a failing course of action is driven by irrational impulses (for example, Staw and Ross 1987a,b, Brockner 1992, Whyte 1986, Moon 2001a). In contrast, decision-dilemma theorists argue that persistence may simply be a rational response to difficult circumstances. In this view escalation should be viewed as a normal business expense, and only deemed irrational if decision-makers ignore information that clearly indicates persistence is futile (Bowen 1987). The third perspective suggests that 'lock-in' can occur mainly as the result of the simple passage of time – a phenomenon known as entrapment (for example, Rubin and Brockner 1975, Drummond 2004).

Indoor market traders were chosen as focal subjects for the research because of their potentially precarious economic situation. Historically, becoming a market trader was an almost guaranteed route to prosperity. Now, competition from supermarkets and chain stores is destroying traders' livelihoods and pensions. Some cut their losses, whereas others remain almost until the bailiffs arrive – why? Moreover, mortality rate amongst new traders is high. Few survive beyond 18 months. Many last only a few weeks. What makes new traders believe they can succeed against the odds?

The purpose of this chapter is answer the main research questions and to suggest directions for future research. In a nutshell, what emerges in the present study suggests that whilst behavioural theorists may exaggerate human irrationality, those theories are by no means superfluous. Before elaborating on this observation and other important findings, it is necessary to mention the limitations of the research. In particular, the present study has not considered the possible impact of individual differences (for example, Meglino and Korsgaard 2004, Greer and Stephens 2001, Moon 2001b) on decisions to persist. For instance, little has been said about the role of formative experiences and other psycho-dynamics in shaping decision-makers strategic preferences (Kisfalvi 2000, Kisfalvi and Pitcher 2003, Stein 2000); or the possible effect of perceived efficacy (for example, Gatewood, Shaver and Gartner 1995, Heath and Tversky 1991); personality (for example, Schaubroeck and Williams 1993) and cultural influences in driving persistence (for example, Greer and Stephens 2001). Another limitation is that market traders represent a conservative setting in which to study escalation. They invest their own money and their resources are relatively limited. Consequently, the effects observed in the present study may understate the potential impact of behavioural influences. Moreover, retrospective accounts are open to the bias of hindsight and retrospective rationalization of decisions. As President Kennedy observed, we can never know for sure what goes through a decision-makers mind because they do not know themselves. For example, Carole can only point to what she 'thinks' pushed her to leave the market.

Addressing the Research Questions

RESEARCH QUESTION 1: WHY DO OWNERS EMBARK UPON VENTURES THAT CLEARLY HAVE LITTLE HOPE OF SUCCEEDING?

Interviews with new traders clearly suggest that escalation may indeed start with bright promises (for example, Staw and Ross 1987a,b, Drummond 2001: Ch. 7, Ch. 9, Hmieleski and Baron, 2009). According to Hmieleski and Baron (2009) misplaced optimism reflects the entrepreneurial personality. The argument is that entrepreneurs have high risk-taking propensity so they see less risk than is normatively appropriate. The present study suggests that the reasons for failure may be even simpler; that is, prospective owners may not see any risk at all because they fail to conduct anywhere near sufficient reality testing. For example, Crystal, Karma and Sally conduct superficial research, only visiting the market on a Saturday and are subsequently shocked by how little trade there is during the week.

Consistent with behavioural theories, the limited reality testing that prospective owners do conduct may reflect self-serving biases (for example, Ross and Staw 1986, Staw and Ross 1987b). For instance, negative cues such as boarded-up stalls tend to be ignored. Moreover, new owners are typically over-confident to begin with. Just because they have a novel idea for business such as David's wholefood cafe and Ann's curried mutton, new owners may believe that they can defeat poor odds. For instance, Anita thought that by selling beautiful things, she would attract enough non-market shoppers to make the business viable. Likewise, Fei and Bob decided that since they were using high-quality ingredients, they might be able to make a go of the business, despite poorly located premises.

RESEARCH QUESTION 2: WHY DO SOME OWNERS EXIT SOONER RATHER THAN LATER WHEN ECONOMIC FEEDBACK IS CONSISTENTLY NEGATIVE WHEREAS OTHERS WAIT UNTIL FORCED TO LEAVE?

Recall that behavioural theorists are unclear about whether irrational persistence is driven by a desire to avoid the ego costs of failure (for example, Staw 1976, Staw and Ross 1978) or the manner in which issues are expressed (framed) (for example, Whyte 1986, 1991 see also Brockner's 1992 review of the literature. An important finding of the present study is that decision-makers are most vulnerable to escalation when the status quo involves a loss. Desperate for income, Silvio opened a second cafe that also failed. Frustrated by the failure of her first shop and unable to obtain suitable premises, Anita contemplates an extremely risky reinvestment in the market. Tanya entertains similar thoughts. Stuck with her loss-making cafe, Sally decides to expand the premises, almost doubling her rent. Taken together these stories have a better 'goodness of fit' with prospect theory than self-justification theory though the status quo may also mean a loss of self-esteem.

Delving into the more detailed findings, the present study has adduced six main escalation drivers:

1. Optimism bias
2. Sunk costs
3. Prohibitive closing costs
4. Perceived salvage value
5. Lowering expectations
6. Decision avoidance

Each of these is discussed in turn.

Optimism bias

Contrary to what behavioural theorists predict, decision-makers soon recognize failure. The main problem is dealing with it (see below). The exception in the present study is Terry. Terry's story is an archetypal instance of a decision-maker refusing to see the future after it had arrived – reinvesting his savings in the business, expecting things to get better after five years of negative returns. Since this is not a statistical survey we cannot say that because we only encountered one such case that true cases of escalation are extremely rare – though they may be. What is clear is that if the decision-makers do entertain such mistaken beliefs, and, have the resources to support their conviction, the results may be highly destructive.

Emotional attachment to sunk costs

Sunk costs can also drive. Omar refuses a good (if tentative) offer for the business because it is less than what his late father paid for it. Richard clings to his investment. Moreover, although experiments have shown that decision-makers who receive training in accounting techniques may be less prone to sunk costs errors (for example, Tan and

Yates 1995), the present study suggests that training may not make much difference when it comes to parting with sunk costs in real life. Richard recognizes that sunk costs are irrelevant from an accounting standpoint, but he cannot write them off.

Recall that Karlsson et al. (2005) found that decision-makers may persist with a course of action even though their information reliably indicates that persistence will not make them any better off – particularly if they had sunk costs. The present study suggests that sunk costs can exert a hold, even though decision-makers know that they will inevitably end up *worse* off. Carole would rather dump stock than sell it cheaply even though she needs the money for housekeeping.

Closing costs

Recall that decisions about whether to quit or continue may be finely balanced because some ventures are almost as expensive to shut down as they are to continue (for example, Staw and Ross 1987a,b, Staw 1997). Barry could not exit immediately because he had redundancy costs and an overdraft to pay. Terry had stock to clear. Moreover, apropos of Karlsson et al., the present study suggests that closing costs may also drive persistence even though decision-makers know that persistence is unlikely to make them any better off. Sally continued with the loss-making cafe rather than pay an exit charge.

Perceived salvage value

It is thought that decision-makers are less likely to persist with a failing venture if it possesses some salvage value (Staw 1997, Simonson and Staw 1992, Ross and Staw 1991). Counter-intuitively the present study suggests that the opposite may sometimes be true. While they wait for a buyer Sana and Omar get into debt. Carole might have fallen into a similar trap but for the 'bombshell' of the proposed rent rise.

Lowering expectations

According to decision-dilemma theorists, decision-makers are driven to persist because it is hard to know when a venture has well and truly failed. Decision-dilemma theorists predict that once it becomes abundantly clear that expectations cannot be met, decision-makers will exit rapidly (for example, Bowen 1987). In contrast, behavioural theorists assume that decision-makers respond to negative feedback by actively reinvesting in the business (for example, Staw 1976, Staw and Ross 1978, Whyte 1986, 1991).

The present study suggests a third possibility. Again apropos Karlsson et al., it is one where decision-makers persist knowing that persistence will actually make them *worse* off. To be more precise, decision-makers may respond to a deteriorating situation by simply lowering their expectations. Initially Peter resolves to live on even thinner air. Sana, Tony and Barry close down loss-making businesses and retreat to the core.

This strategy provides temporary security (Anderson 2003). For instance, Barry comforts himself that things cannot get any worse. Tony assumes that having closed non-performing businesses, they will be 'all right'. Yet although marginal revenues may still exceed marginal costs, persistence may nevertheless become severely suboptimal as a result. Peter becomes ever poorer. Tony has to move to a smaller house. Barry is left with barely a sixteenth of his former wealth. A bigger danger is that the strategy proves maladaptive because it avoids the real problem. The risk is revealed to Sana and Tony when the business suddenly melts down.

Decision avoidance

Recognizing failure is all very well. Decision-makers have to act in order to cap their losses. The present study suggests, however, that decision-makers may lapse into decision avoidance (Anderson 2003 discusses this point). Carole accepts that the business is doomed, but procrastinates for seven months before putting it up for sale, a delay that works against her goal of preserving her savings. Barry vacillates between going and staying. Every time he renews the lease, he risks becoming caught up in a lengthy notice period if trade suddenly melts down and reverting to another 'overdraft situation'.

RESEARCH QUESTION 3: HOW ARE ESCALATION PREDICAMENTS FINALLY RESOLVED?

Clearly no one can reinvest in failing venture indefinitely. How and why do decision-makers decide that 'enough is enough'? The present study has adduced five main ways in which escalation predicaments may be resolved:

1. Overwhelming economic pressure
2. Overwhelming psychological pressure
3. Critical incident occurs
4. Limit setting
5. Critical threshold is reached

Each of these is discussed in turn.

Overwhelming economic pressure

Market forces may be slow to act but act they do. Just as the share price of companies like Enron and Lehman's can tumble uncontrollably, owners can become overwhelmed by economic pressure. Crystal and Ann have no more money. The bailiffs close Omar down. Tony can no longer buy stock. David is obliged to 'do a runner'. For Terry, the situation is 'snowballing'. Barry's two shops are plunging him deeper and deeper into the red. In other words, there is no longer any choice but to quit.

Overwhelming psychological pressure

Owners may exhaust their mental and physical resources before they exhaust their material ones. Sally, worn down by drunks and 'all-day sitters' is about to 'walk it', regardless of the expense. Sana gets fed up and gives notice. Karma suddenly bursts into tears. Alternatively, stress may take an indirect path of influence. Sam has grown tired of long journeys to buy stock. Anita is burned out. Latterly, Tony's wife comes home in tears. Bev and Sue are ground down by litter louts.

Critical incidents

Critical incidents can precipitate withdrawal. The incident may evoke vividness effects that signal virtually beyond doubt 'it's broke' (Bazerman and Watkins 2008: Ch. 4 discuss this point. See also Ross and Staw 1993). For instance, a busy Saturday convinces Fei and Bob that they can never succeed without a gas supply. The 'bombshell' of a rent rise convinces Carole that the business is unsaleable. A devastating bank statement galvanizes Barry into action. A poor Christmas finally forces Terry to recognize that trade is not going to improve.

Critical incidents can also curb persistence by forcing decision-makers to confront their options. Terry finally decides to quit when he discovers he is no longer able to pay the rent on his warehouse. He has to liquidate his stocks in order to avoid getting into debt. Recall that experiments have shown that decision-makers are less likely to persist with an economically poor course of action if persistence requires an active decision, as distinct from where the decision can be made passively (Brockner, Shaw and Rubin 1979). The present study provides field support for this observation. When Barry renews his lease, he makes an active decision to stay, but opts for a shorter term even though it is more expensive. Bev and Sue decide to quit rather than sign a contract. Howard and Tanya pull back for a similar reason.

Limit setting

To paraphrase Anderson (2003) limit setting means the decision-maker defers choice for the time being. Brockner and Rubin (1985: 201) suggest that setting limits curbs escalation because it produces pressure for consistency. It also thought that limit setting can curb persistence because it forces decision-makers be clear about what they expect from the business. Clear expectations may improve decision accuracy and vigilance by giving owners a set of criteria to measure performance (Bowen 1987: 56 see also Simonson and Staw 1992). Limit setting may also make it harder to interpret negative results in a self-serving manner. For example, Henderson, Gollwitzer and Oettingen (2007) found that decision-makers who planned to assess a course of action tended to respect new information.

The present study suggests that setting limits and quitting points do indeed reduce vulnerability to escalation. Moreover, another important effect of setting limits is that they enable decision-makers to gather information before making a decision that is virtually irreversible. More specifically, Peter and Sam put their businesses on probation. Peter then observes the trend whilst Sam experiments with selling cheaper items. Peter subsequently decides to quit before his liabilities become overwhelming. Sam discovers that trade improves slightly but a rent rise renders persistence futile because there is no longer any prospect of making a reasonable profit. As Sam says, finally the decision makes itself.

Critical threshold is reached

Another possibility is that the business reaches a critical threshold of risk or loss (McGarth 1999: 14 discusses thresholds). Much as Tanya and Howard want to expand, they decide that the risk takes them beyond their comfort zone. Likewise, Mike will not risk reinvesting in the market because he sees the danger of placing too many eggs in the metaphorical basket. Carole decides she will not raid her savings.

Entrapment

Entrapment is potentially more insidious than escalation because our theories imply that it happens accidentally. Another important finding to emerge from the present study is that whilst entrapment can happen by accident, sometimes it is avoidable.

RESEARCH QUESTION 4: HOW DOES ENTRAPMENT START?

'Side-bets' can indeed bind decision-makers to economically poor decisions (Becker 1960). Recall that 'side-bets' are extraneous investments that have nothing to do with the original decision but eventually become the main reason for persistence. An important 'side-bet' in the small business context uncovered by the present study is the lure of self-employment as evidenced by Elaine and Barry's stories. Other potentially relevant side-bets include emotional attachment to staff (Elaine), to customers (Nana) and divorce (Richard).

The paradox of continuity

Side-bets happen by accident. More importantly, the present study suggests that entrapment may in theory at least, sometimes be preventable. Recall that entrapment may reflect a paradox. That is, a decision is taken for good reason yet eventually persistence can only make things worse as 'bad' can never be turned to 'good'(Zhang and Baumeister 2006). The present study suggests that entrapment may be caused by continuity, that is, by selling the same lines year in year out. Continuity is initially 'good' because it enables owners to maximize profits. For instance, for several years Carole enjoyed a 'brilliant' trade in reconditioned electrical goods. Nana too rode the crest of a wave, as miner's wives treated themselves to handbags. The fish trade was habitually good to Henry. Yet just as innovative companies like Apple and Dyson can eventually solidify, continuity can eventually become 'bad' if owners ignore important environmental cues like shifts in fashion, or an emerging market for exotic fish.

As to why some owners may ignore important environmental cues, the present study suggests that Brockner et al. 1979 may be correct in predicting that entrapment starts because the cost of not doing something is initially negligible. To be more precise, the present study suggests that what actually happens is that the cost of inaction *seems* so low that it is almost invisible. This is because early on, environmental signals are usually very weak so it is easy to overlook them. Even when those signals become stronger, continuity may still be a tempting option. For instance, despite the downturn, Mike's existing business model is by no means life expired. For instance, he could continue selling raw and cooked meats awhile longer. Some owners might well succumb to this temptation perhaps seeing it as extracting maximum value from their investment in their existing business model. Mike, however, decides to get ahead of the game, unlike his neighbour who opts for the status quo. To put it another way the present study points to prospect theory (Kahneman and Tversky 1979, see also Whyte 1986, Bazerman 1984). To be more precise, somewhat speculatively we suggest that decision-makers may be most vulnerable to entrapment when the status quo involves a gain. Recall that prospect theory predicts that decision-makers are likely to prefer a gain that is certain to one that is merely probable. Henry's reaction to experimenting with exotic fish is a fairly good fit with the theory.

RESEARCH QUESTION 5: WHAT HOLDS ENTRAPPED DECISION-MAKERS IN PLACE?

An important question for research concerned the relative impact of driving and restraining forces, namely the costs of persistence versus the costs of withdrawal (Rubin and Brockner 1975. Recall the parsimonious theory that entrapment is inversely related to cost salience (Brockner, Shaw and Rubin 1979, see also Drummond 2005). In other words, the theory predicts that decision-makers only succumb to 'lock-in' if are oblivious to the costs of persistence. Yet although experiments have shown that people are more likely to quit when opportunity costs are made explicit (Northcraft and Neale 1986), the present study suggests that in reality, knowledge of opportunity costs may make little difference as decision-makers may be well aware of what persistence is costing them. Elaine, for example, knows she has no pension. Barry is reduced to chopping pigs' feet. Sally is subsidising drunks and all day sitters.

The present study reveals that decision-makers are mainly held in place by the cost of quitting. For example, for Richard it is the emotional cost of giving up. For Barry and Elaine it is the loss of self-employment. Nana would be left sitting at home all day. For Sally it is the penalty charge on the lease.

RESEARCH QUESTION 6: HOW IS ENTRAPMENT EXPERIENCED?

Contrary to notions of drifting idly towards eternity (Rubin and Brockner 1975, Drummond 2004), the present study also reveals that decision-makers may be well aware of how they succumbed to 'lock-in'. Mike wishes he had not invested so heavily in the market in the first place. Elaine thought she would have the shop for only three months. Sally did not read the lease properly. Nana realizes that although her stall is in a good position, no one looks because she is not selling branded goods.

To reframe, the present study suggests that the hallmark of entrapment is running out of options. Real options theory is discussed in the next chapter. Here it is sufficient to note that firms can be seen as bundles of options. In this view, a problem for which there is no solution (option) represents a failure of management. For instance, when the Federal Reserve refused to rescue Lehman's and the proposed merger with Barclay's failed, the bank was left with no option but to file for bankruptcy. By the same token, Richard has nothing left to invest. He can only carry on and hope for the best. Likewise having reinvested so heavily, Mike's options are now extremely limited. In time, he may become another Richard. Nana has no other life except the business. Barry has no choice but to keep the shop. This is another way of reiterating the parsimonious theory that escalation only occurs in the absence of alternatives (McCain 1986 discusses this point. See also Karlsson, Gärling and Bonini 2005).

The present study suggests that decision-makers are mainly held in place by the cost of quitting. For example, for Richard it is the emotional cost of giving up. For Barry and Elaine it is the loss of self-employment. Nana would be left sitting at home all day. For Sally it is the penalty charge on the lease.

RESEARCH QUESTION 7: HOW ARE ENTRAPMENT PREDICAMENTS RESOLVED?

Although decision-makers may be driven to persist suboptimally because quitting is too expensive, they are likely to change direction if the costs of persistence become too high.

For all her love of self-employment Elaine has her quit point. She will not incur debt. Richard may have invested heart and soul in the business, but if it can no longer pay his mortgage; he too will quit. Yet if the costs of persistence remain below a critical threshold, decision-makers like Nana and Barry may persist indefinitely until events play themselves out.

Implications for Research

Ideally, case studies raise more questions than they answer. Although part of what emerges in the present study confirms extant theorising and research, some of the findings suggest new directions for research. Seven areas for inquiry are identified namely:

1. Impact of prior commitment
2. Factors affecting risk-taking propensity
3. Impact of alternatives
4. Doing nothing: decision-avoidance
5. Impact of optimism
6. Impact of depression
7. Paradox of irrationality

IMPACT OF PRIOR COMMITMENT

So far, research has mainly focused on how decision-makers respond to negative feedback. It may be fruitful to consider prior commitment to the venture as highly committed individuals may be more prone to escalation that the less committed.

This observation is hardly novel. For instance, it is thought that individuals who are highly committed to an idea may have more their self-worth invested in it and have a bigger expectation of success (for example, Brockner et al. 1992). Likewise, Moon (2001a) found that escalation correlates with achievement striving. More specifically, individuals with high aspiration levels who had worked hard to achieve their goals were four times more likely to persist with difficult projects than low achievement strivers. The present study suggests two more possibilities. First, high and low committed individuals may react differently to identical feedback. Specifically, both Karma and Anita started ventures that were partially successful. Yet Karma's commitment was severely dented on day one when she experienced the burdens of ownership and she soon quit. In contrast, failure only made Anita more determined to persist. Of the two Anita was the most committed. Whereas Karma regarded her incursion into business as an experiment that might lead to 'something', Anita had a clear blueprint for a chain of shops.

Second, the evidence regarding the impact of high payoff is conflicting. Gatewood et al. (1995) found that individuals who expected a big reward were more likely to persist at difficult tasks than those who expected fewer rewards whereas Brockner et al. (1981) found no effect for reward importance (see also Wong 2005). The present study suggests that the issue merits further investigation, as decision-makers may be driven to make ill-advised moves if the stakes are high enough. Silvio opened a second cafe because the first one failed and he needed income. In contrast, Anita, Tanya and Howard were less desperate because their businesses at least generated a basic wage. Silvio had nothing.

FACTORS AFFECTING RISK-TAKING PROPENSITY

Risk-taking propensity is thought to be a broadly stable but potentially changeable entity (for example, Sitkin and Pablo 1992). The present study suggests that it may be more changeable than we realize. For example, the stories of Silvio, Anita and Tanya suggest that risk-taking propensity is increased by frustration and disappointment. Conversely Henry's reaction to experimenting with exotic fish suggests that the experience of success reduces risk-taking propensity.

IMPACT OF ALTERNATIVES

Recall that the role of alternatives in curbing escalation is unclear (for a review see Hantula and Crowell 1994). Taken together the various studies suggest that alternatives are most likely to curb escalation if they are clearly visible and appealing. For example, Goltz (1999) found that alternatives only curb persistence if they yield distinctly positive outcomes.

The most dramatic evidence concerning the impact of alternatives in the present study is Karma's sudden realization that she could go to college. Karma's reaction suggests that alternatives are indeed most likely to curb escalation if they are both salient and highly attractive. Yet it is unclear why. For instance, do alternatives make the opportunity costs of persistence salient, as McCain suggests? Or is it that they reduce fear of the unknown as Peter's reaction to being unemployed suggests? Moreover, do alternatives always need to be explicit? Carole quit even though her alternatives existed only in shadow form.

A creative way of exploring the role of alternatives is to imagine what would be required for a *perfect* relationship between alternatives and de-escalation (Wicker 1985: 1096). For instance, we imagine that the alternative would need to offer distinctly better returns, for no risk. Switching costs (emotional and financial) would need to be zero. The salvage cost of the existing venture would need to be high. In other words, as Wicker notes, the real purpose of the exercise is to identify factors that could constrain or heighten the impact of alternatives.

Another creative angle would be to play with the question and imagine the circumstances in which decision-makers would de-escalate in the *absence* of alternatives. The present study offers some clues. Specifically, Bev and Sue quit even though they have no definite alternative lined up, because they know they cannot survive the winter. Elaine and Richard have quitting points. Taken together their stories suggest that alternatives are immaterial if persistence becomes too costly.

DOING NOTHING: DECISION AVOIDANCE

Delay can be productive. For instance, Ann recognized failure on day one but persisted for seven months. If Ann had quit immediately, she would have lost a valuable learning opportunity. By persisting Ann learned about the importance of cash flow and opening hours. Escalation theorists see failure negatively. Research might consider the positive possibilities (McGarth 1999 discusses this point).

Delay can also serve an emotionally useful purpose, including temporary security (for example, Anderson 2003), minimization of regret (e.g., Ku 2008b) and enable anticipatory grieving (Shepherd et al. 2009). Yet the long-term costs of delay may outweigh any short-term benefits. For instance, Anderson suggests that where decision-makers are faced with two costly choices, like quitting or continuing with an unprofitable business, the temptation to retreat into avoidance is heightened. Carole's story exemplifies this point. Likewise, Staw (1997) notes that decision-makers may use objective factors like closing costs in order to postpone the inevitable. We need to know more about decision avoidance and in particular the potentially crucial gap between recognizing a venture has no future and ending it.

IMPACT OF OPTIMISM

Recall Arkes and Hutzel (2000) found that over-optimism is a consequence of investment. That is, having embarked upon research and development decision-makers tend to become more optimistic about success. Sally's story offers field confirmation of this important finding. That is, when Sally decides to keep the cafe she reinvests in order to make the best of it. The belief that the business had turned a corner, 'we're getting there', was irrational because it was based on overweighing Christmas takings when experience should have told Sally that these were atypical. Such optimism is dangerous if it encourages further investment. Are decision-makers more prone to optimism bias when, like Sally, they are forced to persist?

IMPACT OF DEPRESSION

Richard's greengrocery survived. After the divorce was concluded Richard made some changes to the business. He replaced the security camera. He sacked poorly performing staff, recruited employees and trained them to meet his standards. He also revamped a big unprofitable display and introduced new lines consisting of pre-packed fruit and vegetables to become more of a convenience store. In the result, the business recovered sufficiently to make it a rewarding experience once more.

Those options were always open to Richard but when first interviewed he was depressed. Moon et al. (2003) discovered that anxiety heightens escalation, whereas depression correlated negatively with escalation. Intuitively this result makes sense because depressed individuals tend to be preoccupied with thoughts of loss and failure. Moreover, a hallmark of depression is helplessness, where individuals doubt their ability to influence outcomes and regard success largely as a matter of luck (Moon et al. 2003). Another hallmark of depression, however, is inactivity. The present study suggests that rather than de-escalate, decision-makers may simply stall. To some extent inaction may a good thing. Depression can enable individuals to conserve resources (for example, Taylor 1980). It may also stop them from making irreversible decisions in a precipitate fashion.

Inactivity can be dangerous, however. For instance, front line troops who have been in battle for long periods, seeing their comrades being killed and themselves having no hope of leave or transfer, may be unable to make decisions necessary to protect their lives (Anderson 2003: 139, citing Janis 1989). So whilst anxious individuals may actively reinvest to stave off failure, Richard's story suggests that depressed individuals may stand by helplessly (Moon et al. 2003). Future research might explore how and why depression may prevent decision-makers taking important actions. For instance, the present study suggests that decision-makers may see a problem like a broken security camera but not act upon it. Likewise, opportunities may be staring them in the face, but either they do not see it or they see it but do not act upon it. Which is it?

THE PARADOX OF IRRATIONALITY

Finally in this chapter, there is the issue of rationality itself. Economics teaches that the only defensible approach to decision-making is algorithmic, that is, one that depicts decision-makers diligently searching for options, analysing them exhaustively and objectively before choosing the course of action offering the greatest utility. In this view, emotion is a destructive influence on decision-making. Likewise, many psychologists believe that for individuals to be effective, they must be in touch with reality (Taylor and Brown 1988 discuss this point).

Although emotion can cloud judgement, it can also be highly beneficial. Karma's emotional outburst clears the way for a productive change of direction. It was no bad thing that Sana got 'fed up' and gave notice. Howard is partly motivated by a thirst for revenge. Whilst revenge can be calamitous (for example, Teger 1980), it energizes Howard and fuels his ambitions to expand. Moreover, although Howard's perception of owning three businesses may be partly an illusion, that illusion makes him feel that he is already successful and helps to prevent him from overreaching himself. Sam and Terry's absurd attitude towards the Council may be irrational but it reduces the psychological pain of failure.

Besides, rational approaches to decision-making are not always possible. Decision-makers may have no alternative but to press on with the one option that is available to them and hope for the best (Lipshitz 1995 discusses this point). Surprising things do happen. Given her ambition and determination, had she been offered the big stall, Anita might have succeeded. We need to know more about the potentially beneficial impact of emotion on decision-making. In particular, the present study suggests that there may be a fine line between the commitment that is needed to found a successful business (for example, Brunsson 1985) and inordinate risk-taking. How may decision-makers know when that line has been reached?

Summary

The present study has focused upon escalation of commitment. The main research question was why decision-makers can become 'locked in' to an economically poor course of action. More specifically why do some owners of failing businesses exit sooner rather than later whereas persisting to the bitter end, particularly if they know that persistence is unlikely to make them any better off and may even make things worse. What emerges suggests that decision-makers are most vulnerable to suboptimal persistence when the costs of changing direction are high. A more fundamental cause of 'lock-in', however, is a lack of alternatives.

Although escalation and entrapment are surrounded by an air of inexorability, 'lock-in' is by no means inevitable. Decision-makers can protect themselves by setting clear expectations, tracking results against expectations, and, if expectations consistently fail, exiting sooner rather than later, regardless of cost. In other words, decision-makers can best protect themselves by taking charge rather than merely waiting upon events.

10 *Beyond Magic Thinking: Making Better Decisions – 10 Lessons For Practice*

The word 'risk' derives from the early Italian risicare which means 'to dare'. In this sense, risk is a choice rather than a fate.

(Bernstein 1998: 8)

Introduction

Although it is axiomatic that all decisions involving uncertainty run the risk of failure, many of the losses suffered by the traders we met earlier in this book could have been avoided. As Bernstein notes, failure is not always the result of a malignant fate. Misfortune can strike at random but more often misfortune reflects the risks that we *choose* to take. If caught for speeding in a motor car, we may feel we have been unlucky. Yet we chose to break the speed limit in the first place just as people choose to open businesses with very little capital and experience and choose to keep them open or close them down.

This chapter considers the implications of the present study for practice. It is divided into two main parts. The first part considers measures to help prevent escalation and entrapment. The second part considers what can be done to minimize the losses incurred by decision-makers who become caught up in escalation and entrapment scenarios.

Part One: Preventing Escalation and Entrapment

LESSON 1: WHAT ARE YOU GETTING INTO?

The most important advice to decision-makers is *'think'*. Think first of all about what you may be getting into. Emphatically, we are not suggesting that decision-makers avoid risk at all costs. Economics is sometimes called the dismal science. One of the science's more optimistic prognostications is that risk-taking is the key to economic growth and prosperity. It has to be the right risk at the right time, however. We merely urge decision-makers to pause for long enough to consider how their putative decisions might play out in practice and what commitments they make be shouldering.

Beware compromise

Compromise is inevitable in decision-making. It is precisely because resources are scare that choices have to be made. Seldom do decision-makers have all the time and all the resources they need. Indeed, the essence of management is 'making do'. Yet some compromises are dangerous. Although the proverb states that half a loaf is better than no bread, compromising on factors that are mission-critical such a location only wastes resources. In large firms, how often are budgets trimmed, resources pared down and protesting managers told to get on with the job? Under-resourcing projects guarantees failure. So it might be better not to undertake them in the first place. The ancient military philosopher advises commanders only to fight battles that are already won (for example, Griffith 1971, Minford 2002). Getting mission critical factors right is more than half the battle.

Patience is the key. Just as it is better to wait for the waters to subside instead of trying to cross a flooding river, decision-makers might be well advised to exercise patience. Patience does not necessarily mean waiting indefinitely for something to happen. It simply means that a decision is not regarded as time-critical. Anita's frustration arises because she has set overly ambitious timescales. Likewise, if Silvio had taken his time and waited until more suitable premises became available, he could have spared himself two expensive failures. As the saying goes in poker, money has a habit of flowing from the impatient to the patient.

What will definitely happen?

It is important to think about how a decision might play out in practice. The future may be hidden but there are certainties as well as uncertainties. A question that decision-makers should pose is what will *definitely* happen if this decision is implemented (for example, De Bono 2000 Ch. 19)? For instance, as soon as a venture opens for business there will be a relentless stream of expenses to be met. Where are the resources going to come from? In 2006 Cadbury chose to market chocolate bars that were contaminated by salmonella. The level of contamination was thought to be extremely low but a question that Cadbury should have dwelt upon was what would definitely happen if even one customer contracted salmonella? In fact, that is precisely what did happen. Cadbury were subsequently prosecuted and forced to recall millions of bars of chocolate. If Cadbury had paused for long enough to consider what they might be getting into, they might have decided not to take the risk. More recently Toyota de-emphasized quality standards in a bid to become the world's largest car manufacturer. The decision is proving counter-productive because some of the main reasons for buying a Toyota vehicle were quality and reliability.

Beware overreach

Anita and to a lesser extent Tanya were in danger of overreaching themselves by expanding too far and too soon. Silvio's decision to open another cafe was also a mistake. Overreach happens where ambition significantly outstrips resources causing owners and companies to overbalance. For example, Porsche's audacious bid for VW that rebounded and cost Porsche their independence.

Overreach can reflect linear intuitive thinking. Recall that the managers of the brewery assumed that an eight-fold increase in production would mean an eight-fold increase in profits, only to discover that the margins on large scale production were much slimmer than they expected. Likewise, running two businesses may not require twice as much effort but four times more.

The recommendation for practice is to confine ambitions to what is achievable. Tanya does this well. She is ambitious to expand but considers what will definitely happen if she opens a second business. As a result of thinking how the decision might play out in practice, she realizes that the day-to-day practicalities could prove difficult and even destroy two businesses. She chooses not to take the risk. Instead she exercises patience and decides to await a better opportunity. Like politics, good decision-making is the art of the possible.

What assumptions are you making?

Assumptions are inevitable in decision-making. The trouble is that assumption has a habit of masquerading as fact. Every time we switch on the kettle we assume that the water will boil, but it is an assumption. David assumed that hordes of customers would immediately flock to his cafe. He never stopped to think that this assumption might be wrong. Was Lehman any different when revaluing (mark to market) their sub-prime loan portfolio, an exercise that the media subsequently dubbed 'mark to mirage'? At the time of writing, Apple were about to launch a new tablet computer. Although it is widely predicted that this much vaunted device will prove extremely popular, there are no guarantees. This one may be different, but so far, tablet computers have been 'also rans' in the market.

The lesson for practice is to review key assumptions, particularly those that seem rock solid certain, and consider whether you could be mistaken. Silvio, for example, was sure that customers would follow when he moved to a new location. They didn't, but Silvio never stopped to think whether his assumption might prove to be wrong.

LESSON 2: REALITY TESTING

The successful Korean electronics firm HTC originally made mobile phones and other electronic devices for other companies before becoming a leading manufacturer in their own right. In other words, HTC's experience created a shadow option. Real options theory is discussed later in this chapter. Here it is sufficient to note that the experience gained by HTC working at the behest of others helped to ensure the success of their own products. Gaining experience is a better form of reality testing than merely planning precisely because it is real and offers an opportunity to learn at limited cost. If Karma had worked in her parents mobile delicatessen she might have been better prepared for the physical challenges of running a business. Likewise, Sally's idyll of running a cafe did not include the stream of drunks and all-day sitters that patronized her establishment.

Sally may have been disillusioned but she planned to start another business. Asked what she had learned from the first episode, Sally replied, 'Go into everything.' There was no need for new traders to experience unpleasant surprises over the expenses involved in running a business. That information could have been discovered beforehand and factored into the equation. Large firms employ legions of financial specialists to calculate costs and benefits but they too get it wrong. In the early 1990s Persil launched a new soap powder. The decision was a public-relations disaster because the new powder rotted fabric. The disaster happened because Persil became so absorbed in the marketing of the new product that they failed to test adequately chemical constituents of the new powder. Recall too the example of the film *Titanic*. The project became an escalation scenario because the costs were seriously underestimated in the first place.

LESSON 3: TOO LITTLE RISK CAN BE WORSE THAN TOO MUCH

That said, there may be a price to be paid for *not* taking a risk. For example, as Jim gracefully acknowledged, if he had not moved in to selling exotic fish the business would now be defunct.

Pubs in the UK are closing at the rate of about 40 a week. Many newspapers worldwide are struggling to survive. Is there any future for businesses like these, and if, so, what is that future?

Perhaps it is the wrong question because no one really knows. More importantly, why wait to find out? Ken could teach big business a lesson. He seized uncertainty by the scruff of the neck and revamped the business while he still had the resources to do it. Instead of following a trend, in a small way, Ken created one by raising the standards bar for market stalls. Likewise, Indian restaurants sprang up in the late 1950s to feed migrants working nightshifts in textile mills. With their bare Formica tables, they provided a low-cost amenity – where designer decor and even cutlery were surplus to requirements. Successful chains of Indian restaurants like Gaylord and Bombay Brasserie have prospered because they recognized that more could be achieved by going above and beyond the basic. Like Ken, they became industry leaders. It is the difference between dreading the arrival of a Black Swan (a rare and extreme event) and becoming a Black Swan (Taleb 2008: 298).

Goldman Sachs did a similar thing in the early 1990s. In December 1990 Steve Friedman and Bob Rubin were named senior partners and co-chairmen of the management committee. Their ambitious vision involved expanding the firm to offer the full range of expertise, capable of competing with the biggest investment banks and offering new services. Many of the partners opposed the idea ('going to be a disaster is this') particularly as Goldman's boutique model had served the firm well:

> Goldman Sachs, with its sixty-five hundred employees, was highly successful, and the partnership was by its nature conservative. After a decade of astounding prosperity, the impetus for change was low. 'We were moving too slowly, or not at all, to face some serious competitive threats … and with too much self-satisfaction,' Friedman remembers. 'Too many things were on autopilot and were not re-examined. If we waited to fix them it might get too late.' (Endlich 1999: 188)

Adapt to survive

Some of the more prosperous market traders have succeeded by taking a low-key approach to fixing things; that is, by making small low risk adaptations. Not everything works, but if an experiment fails, the damage is slight. For example, some greengrocer's have survived by capitalizing on healthy eating campaigns, selling packs containing five small portions of fruit for 99p and obtaining contracts to supply local offices with the same. Some market cafes have broken the 'greasy spoon' stereotype by achieving high 'scores on the door' for hygiene.

Above all, unlike traders who have become trapped in dying businesses trend setters have moved with the times. Recall that entrapment can happen because the cost of *not* doing something is initially very low. Woolworths, like many market traders came to rely increasingly upon Christmas profits for survival. Eventually Christmas never came to Woolworths just as it eventually eluded traders like Tony, and in November 2008, the venerable retail giant closed. A decade earlier Marks and Spencer came close to nemesis. In both cases, the roots of collapse lay in earlier success, that is, a determination to stick to a tried and tested model even though it no longer met customer expectations. For example, Marks and Spencer refused to acknowledge that their policy of offering exchanges rather providing changing rooms, and accepting only their own credit card, no longer cut the mustard until the firm was on the verge of collapse. As Steve Friedman put it, 'If you are not constantly working for constructive strategic change, then you are the steward of something which must erode' (Endlich 1999: 188). Microsoft seemed omnipotent until firms like Google and Yahoo! transformed the centre of gravity in the industry.

Part Two: Measures for Dealing with Escalation

Avoiding escalation and entrapment can be easier said than done. If a venture shows signs of faltering, the sooner decision-makers implement damage limitation measures the better.

Until decision-makers can make sense of a problem, there is no decision to make (Weick 1995). Yet as we saw in the present study, the way in which we make sense of things is not a neutral exercise, but one that is highly subjective and influenced by self-serving biases. Barry the butcher, for example, sees the downturn but insists that things cannot get any worse. It was a comforting assessment but it reflected wishful thinking. If Barry had correctly identified the 'problem behind the problem', that is, a potentially irreversible downwards trend, he might have been able to make a timely exit instead of enduring the ignominy of selling pigs' feet.

It is even harder for large firms to diagnose problems accurately because information passes through so many filters (for example, Starbuck 1983 see also Brown 1978). Mangers can only treat what others call reality as a myth, that is, partly true and therefore partly untrue (for example, Hedberg and Jönsson 1977).

LESSON 4: SET CLEAR EXPECTATIONS

Howard may have been helped by not setting precise targets but he is an exception. Setting expectations enables decision-makers to recognize failure sooner rather than later. For example, Karma recognized within six months that the business had stalled and Carole realized the writing was on the wall when her expectation of using profits to build her savings failed. In contrast, without an outcome standard, Crystal was at the mercy of events.

Of course it is no good having targets and other outcome standards unless decision-makers stick to them. (The only way the US could exit from Vietnam was by lowering their expectations from 'victory' to 'peace with honour' – a graceful admission of defeat.) Lowering one's expectations might seem like a sensible adaptive strategy but as we saw with Sana and Tony, the end result may be a progressive collapse – or in large firms a hostile takeover bid. Likewise without clear expectations and milestones complex projects quietly slip, one day at a time.

Create a crisis

Recall critical incidents can precipitate de-escalation by forcing decision-makers to confront their options. Decision-makers could benefit from engineering critical incidents into their decision-making procedures. For example, zero-based budgeting where projects are only funded one phase at a time is used in some high risk industries like pharmaceuticals. Funding is only renewed at each stage if the project passes a rigorous assessment. Another advantage of imposing such controls is that they force decision-makers to make an active decision to persist. Recall that investment in failing projects tends to be higher where decisions can be made passively as distinct from where they must be made actively (Brockner, Shaw and Rubin 1979).

LESSON 5: READ THE ROAD AHEAD

Peter Norris, former chief executive of Barings, observed that it is impossible to stop rogue trading. What matters is how long it takes to detect it. The same goes for impending bankruptcy. The sooner decision-makers can recognize the inevitable, the sooner they can arrest the decline. It is particularly important in a small business because the scope for creative accounting is limited. In the mid 1990s Spring Ram solved their immediate financial problems by booking orders as actual sales. More recently Enron created a company to dump their losses into. By contrast, small businesses can go under very rapidly, 'really really disaster' – as owners like Tony and Sana discovered.

In the present study, the owners who suffered least financial damage and least emotional angst were those like Peter who read the road ahead and took action to stem the losses. Peter did not wait for things to get worse before exiting. He saw a consistently downwards trend and decided to quit before he got into debt. Another tell-tale sign is diminishing returns on the capital employed. Has the business reached a point where it would be possible to earn more money by investing that money in the bank? Another way of distinguishing signal from noise is to pay attention to stress levels. More specifically, rising stress levels may be the outcroppings of serious problems.

LESSON 6: ACT SWIFTLY

Although National Express should have known better than try where Sea Containers failed, the difference between the two companies was that National Express recognized failure sooner rather than later and handed the keys back.

Napoleon observed than in war, speed is all important. Without it: nothing. It is a good maxim for business. It is no good recognizing a problem unless decision-makers act upon their diagnosis. Carole, for example, knew the business was doomed but carried on, 'business as usual' for months before quitting. Large firms can be slow to act too. For instance, construction of the new Denver airport baggage system even though project managers suspected that the project was seriously flawed (Monteaglre and Keil 2000). Another possibility is to set quitting points. Both Sam and Peter mitigate their losses by doing precisely that.

LESSON 7: THE BUSINESS MAY HAVE FAILED – YOU HAVEN'T

Thomas Edison, inventor of the light bulb, was nothing if not persistent. He tried over 700 times to get his new invention to work. One of Edison's detractors scornfully observed that Edison had failed over 700 times. Edison retorted that he was not a failure. He had simply learned 700 ways not to do it.

The same goes for exiting business ventures. Instead of seeing quitting as 'giving in' (Sam) as being weak and pathetic (Karma), think of it (a) as a learning experience; and (b) as redirecting resources (strategy) in a more profitable direction. Strategy is about what you *don't* do, as well as what you do. For instance, the owner of the *London Evening Standard* decided that if the newspaper was to survive, charging readers was no longer an option.

Don't blame others

One thing that unites traders who make a timely exit is that they avoid blaming others for their misfortunes. Recall that blaming others can be productive if passing responsibility frees decision-makers' to deal with their predicament. To go on blaming others is not productive, however, because it means that the decision-maker never learns from their mistakes. How can they when it is someone else's fault?

Several of the owners we interviewed planned to restart in business, For example, Ann took a temporary job, made arrangements to repay her debts and then set about looking for premises to open another take away:

> I don't feel like a failure in any way. I just felt disappointed because to me it's the best thing I've ever done. I mean I was the first black person to take food in the market you know, cooked food … I'm not the first black person to go on the market but I'm the first black person to take a cafe. I feel proud of that even though it didn't last long. (Ann)

It is important not to read too much into failure. Richard Branson has repeatedly failed to secure the contract to run the UK National Lottery but that does not make him a failure. For all we know we may have interviewed a future founder of a chain like KFC or Burger King – perhaps more than one.

LESSON 8: KEEP YOUR OPTIONS OPEN

Decision-makers can only redirect resources if they have resources to redirect. In other words, if they keep their options open. Real options are toehold investments that enable but do not compel decision-makers to take a certain course of action in the future. For example, a company may buy the rights to a goldmine but mine only if the price of gold reaches a certain level so that mining becomes economically justified. Options are thus a way of providing for the future instead of trying to second guess it. The beauty of purchasing an option is that the loss is confined to the purchase price, whereas the potential gain is unlimited (for example, Janney and Dess 2004, Zardkoohi 2004, Denison 2009).

Economics teaches that decisions that create real options are more profitable than decisions that involve exercising them. For example, wildcat oil exploration firms like Tullow and Heritage make money by selling their discoveries to the big oil producing companies who effectively purchase an option to commence drilling immediately or at some time in the future – or not at all. Carole's decision to quit with her savings more or less intact was wise because it created options – including the possibility of opening another business.

As Carole also recognized, part of the value of an option is lost if the timing is wrong. For example, even if the price of gold reaches the strike price, decision-makers may wait to see if that price is maintained before exercise the option to mine. Yet by the time mining actually commences, the bull run in the gold market may be almost over. Indeed, Carole lost part of the value of her options because of the 15-month delay between recognizing that the business probably had no future and finally quitting.

Options are most valuable in times of high uncertainty. Companies worried that a contract might be cancelled sometimes employ staff on a consultancy basis. It costs more but it means they can rid immediately themselves of surplus labour if the need arises. Barry the butcher too purchases a kind of immediate exit option when he decides to extend the lease for only three months instead of six.

Quitting can become easier if decision-makers are willing to count the cost of persistence. This is because losses out of pocket are felt more keenly than revenues foregone (for example, Kahneman and Tversky 1982, Northcraft and 1984). For instance, Elaine and Peter should count every year spent in self-employment as a loss of one year's pensionable service. Likewise, Barry might have been less enthusiastic about the joys of self-employment if he sees that it costing him at least £3 an hour (actual earnings versus UK statutory minimum wage).

Additionally, new owners may fail is because they overcommit early on. Howard is the exception that exemplifies the rule. By starting outdoors, Howard's losses (if any) were confined to the price of the stock (less any salvage value), and the cost of a day's rent (£20) whereas his gains were potentially unlimited. Interestingly sophisticated organizations can make the same mistake. For example, Citibank pioneered the use of an electronic card to monitor consumer purchases in supermarkets. Instead of limiting potential losses by running a pilot project, Citibank invested over $100 in a full-blown scheme. When take-up proved slower than expected, Citibank then lurched to the other extreme and shut it down. Since Citibank sold off the assets and made specialist staff redundant, they learned nothing from the exercise. In the end, it was their rivals who profited (McGarth 1999).

Discounting the future

Recall that running out of options is a hallmark of entrapment. This is also Anita's problem. She has run out of rational options so she contemplates more doubtful possibilities. Organizations (including small businesses) can be seen as bundles of options. In this view, a problem for which there is no solution represents a failure to manage. To put it another way, decision-makers should be careful about making decisions that destroy options.

Something that can result in options being destroyed is a judgemental bias known as discounting the future (Bazerman and Watkins 2008: 85). Discounting the future refers to our innate preference as human beings for short-term considerations instead of evaluating options from a long-term perspective. For example, would you prefer £10,000 now or £12,000 in two year's time? Given current interest rates, clearly £12,000 in two years time is the option that offers maximum benefit but we may be tempted to forgo it to obtain immediate gratification. Likewise, overfishing results in immediate profits at the expense of the long-term viability of the fishing industry. In the present study, Carole's decision to show solidarity with other traders boosted her esteem initially but the consequent loss of £6,000 was a blow to her finances and she now regrets the decision. The point is, when we discount the future at high levels we may regret it later. 'I have *no pension*,' says Elaine. The (predictable) future has arrived and it is so bleak that she dare not think about it.

LESSON 9: TIME VERSUS MONEY

When it comes to counting the costs of persistence, although it is axiomatic in business that time *is* money, the two are not of equal value. Time is the more valuable resource. Money can be replenished whereas a moment of elapsed time is gone forever. Yet despite what has been said in the literature about decision-makers 'throwing good money after bad' research has shown that we may be more willing to reinvest time (rather than money) to salvage money (Heath 1995). Sally was completely disillusioned with the cafe after a year. Yet she spent another year working for nothing, subsiding unpleasant customers and damaging her physical and mental health rather than part with money that she and her husband could comfortably afford.

It is easy to understand why decision-makers like Sally make those choices. Investing money requires an active decision to persist whereas time can be invested passively. Yet there is nothing to stop decision-makers from reviewing their options, their expectations and generally taking stock. Those who are content to 'drift idly towards eternity' should note Queen Elizabeth I's dying words, 'All my riches for a moment of time' (Oxford Dictionary of Quotations 1993).

LESSON 10: WHEN IS THE BEST TIME TO QUIT?

The traders that we most wanted to interview were the ones who were no longer there; that is, those who sold out years earlier when stalls were 'gold dust'. Escalation theory stresses the importance of changing direction when things are going badly. Yet economics also teaches that it may be wise, in certain circumstances, to change direction when things are going well. To be more precise, economics teaches that, if an opportunity arises that offers a better return on investment, all else equal, we should switch, even though it means giving up on a successful venture (Northcraft and Wolf 1984). For example, merchant bankers were originally merchants who used their good reputation to guarantee bills issued by lesser merchants. They discovered that they could make more money from their financial activities than from being merchants so they gradually became full time bankers. More recently, Tullow Oil abandoned over £300 million of investment in North Sea explorations to new opportunities in Uganda and Ghana. Tullow were promptly rewarded with an 827 per cent rise in share price and listing in the FTSE 100 index. Whether those gains will be realized remains to be seen, but Tullow's decision shows what can happen when companies follow economic wisdom.

Besides, nothing lasts forever. Nothing is immune from erosion whether it is a little whelk bar or a multi-billion pound concern like Woolworths. Barry, the butcher, recalls how the first ominous note was sounded by his accountant – 10 years before the arrival of the devastating bank statement:

> He said to me, 'Where do you think you'll be in 10 years time?'

> I was flying high at that point. I said, 'Well, what do you mean?'

> He said, 'Where do you think you'll be in 10 years time?'

> I said, 'Well I hope I'll still be in business and making a living.'

> But you do, you think it's never going to end. (Barry)

But it did end: if Barry had sold the shops 10 years earlier while they were still worth something, he might still be enjoying a Ferrari lifestyle or at least not be chopping pigs' feet for less than the UK minimum wage. Nothing is forever no matter how rock solid it may seem, whether it is Microsoft's domination of computer operating systems, the building boom in Dubai, or florists transporting their takings in buckets and grocers doing a roaring trade in pork pies. Incidentally, the neighbouring trader who said Mike was mad to invest is no longer there.

Returning to the traders who left early, some will have retired from business in the ordinary way. Others may have sold for personal reasons. But did some recognize that the good times would end? If so, how did they recognize it?

We will probably never know the answer to these two questions. The timing of those decisions does suggest, however, that the best time to quit a *successful* venture is about half-past eleven on the metaphorical clock. Self-discipline is essential because it means letting someone else reap part of what has been sown. Yet as Joe Kennedy (father of assassinated president John Kennedy) observed when he quit playing financial markets before the stock market crash of 1929, only a fool holds out for top dollar.

Epilogue

We stood near to the spot on Leeds market where Michael Marks first opened his penny bazaar. It was a cold Wednesday afternoon: half-day closing. The outdoor market had been swept clean and tidy except for a red chilli that had been left behind. Short of a 'black swan' appearing over the horizon the future for markets is bleak. Some have shrunk to a fraction of their former selves. Others have been turned into shopping malls charging huge rents that only big stores can afford. What would Michael Marks have made of it all? What would he have said to beleaguered traders?

Yet for all Michael Marks's entrepreneurial spirit and energy, it was actually Tom Spencer who played a decisive role in creating the modern retail chain by investing £300 to finance expansion. Spencer took a huge risk because the money represented his life savings. Moreover, in 1894 there was no welfare state to fall back on. He could easily have ended up destitute. Yet it proved to be one of the most successful gambles in business history. Spencer became equal partner in a firm that still bears his name though he only worked in it for nine years before retiring to the country and cheerfully drinking himself to death. Mark's survived Spencer by only a few months. He dropped dead at the relatively young age of 48 from overwork. If we only knew what guided that decision?

It would be unusual social sciences practice to interview the dead. Where shall we await his ghost? Recall the little whelk stall that once throve amazingly: the one that stood between the gents' toilets and the pub. It doesn't sound very nice, but judging by Tom Spencer's habits, it has got to be lucky.

Perhaps the pub was called the Black Swan.

Appendix

Table A.1 Summary of interviews

Name used in book	Details of business	Outcome
Chapter 3: David	Wholefood cafe	New venture. Closed after approximately 2 months.
Chapter 3: Fei and Bob	Oriental takeaway and cafe	New venture. Closed after approximately 4 months.
Chapter 3: Ann	Takeaway specializing in curried mutton	New venture. Closed after approximately 6 months.
Chapter 3: Jim	Fishmonger	Experienced owner buys another business that disappoints.
Chapter 3: Silvio	Cafe owner	Experienced owner starts 2 new businesses that fail.
Chapter 5: Crystal	Gift shop	New venture. Closed after 16 months.
Chapter 5: Tony	Owned multiple shops over 30 years	Goes from 4 shops to none in 2 years.
Chapter 5: Sam	Owns 2 shops: linen stall and paint shop	Closes paint shop after 6 years.
Chapter 5: Omar	Greengrocer	Closed after 16 years. Premises repossessed.
Chapter 5: Sana	Clothes stall	Closes last remaining business after 20 years.
Chapter 5: Terry	Owns 2 shops (formerly 3): frozen foods, perfume and make-up	Closes down after 30 years.
Chapter 5: Sally	Cafe	New venture. Sold after 2 years.
Chapter 4: Anita	Gift shop	New venture. Closed after approximately 15 months.
Chapter 4: Tanya	Nail bar	New venture that disappoints. Pulls back from second shop.
Chapter 4: Howard	Camping gear and outdoor clothing	New venture plus expansion.

Table A.1 continued   Summary of interviews

Name used in book	Details of business	Outcome
Chapter 6: Henry	Fishmonger	Reluctant to experiment with new lines.
Chapter 6: Mike	Grocer	Makes a huge reinvestment to avoid entrapment.
Chapter: 6: Richard	Greengrocer	Trapped in poorly performing business.
Chapter 6: Elaine	Clothes	Trapped in a poorly performing business.
Chapter 6: Barry	Butcher	Trapped in a poorly performing business.
Chapter 6: Nana	Clothes	Persists with a poorly performing business.
Chapter 7: Karma	Delicatessen	Closes a poorly performing business.
Chapter 7: Bev and Sue	Jewellery	Closes a poorly performing business after 4 months.
Chapter 7: Peter	Toys	Closes a poorly performing business after 8 years.
Chapter 7: Carole	White goods and dry-cleaning	Closes down a poorly performing business and exits market after more than 30 years as a trader.

References

Abdelsamad, M.H. and Kindling, A.T. 1978. Why small businesses fail. *Advanced Management Journal*, 43, 24–32.

Amsel, A. 1958. The role of frustrative non-reward in non-continuous reward situations. *Psychological Bulletin*, 55, 102–119.

Amsel, A. 1968. Secondary reinforcement and frustration. *Psychological Bulletin*, 69, 278.

Anderson, C.J. 2003. The psychology of doing nothing: forms of decision avoidance result from reason and emotion. *Psychological Bulletin*, 129, 139–167.

Arkes, H.R. 1996. The psychology of waste. *Journal of Behavioural Decision-Making*, 9, 213–224.

Arkes, H.R. and Blumer, C. 1985. The psychology of sunk costs. *Organisational Behaviour and Human Performance*, 35, 124–40.

Arkes, H.R. and Hutzel, L. 2000. The role of probability of success estimate in the sunk cost effect. *Journal of Behavioral Decision-Making*, 13, 295–306.

Armstrong, J.S., Coviello, N. and Safranek, B. 1993. Escalation bias: does it extend to marketing? *Journal of Academy of Management Science*, 21, 247–253.

Aspinwall, L.G. and Richter, L. 1999. Optimism and self-mastery predict more rapid disengagement from unsolvable tasks in the presence of alternatives. *Motivation and Emotion*, 23, 221–242.

Bacharach, S.B. 1989. Organizational theories: some criteria for evaluation. *Academy of Management Review*, 14, 496–515.

Baron, J. 1988. *Judgement Misguided: Intuition and Error in Public Decision-Making*. New York: Oxford University Press.

Baron, R.A. 2000. Counterfactual thinking and venture formation: the potential effects of thinking about 'what might have been'. *Journal of Business Venturing*, 15, 79–91.

Barton, S.L., Duchon, D. and Dunegan, K.J. 1989. An empirical test of Staw and Ross's prescriptions for the management of escalation of commitment behaviour in organizations. *Decision Sciences*, 3, 532–544.

Bazerman, M.H. 1984. The relevance of Kahneman and Tversky's concept of framing to organization behaviour. *Journal of Management*, 10, 333–343.

Bazerman, M.H. 2004. *Judgement in Managerial Decision-Making*. New York: Wiley.

Bazerman, M.H., Beekun, R.I. and Schoorman, F.D. 1982. Performance evaluation in a dynamic context: a laboratory study of the impact of the prior commitment to the rate. *Journal of Applied Psychology*, 67, 873–876.

Bazerman, M.H. and Watkins, M.D. 2008. *Predictable Surprises*. Harvard University Business Press.

Becker, H.S. 1960. Notes on the concept of commitment. *American Journal of Sociology*, 66, 32–40.

Beeler, J.D. and Hunton, J.E. 1997. The influence of compensation method and disclosure level on information search strategy and escalation of commitment. *Journal of Behavioral Decision-Making*, 10, 77–91.

Bernstein, P.L., 1998. *Against the Gods: The Remarkable Story of Risk*. Chichester: Wiley.

Bhide, A., 2000. *The Origin and Evolution of New Businesses*. New York: Oxford University Press.

Boehne, D.M. and Pease, P.W. 2000. Deciding whether to complete or terminate an unfinished project: a strong test of the project completion hypothesis. *Organizational Behavior and Human Decision Processes*, 81, 178–194.

Bowen, M.G. 1987. The escalation phenomenon reconsidered: decision dilemmas or decision errors. *Academy of Management Review*, 12, 52–66.

Bragger, J.D., Bragger, D.H., Hantula, D.A. and Kirnan, J.P. 1998. Hysteresis and uncertainty: the effect of information on delays to exit decisions. *Organizational Behavior and Human Decision Processes*, 74, 229–253.

Brecher, E.G. and Hantula, D.A. 2005. Equivocality and escalation: a replication and preliminary examination of frustration. *Journal of Applied Social Psychology*, 35, 2606–2619.

Brockner, J. 1992. The escalation of commitment to a failing course of action: toward theoretical progress. *Academy of Management Review*, 17, 39–61.

Brockner, J., Shaw, M.C. and Rubin, J.Z. 1979. Factors affecting withdrawal from an escalating conflict: quitting before it's too late. *Journal of Experimental Social Psychology*, 15, 492–503.

Brockner, J., Rubin, J.Z. and Lang, E. 1981. Face-saving and entrapment. *Journal of Experimental Social Psychology*, 17, 68–79.

Brockner, J. and Rubin, J.Z. 1985. *Entrapment in Escalating Conflicts*. New York: Springer-Verlag.

Brockner, J., Houser, R., Birnbaum, G., Lloyd, K., Deitcher, J., Nathanson, S. and Rubin, J.Z. 1986. Escalation of commitment to an ineffective course of action: the effect of feedback having negative implications for self-identity. *Administrative Science Quarterly*, 31, 109–126.

Brockner, J., Tyler, T.R. and Cooper-Schneider, R. 1992. The influence of prior commitment on reactions to perceived unfairness: the higher they are, the harder they fall. *Administrative Science Quarterly*, 37, 241–261.

Brown, R.H. 1978. Bureaucracy as praxis: toward a political phenomenology of formal organizations. *Administrative Science Quarterly*, 23, 365–382.

Brown, R.H. 1989. *Social Science as Civic Discourse*. Chicago: University of Chicago Press.

Brunsson, N. 1985. *The Irrational Orgnaization*. Chichester: Wiley.

Burgess, A.W. and Holstrom, L. 1979. *Rape: Crisis and Recovery*. Bowie, MD: Brady.

Camerer, C.F. and Weber, R.A. 1999. The econometrics and behavioural economics of commitment: a re-examination of Staw and Hoang's NBA data. *Journal of Economic Behaviour and Organization*, 39, 59–82.

Caminiti, S. 1987. He put the kick back into Coke. *Fortune*, 26 October, 48.

Carter, N., Gartner, W. and Reynolds, P. 1996. Exploring start-up event sequences. *Journal of Business Venturing*, 11, 151–166.

Chell, E. 1998. The critical incident technique, in *Qualitative Methods in Organizational Research: A Practical Guide*, edited by G. Symon and C. Cassell. London: Sage, 51–72.

Chell, E. 2001. *Entrepreneurship, Innovation and Change*. London: Thomson Learning.

Chell, E. and Pittaway, L. 1998. A study of entrepreneurship in the restaurant and cafe industry: exploratory work using the critical incident technique as a methodology. *Hospitality Management*, 17, 23–32.

Cohen, M.D., March, J.G. and Olsen, J.P. 1972. A garbage can model of organizational choice. *Administrative Science Quarterly*, 17, 1–25.

Coleman, M.D. 2009. Sunk cost and commitment to dates arranged online. *Current Psychology*, 28, 45–54.

Conlon, E.J. and Parks, J.M. 1987. Information requests in the context of escalation. *Journal of Applied Psychology*, 72, 344–350.

Conlon, E.J. and Garland, H. 1993. The role of project completion information in resource allocation decisions. *Academy of Management Journal*, 36, 402–413.

Crocker, J. and Park, L.E. 2004. The costly pursuit of self-esteem. *Psychological Bulletin*, 130, 392–414.

Dane, E. and Pratt, M.G. 2007. Exploring intuition and its role in managerial decision making. *Academy of Management Review*, 32(1), 33–54.

De Bono, E. 1990. *Lateral Thinking for Management*. Penguin: Harmondsworth.

De Bono, E. 2000. *Six Thinking Hats*. Harmondsworth: Penguin.

Defence Procurement. 2006. London: TSO.

Deming, E. 1986. *Out of the Crisis*. Cambridge, MA: Cambridge University.

Denison, C.A. 2009. Real options and escalation of commitment: a behavioural analysis of capital investment decisions. *Accounting Review*, 84, 133–155.

Drummond, H. 1994. Escalation in organizational decision-making: a case of recruiting an incompetent employee. *Journal of Behavioral Decision Making*, 7, 43–55.

Drummond, H. 1995. De-escalation in decision-making: a case of a disastrous partnership. *Journal of Management Studies*, 32, 265–281.

Drummond, H. 1996. *Escalation in Decision-Making: The Tragedy of Taurus*. Oxford University Press.

Drummond, H. 1997. Giving it a week and then another week: a case of escalation in decision-making. *Personnel Review*, 26, 99–113.

Drummond, H. 2001. *The Art of Decision-Making: Mirrors of Imagination: Masks of Fate*. Chichester: Wiley.

Drummond, H. 2004. See you next week? A study of entrapment in a small business. *International Small Business Journal*, 22, 487–502.

Drummond, H. 2005. What you never have: the risks of premature termination. *Journal of Information Technology*, 20, 153–170.

Drummond, H. 2008. *The Dynamics of Organizational Collapse: The Case of Barings' Bank*. London: Routledge.

Drummond, H. and Chell, E. 2002. Life's chances and choices, a study of entrapment in career decisions with reference to Becker's side bets theory. *Personnel Review*, 30, 186–202.

Dubin, R. 1976. Theory building in applied area, in *Handbook of Industrial and Organizational Psychology*, edited by M.D. Dunnette. Chicago: Rand McNally, 17–40.

Dunegan, K.J. 1993. Framing, cognitive models and image theory: toward an understanding of a glass half full. *Journal of Applied Psychology*, 78, 419–503.

Dyer, W.G. and Wilkins, A.L. 1991. Better stories, not better constructs, to generate better theory: a rejoinder to Eisenhardt. *Academy of Management Review*, 3, 613–619.

Eisenhardt, K.M. 1989. Building theories from case study research. *Academy of Management Review*, 14, 532–550.

Eisenhardt, K.M. 1991. Better stories and better constructs: the case for rigor and comparative logic. *Academy of Management Review*, 16, 620–627.

Endlich, L. 1999. *Goldman Sachs: The Culture of Success*. London: Time Warner.

Fantino, E., Navarro, A. and Stolarz-Fantino, S. 2008. Multiple causes of the sunk cost effect. In *Psychology of Decision-Making: Legal and Healthcare Settings*, edited by G.R. Burtold. Hauppuge, New York: Nova Science, 141–157.

Fay, S. 1982. *Beyond Greed*. New York: Viking.

Ferraro, F., Pfeffer, J. and Sutton, R.I. 2005a. Economics language and assumptions: how theories can become self-fulfilling. *Academy of Management Review*, 30, 8–24.

Ferraro, F., Pfeffer, J. and Sutton, R.I. 2005b. Prescriptions are not enough. *Academy of Management Review*, 30, 32–35.

Festinger, L. 1957. *A Theory of Cognitive Dissonance*. Evanston, IL: Row, Peterson.

Fisher, J. and Ury, W. 1983. *Getting to Yes*. London: Hutchinson.

Forlani, D. and Mullins, J.W. 2000. Perceived risks and choices in entrepreneurs' new venture decisions. *Journal of Business Venturing*, 15, 305–322.

Fox, F. and Staw, B.M. 1979. The trapped administrator: the effects of job insecurity and policy resistance upon commitment to a course of action. *Administrative Science Quarterly*, 24, 449–471.

Funder, D.C. 1987. Errors and mistakes: evaluating the accuracy of social judgement. *Psychological Bulletin*, 101, 75–90.

Garland, H. 1990. Throwing good money after bad: the effect of sunk costs on the decision to escalate commitment to an ongoing project. *Journal of Applied Psychology*, 75, 728–731.

Garland, H., Sandefur, C.A. and Rogers, A.C. 1990. De-escalation of commitment in oil exploration: when sunk costs and negative feedback coincide. *Journal of Applied Psychology*, 75, 721–727.

Garland, H. and Newport, S. 1991. Effects of absolute and relative sunk costs on the decision to persist with a course of action. *Organizational Behavior and Human Decision Processes*, 48, 55–69.

Gartner, J.D. 2005. America's manic entrepreneurs. *American Enterprise*, 16, 18–21.

Gatewood, E.J., Shaver, K.G. and Gartner, W.B. 1995. A longitudinal study of cognitive factors influencing start-up behaviours and success at venture creation. *Journal of Business Venturing*, 10, 371–391.

Gatley, D. 1980. Individual discount rates and the purchase and utilization of energy – using durables. *Bell Journal of Economics*, 11, 373–374.

Glaser, B.G. and Strauss, A.L. 1968. *Discovery of Grounded Theory*. London: Weidenfeld and Nicolson.

Goltz, S. 1992. A sequential learning analysis of decisions in organizations to escalate investments despite continuing costs or losses. *Journal of Applied Behavior Analysis*, 25, 561–574.

Goltz, S. 1993. Examining the joint roles of responsibility and reinforcement history in recommitment. *Decision Sciences*, 24, 977–994.

Goltz, S. 1999. Can't stop on a dime: the roles of matching and momentum in persistence of commitment. *Journal of Organization Behavior Management*, 19, 37–63.

Greer, C.R. and Stephens, G.K. 2001. Escalation of commitment: a comparison of differences between Mexican and US decision-makers. *Journal of Management*, 27, 51–78.

Griffith, S.B. 1971. *Sun Tzu: The Art of War*. Oxford University Press.

Griffiths, M.D. 1990. The cognitive psychology of gambling. *Journal of Gambling Studies*, 6, 31–43.

Hantula, D.A. and Crowell, C.R. 1994. Intermittent reinforcement and escalation processes in sequential decision-making: a replication and theoretical analysis. *Journal of Organizational Behavior Management*, 14, 7–36.

Harford, T. 2007. *The Undercover Economist*. Harmondsworth: Penguin.

Heath, C. 1995. Escalation and de-escalation of commitment in response to sunk costs: the role of budgeting in accounting. *Organization Behaviour and Human Decision Processes*, 62, 38–54.

Heath, C. and Tversky, A. 1991. Preference and belief: ambiguity and competence in choice under uncertainty. *Journal of Risk and Uncertainty*, 4, 5–28.

Hedberg, B.L.T. and Jönsson, S.A. 1977. Strategy Formulation on a Discontinuous Process. *International Studies on Management and Organization* 7, 88–109.

Henderson, M.D., Gollwitzer, P.M. and Oettingen, G. 2007. Implementation intentions and disengagement from a failing course of action. *Journal of Behavioral Decision-Making*, 20, 81–102.

Hmieleski, K.M. and Baron, R.A. 2009. Entrepreneur's optimism and new venture performance: a social cognitive perspective. *Academy of Management Journal*, 52, 473–488.

Ivancevich, J.M. and Matteson, M.T. 1980. *Stress at Work*. Glenview IL: Scott Foresman.

Janis, I.L. 1989. *Crucial Decisions: Leadership in Policy and Crisis Management*. New York: Free Press.

Janney, J.J. and Dess, G.G. 2004. Can real-options analysis improve decision-making? Promises and pitfalls. *Academy of Management Executive*, 18, 60–75.

Jeffrey, C. 1992. The relation of judgement, personal involvement and experience in the audit of bank loans. *Accounting Review*, 67, 802–819.

Kahneman, D.H. and Tversky, A. 1972. Subjective probability: a judgement of representativeness. *Cognitive Psychology*, 3, 430–454.

Kahneman, D. and Tversky, A. 1979. Prospect theory: an analysis of decision under risk. *Econometrica*, 47, 263–291.

Kahneman, D. and Tversky, A. 1982. The psychology of preferences. *Scientific American*, 246, 162–170.

Kahneman, D., Slovic, P. and Tversky, A. 1982. *Judgment Under Uncertainty: Heuristics and Biases*. New York: Cambridge University Press.

Kahneman, D. and Frederick, F. 2002. Representativeness revisited: attribute substitution in intuitive judgement, in *Heuristics and Biases: The Psychology of Intuitive Judgement*, edited by T. Gilovich, D. Griffin and D. Kahneman. Cambridge University Press, 49–81.

Karlsson, N., Julisson, A., Grankivist, G. and Gärling, T. 2002. Impact of decision goal on escalation. *Acta Psychologia*, 111, 309–322.

Karlsson, N., Gärling, T. and Bonini, N. 2005. Escalation of commitment with transparent future outcomes. *Experimental Psychology*, 52, 67–73.

Karlsson, N., Juliusson, E.A. and Gärling, T. 2005. A conceptualisation of task dimensions affecting escalation of commitment. *European Journal of Cognitive Psychology*, 17, 835–858.

Kirby, S.L. and Davis, M.A. 1998. A study of escalation of commitment in principal-agent relationship: effects of monitoring and personal relationship. *Journal of Applied Psychology*, 83, 206–217.

Kisfalvi, V. 2000. The threat of failure, the perils of success and CEO character: sources of strategic persistence. *Organization Studies*, 21, 611–639.

Kisfalvi, V. and Pitcher, P. 2003. The influence of CEO character and emotions on top management team dynamics. *Journal of Management Inquiry*, 12, 42–66.

Ku, G. 2008a. Before escalation: behavioural and affective forecasting in escalation of commitment. *Personality and Social Psychology Bulletin*, 34, 1477–1491.

Ku, G. 2008b. Learning to de-escalate: the effects of regret in escalation of commitment. *Organizational Behavior and Human Decision Processes*, 105, 221–232.

Ku, G., Galinsky, A.D. and Murnigham, J.K. 2006. Starting low but ending high: a reversal of the anchoring effect in auctions. *Journal of Personality and Social Psychology*, 90, 975–986.

Langer, E.J. 1975. The illusion of control. *Journal of Personality and Social Psychology*, 32, 311–328.

Langer, E.J. 1983. *The Psychology of Control*. Sage: Beverly Hills.

Lipshitz, R. 1995. The road to desert storm. *Organization Studies*, 16, 243–263.

Lowenstein, G. and Thaler, R.H. 1989. Inter-temporal choice. *Journal of Economic Perspectives*, 3, 197–201.

Mähring, M. and Keil, M. 2008. Information technology project escalation: a processes model. *Decision Sciences*, 39, 239–272.

McCain, B.E. 1986. Continuing investment under conditions of failure: a laboratory study of the limits of escalation. *Journal of Applied Psychology*, 71, 280–284.

McCarthy, A.M., Schoorman, F.D. and Cooper, A.C. 1993. Reinvestment decisions by entrepreneurs – rational decision making or escalation of commitment. *Journal of Business Venturing*, 8, 9–24.

McGarth, R.G. 1999. Falling forward: real options, reasoning and entrepreneurial failure. *Academy of Management Review*, 1999, 24, 13–30.

Meglino, B.M. and Korsgaard, M.A. 2004. Considering rational self-interest as a disposition: organizational implications of other orientation. *Journal of Applied Psychology*, 89, 946–959.

Mills, C.W. 1959. *The Sociological Imagination*. Oxford University Press.

Minford, J. 2002. *The Art of War: Sun-Tzu*. Harmondsworth: Penguin.

Mintzberg, H. 1994. *The Rise and Fall of Strategic Planning*, Boston: Free Press.

Money down the drain. *Time*, 25 June, 26.

Monteaglre, R. and Keil, M. 2000. De-escalating information technology projects: lessons from the Denver international airport. *MIS Quarterly*, 24, 417–447.

Moody, E.A. 1974. William of Ockham in *Dictionary of Scientific Biography*. New York: Scribner.

Moon, H. 2001a. Looking forward and looking back: integrating completion and sunk cost effects within and escalation-of-commitment progress decision. *Journal of Applied Psychology*, 86, 104–113.

Moon, H. 2001b. The two phases of conscientiousness: duty and achievement striving in escalation of commitment dilemmas. *Journal of Applied Psychology*, 86, 533–540.

Moon, H., Hollenbeck, J.R., Humphrey, S.E. and Maue, B. 2003. The tripartite model of neuroticism and the suppression of depression and anxiety within an escalation of commitment dilemma. *Journal of Personality*, 71, 347–367.

Mullins, J.W. and Forlani, D. 2004. Missing the boat or sinking the boat: a study of new venture decision-making. *Journal of Business Venturing*, 20(1), 47–69.

Nisbett, R.E. and Ross, L. 1980. *Human Inference: Strategies and Shortcomings of Social Judgment*. Englewood Cliffs, NJ: Prentice-Hall.

Northcraft, G. and Wolf, G. 1984. Dollars sense and sunk costs: a life cycle model of resource allocation decisions. *Academy of Management Review*, 225–234.

Northcraft, G. and Neale, M.A. 1986. Opportunity costs and framing of resource decisions. *Organizational Behavior and Human Decision Processes*, 37, 348–356.

O'Reilly, C.A. III. and Caldwell, D.F. 1981. The commitment and job tenure of new employees: some evidence of post decisional justification. *Administrative Science Quarterly*, 26, 597–616.

Parks, J.M. and Conlon, E.J. 1990. Justification and the process of information. *Journal of Applied Social Psychology*, 20, 703–723.

Peters, T. and Waterman, R.H. 1982. *In Search of Excellence: Lessons from America's Best Run Companies*. New York: Harper and Row.

Pfeffer, J. 1974. The ambiguity of leadership. *Academy of Management Review*, 2, 104–112.

Pfeffer, J. and Fong, C.T. 2005. Building organization theory from first principles: the self-enhancement motive and understanding power and influence. *Organization Science*, 16, 372–388.

Platt, J. 1973. Social traps. *American Psychologist*, August, 641–651.

Popper, K.R. 1959. *The Logic of Scientific Discovery*, London: Hutchinson.

Pratt, M.E. 2009. For the lack of a boilerplate: tips on writing up (and reviewing) qualitative research. *Academy of Management Journal*, 52, 856–862.

Reid, R.L. 1986. The psychology of the near miss. *Journal of Gambling Behavior*, 2, 32–39.

Ross, J. and Staw, B.M. 1986. Expo 86: an escalation prototype. *Administrative Science Quarterly*, 31, 379–391.

Ross, J. and Staw, B.M. 1991. Managing escalation processes in organizations. Journal of Management Issues, 3, 15–30.

Ross, J. and Staw, B.M. 1993. Organizational escalation and exit: lessons from the Shoreham nuclear power plant. *Academy of Management Journal*, 36, 701–732.

Rubin, J.Z. and Brockner, J. 1975. Factors affecting entrapment in waiting situations: the Rosencrantz and Guildenstern effect. *Journal of Personality and Social Psychology*, 31, 1054–1063.

Sabini, J. and Silver, M. 1982. *Moralities of Everyday Life*, New York: Oxford University Press.

Salancik, G.R. 1977. Commitment is too easy. *Organizational Dynamics*, 62–80.

Sandelands, L.E., Brockner, J. and Glynn, M.A. 1988. If at first you don't succeed, try, try again: effects of persistence-performance contingencies, ego-involvement, and self-esteem on task persistence. *Journal of Applied Psychology*, 73, 208–216.

Schaubroeck, J. and Williams, S. 1993. Type A behaviour pattern and escalating commitment. *Journal of Applied Psychology*, 5, 862–867.

Schaubroeck, J. and Davis, E. 1994. Prospect theory predictions when escalation is not the only chance to recover sunk costs. *Organizational Behavior and Human Decision Processes*, 57, 59–82.

Scheier, M.F., Carver, C.S. and Bridges, M.W. 2001. Optimism, pessimism and psychological well-being, in *Optimism and Pessimism: Implications for Theory, Research and Practice*, edited by E.C. Chang. Washington: American Psychological Association, 189–216.

Schoorman, F.D. 1988. Escalation bias in performance appraisals: an unintended consequence of supervisor participation in hiring decisions. *Journal of Applied Psychology*, 73, 58–62.

Schoorman, F.D., Mayer, R.C., Douglas, C.A. and Hetrick, C.T. 1994. Escalation of commitment and the framing effect: an empirical investigation. *Journal of Applied Social Psychology*, 24, 509–528.

Schwenk, C.R. 1986. Information, cognitive biases and commitment to a course of action. *Academy of Management Review*, 11, 290–310.

Schultz-Hardt, S., Thurow-Kröning, B. and Frey, D. 2009. Preference-based escalation: a new interpretation for the responsibility effect in escalating commitment and entrapment. *Organizational Behavior and Human Decision Processes*, 108, 175–186.

Schwenk, C. and Tang, M-J.E. 1989. Economic and psychological explanations for strategic persistence. *Journal of Management Science*, 17, 559–570.

Shepherd, D.A. 2003. Learning from failure. *Academy of Management Review*, 28(2), 318–328.

Shepherd, D.A., Wiklund, J. and Haynie, J.M. 2009. Moving forward: balancing the financial and emotional costs of failure. *Journal of Business Venturing*, 24, 134–148.

Shubik, M. 1971. The dollar auction game: a paradox in non-cooperative behaviour and escalation. *Journal of Conflict Resolution*, 15, 109–111.

Sieck, W.R. and Arkes, H.R. 2005. The recalcitrance of over-confidence and its contribution to decision aid neglect. *Journal of Behavioral Decision-Making*, 18, 29–53.

Simons, D.J. and Chabris, C.F. 1999. Gorillas in our midst: sustained inattentional blindness for dynamic events. *Perception*, 28, 1059–1074.

Simonson, I. and Staw, B.M. 1992. Decision strategies, a comparison of techniques for reducing commitment to losing courses of action. *Journal of Applied Psychology*, 77, 419–426.

Singer, M.S. and Singer, A.E. 1985. Is there always escalation of commitment? *Psychological Reports*, 56, 816–818.

Sitkin, S.B. and Pablo, A.L. 1992. Re-conceptualizing the determinants of risk behaviour. *Academy of Management Review*, 17, 9–39.

Sitkin, S.B. and Weingart, L.R. 1995. Determinants of risky decision-making behaviour: a test of the mediating role of risk perceptions and propensity. *Academy of Management Journal*, 38, 1573–1593.

Starbuck, W.H. 1983. Organizations as action generators, *American Sociological Review*, 48, 91–102.

Staw, B.M. 1976. Knee-deep in the big muddy: a study of escalating commitment to a chosen course of action. *Organizational Behavior & Human Decision Processes*, 16, 27–44.

Staw, B.M. 1981. The Escalation of Commitment to a Course of Action. *Academy of Management Review*, 6, 577–587.

Staw, B.M. 1997. Escalation research: An update and appraisal, in *Organizational Decision Making*, edited by Z. Shapira. Cambridge University Press, 191–215.

Staw, B.M. and Ross, J. 1978. Commitment to a policy decision: a multi-theoretical perspective. *Administrative Science Quarterly*, 23, 40–46.

Staw, B.M., Sandelands, L.E. and Dutton, J.E. 1981. Threat rigidity effects in organizational behavior: a multi-level analysis. *Administrative Science Quarterly*, 26, 501–524.

Staw, B.M. and Ross, J. 1987a. Behaviour in escalation situations: antecedents, prototypes and solutions, in *Research in Organization Behaviour*, edited by L.L. Cummings and B.M. Staw. London: JAI Press, 9, 39–78.

Staw, B.M. and Ross, J. 1987b. Knowing when to pull the plug. *Harvard Business Review*, March/April, 65–72.

Staw, B.M. and Ross, J. 1988. Good money after bad. *Psychology Today*, February, 30–33.

Staw, B.M. and Ross, J. 1989. Understanding behavior in escalation situations. *Science*, 246, 216–220.

Staw, B.M. and Hoang, H. 1995. Sunk costs in the NBA: why draft order affects playing time. *Administrative Science Quarterly*, 40, 474–494.

Staw, B.M., Barsade, S.G. and Koput, K.W. 1997. Escalation at the credit window: a longitudinal study of bank executives' recognition and write-off of problem loans. *Journal of Applied Psychology*, 82, 130–142.

Stein, M. 2000. The risk-taker as shadow: a psychoanalytic view of the collapse of Barings. *Journal of Management Studies*, 37, 1215–1259.

Stotz, O. and von Nitzsch, R. 2005. The perception of control and the level of overconfidence: evidence from analyst earnings estimates and price targets. *Journal of Behavioral Finance*, 6, 121–128.

Suddaby, R. 2006. What grounded theory is not. *Academy of Management Journal*, 49, 633–642.

Sutton, R.I. and Staw, B.M. 1995. What theory is *not*. *Administrative Science Quarterly*, 40, 371–384.

Taleb, N.N. 2008. *The Black Swan: The Impact of the Highly Improbable*. Harmondsworth: Penguin.

Tan, H.-T. and Yates, J.F. 1995. Sunk cost effects: the influences of instruction and future return estimates. *Organizational Behavior and Human Decision Processes*, 63, 311–319.

Taylor, S.E. 1980. *Positive Illusions*. New York: Basic Books.

Taylor, S.E. and Brown, J. 1988. Illusion and well being: a social psychological perspective on mental health. *Psychological Bulletin*, 103, 193–210.

Teger, A.I. 1980. *Too Much Invested to Quit: The Psychology of the Escalation of Conflict*. New York: Pergamon.

The Concise Oxford Dictionary of Quotations. 1993. Oxford University Press Press.

Treasury Committee. 1996. *Barings Bank and International Regulation: Minutes of Evidence*, 15 May, London, HMSO.

Tweedale, G. 1995. *Steel City: Entrepreneurship, Strategy and Technology in Sheffield 1793–1993*. Oxford: Clarendon.

Tversky, A. and Kahneman, D. 1974. Judgement under uncertainty: heuristics and biases. *Science*, 185, 1124–1131.

Weick, K.E. 1974. Amendments to organizational theorizing. *Academy of Management Journal*, 487–502.

Weick, K.E. 1989. Theory construction as disciplined imagination. *Academy of Management Review*, 14, 516–531.

Weick, K.E. 1990. The vulnerable system: an analysis of the Tenerife air disaster. *Journal of Management*, 6, 571–593.

Weick, K.E. 1995. *Sense Making in Organizations*. Beverly Hills: Sage.

Weick, K.E. and Sutcliffe, K.M. 2001. *Managing the Unexpected: Assuring High Performance in an Age of Complexity*, San Francisco: Jossey-Bass.

Whyte, G. 1986. Escalating commitment to a course of action: a re-interpretation, *Academy of Management Review*, 11, 311–321.

Whyte, G. 1991a. Diffusion of responsibility: effects on the escalation tendency. *Journal of Applied Psychology*, 76, 408–415.

Whyte, G. 1991b. Decision failures: why they occur and how to prevent them. *Academy of Management Executive*, 5, 23–32.

Whyte, G. 1993. Escalating commitment in individual and group decision making: a prospect theory approach. *Organizational Behavior and Human Decision Processes*, 54, 430–455.

Whyte, G., Saks, A.M. and Hook, S. 1997. When success breeds failure: the art of self-efficacy in escalating commitment to a losing course of action. *Journal of Organizational Behaviour*, 18, 415–432.

Wicker, A.R. 1985. Getting out of our conceptual ruts: strategies for expanding conceptual frameworks. *American Psychologist*, 10, 1094–1103.

Wong, K.F.E. 2005. The role of risk in making decisions under escalation situations. *Applied Psychology: An International Review*, 54, 584–607.

Wong, K.F.E. and Kwong, J.Y.Y. 2007. The role of anticipated regret in escalation of commitment, *Journal of Applied psychology*, 92, 545–552.

Zardkoohi, A. 2004. Do real options lead to escalation of commitment? *Academy of Management Review*, 29, 111–119.

Zhang, L. and Baumeister, R.F. 2006. Your money or your self-esteem: threatened egotism promotes costly entrapment in losing endeavours. *Personality and Social-Psychology Bulletin*, 32, 881–893.

Index